Carom Billiards: Cross-Corner Diagonal Patterns

3-Cushion Billiards Championship Shots

From International Competitions
(Test Yourself against Professional Players)

Allan P. Sand
PBIA Certified Instructor

ISBN 978-1-62505-224-7
PRINT 7x10

ISBN 978-1-62505-417-3
PRINT 8.5x11

First edition

Copyright © 2016 Allan P. Sand

All rights reserved under International and Pan-American Copyright Conventions.

Published by Billiard Gods Productions.
Santa Clara, CA 95051
U.S.A.

For the latest information about books and videos, go to: http://www.billiardgods.com

Acknowledgements
Wei Chao created the software that was used to create these graphics.

Table of Contents

Introduction **1**
About the Graphic Layouts 1
Table Setup 2
Purpose of the Layouts 2
A: Simple Diagonals **3**
A: Group 1 3
A: Group 2 8
A: Group 3 13
A: Group 4 18
A: Group 5 23
A: Group 6 28
B: Simple Modified Diagonals **33**
B: Group 1 33
B: Group 2 38
B: Group 3 43
C: Parallel Diagonals **48**
C: Group 1 48
C: Group 2 53
C: Group 3 58
C: Group 4 63
C: Group 5 68
D: Double Diagonals **73**
D: Group 1 73
D: Group 2 78
D: Group 3 83
D: Group 4 88
D: Group 5 93
D: Group 6 98
D: Group 7 103
E: Double Modified Diagonals **108**
E: Group 1 108
E: Group 2 113
E: Group 3 118
E: Group 4 123
E: Group 5 128
E: Group 6 133
F: Triple Diagonals **138**
F: Group 1 138
F: Group 2 143
F: Group 3 148

Other books by the author ...

- 3 Cushion Billiards Championship Shots (a series)
- Carom Billiards: Some Riddles & Puzzles
- Carom Billiards: MORE Riddles & Puzzles
- Why Pool Hustlers Win
- Table Map Library
- Safety Toolbox
- Cue Ball Control Cheat Sheets
- Advanced Cue Ball Control Self-Testing Program
- Drills & Exercises for Pool & Pocket Billiards
- The Art of War versus The Art of Pool
- The Psychology of Losing – Tricks, Traps & Sharks
- The Art of Team Coaching
- The Art of Personal Competition
- The Art of Politics & Campaigning
- The Art of Marketing & Promotion
- Kitchen God's Guide for Single Guys

Introduction

This is one of a series of Carom Billiards books that show how professional players select shots, based on the table layout. All of these shots have been mapped out based on shots played at international competitions.

This book contains a wide variety of examples of the CB patterns travels cross corner.

These shots put you inside the head of the player beginning with the ball positions (shown in the first table layout). The second table layout shows the shooting decision and the results of the player's choice.

About the Graphic Layouts

There are two graphics for each shot. The first graphic shows the ball positions on the table. The ball labeled "A" is always the player's CB. The first graphic the ball positions on the table. The second graphic shows how the shot was played.

Each table graphic in this book is a black & white representation of a standard 5 x 10 carom billiards table. Balls are represented with these three symbols.

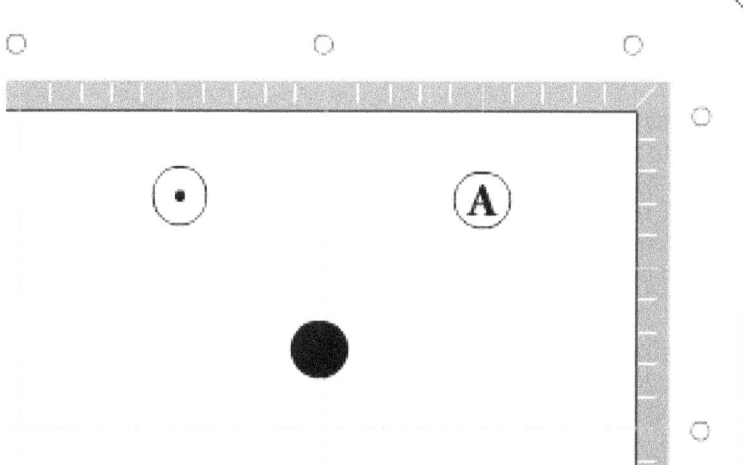

(A) The white "A" ball "A" is ALWAYS the shooter's cue ball.

(•) The white "center dot" ball is always the opponent's cue ball.

● This is the red Object Ball, represented in the layouts as the black ball.

Each shot is represented with two layouts on each page. The first layout shows the ball position setup BEFORE the shot. The second layout shows the ball pathways that the balls travel during the shot.

Table Setup

1. Use donuts (paper reinforcement rings) to mark positions for the carom balls. These are available at any office supply store.

2. Place chalk cubes at the locations where the CB contacts each rail.

When you play the shot, observe where the CB pattern and each rail contact. You may need several attempts as you make adjustments to the CB spin to properly follow the pattern.

Purpose of the Layouts

These are examples of shots that champion 3-cushion players from all over the world had to play. The first graphic provides the layout. The second graphic provides the results of their shooting solution. These layouts are provided for two purposes.

- Use the first layout as a mental exercise. The player picked one, but there are many possibilities. From the comfort of your armchair, you can consider multiple options, and work out the pattern using the spin and speed you would have applied. These help stretch and extend your skills in tactical analysis. Then consider how the player decided how to shoot the shot. From the patterns you can determine how the CB was played and the type of applied spin. It's helpful to use a pointer (or your finger) to trace the pattern as you work out how the shot was played.

- The second purpose is to take these layouts to the practice table. Position the paper reinforcement rings in place for each ball. You are going to shoot the layout many times, so these donuts help mark the ball positions for each attempt. BEFORE you experiment with your own "solutions", shoot the pattern until you can easily duplicate the paths. This means you will do a lot of experimentation to find the spin/speed used by the original player. Only AFTER you understand and can execute the pattern should you experiment with your own ideas.

This combination of mental analysis and practical table practice will boost your growth as an intelligent and thinking carom billiards player.

A: Simple Diagonals

These are a set of shots that travel from one corner towards the opposite corner. These are simple patterns. The CB cross the table from one corner to the opposite corner.

A: Group 1

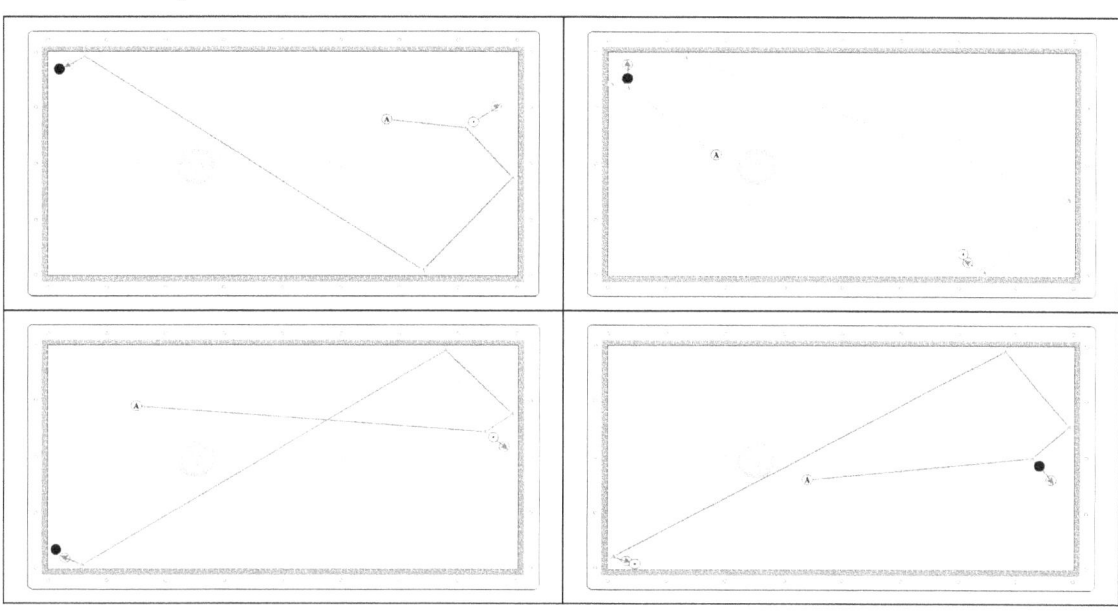

Analysis:

A:1a. _____

A:1b. _____

A:1c. _____

A:1d. _____

Carom Billiards: Cross-Corner Diagonal Patterns

A:1a – Setup

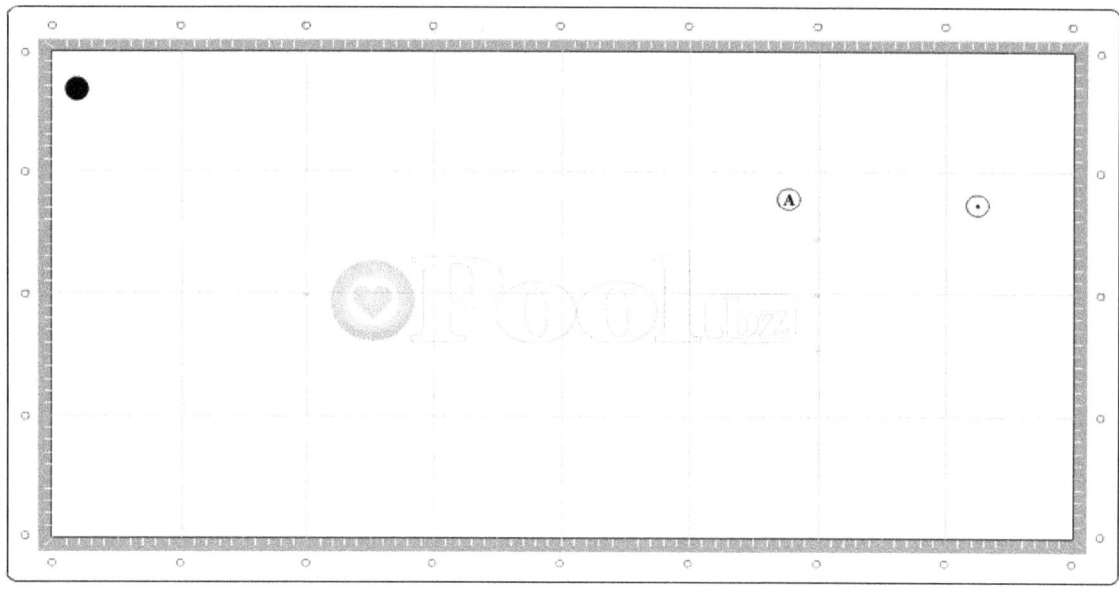

Shot Pattern

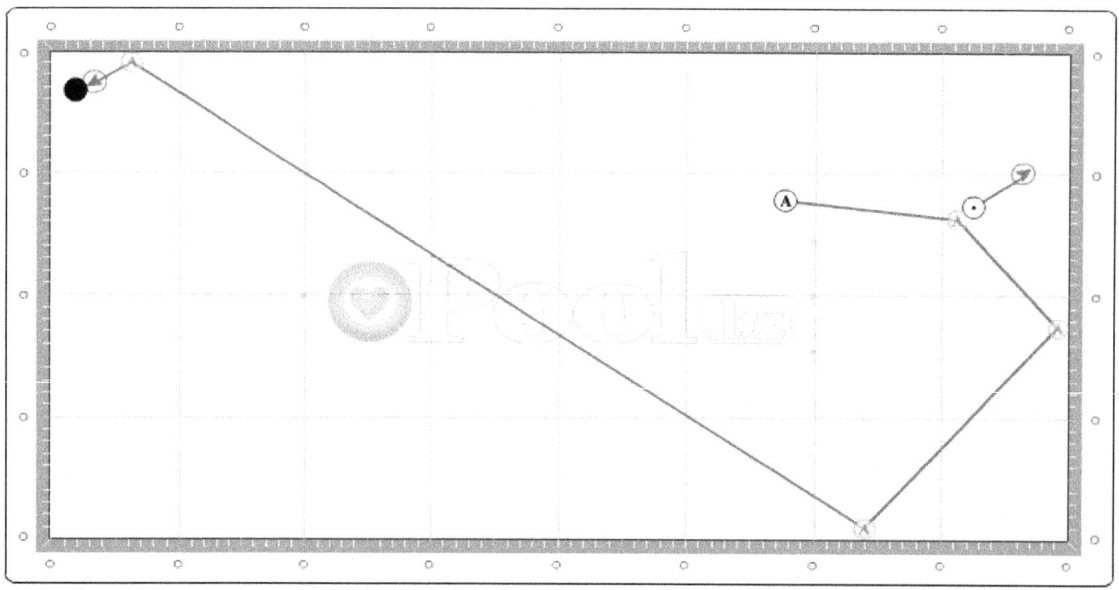

A:1b – Setup

Shot Pattern

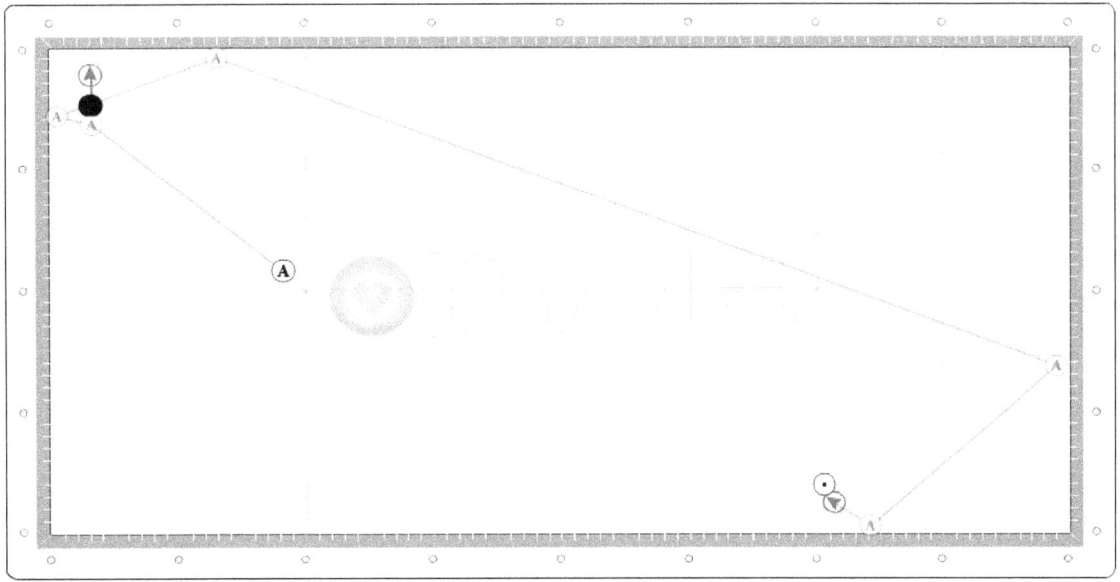

A:1c – Setup

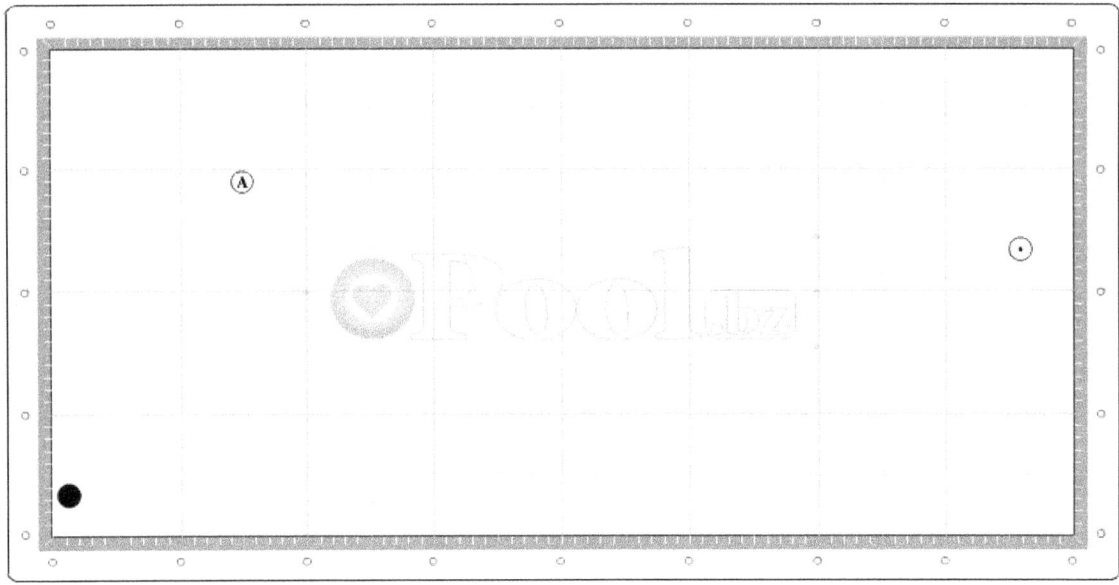

Shot Pattern

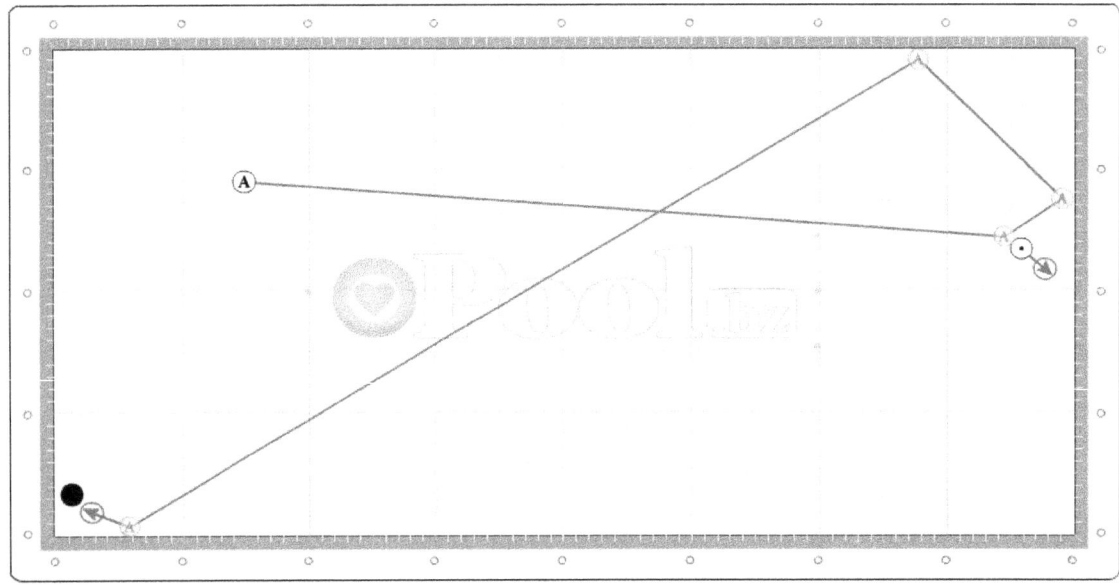

A:1d – Setup

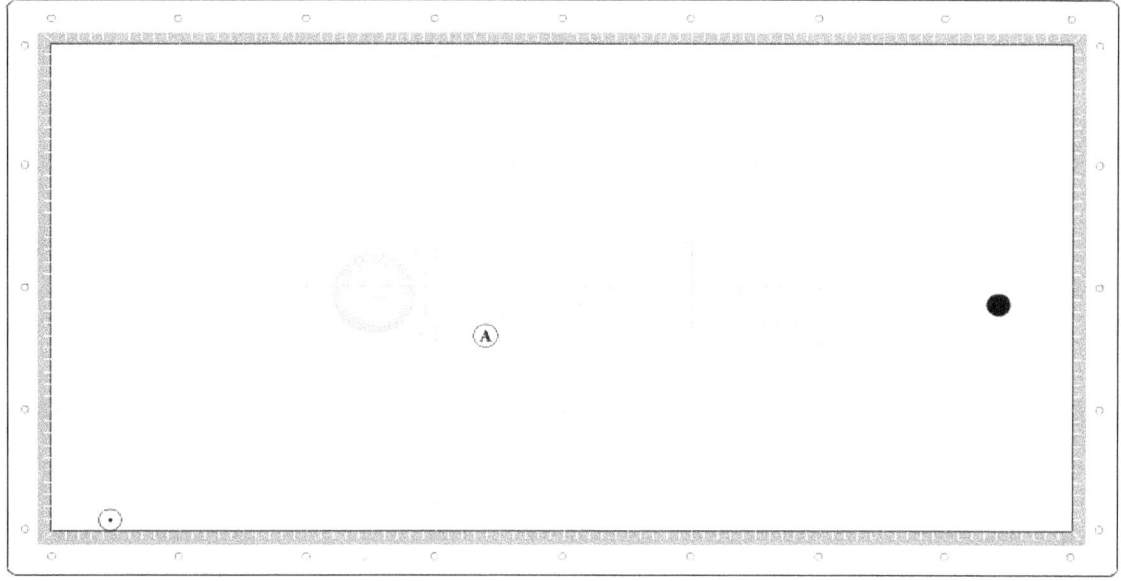

Shot Pattern

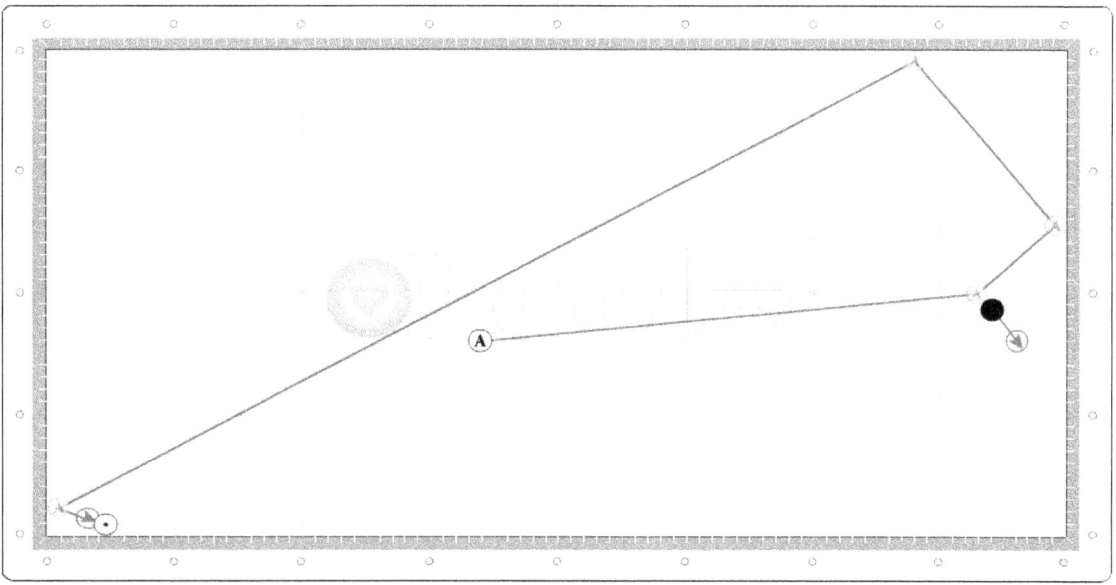

A: Group 2

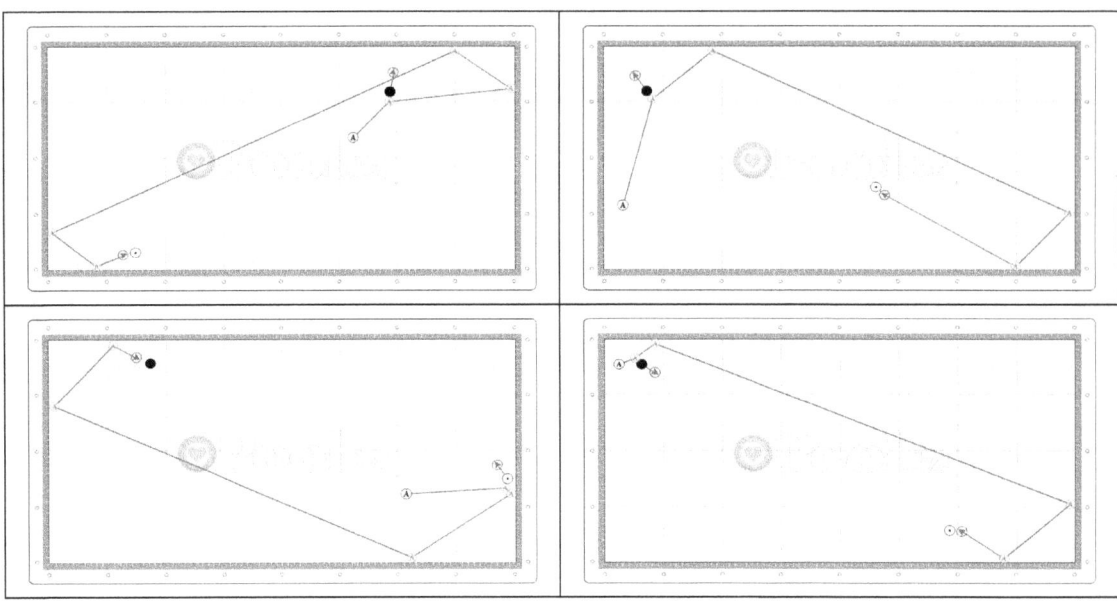

Analysis:

A:2a. _____

A:2b. _____

A:2c. _____

A:2d. _____

A:2a – Setup

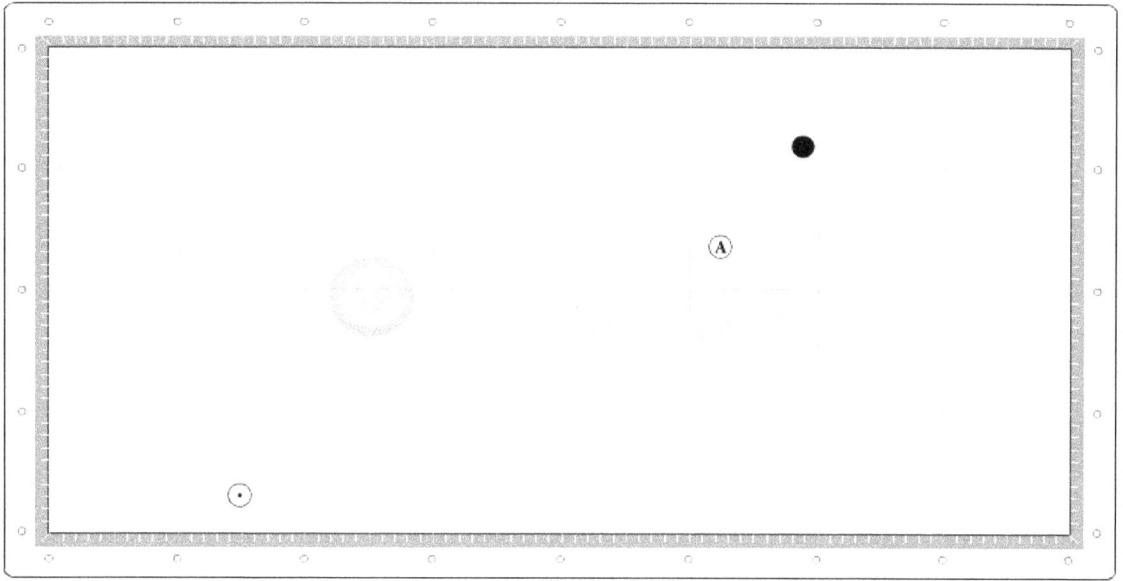

Shot Pattern

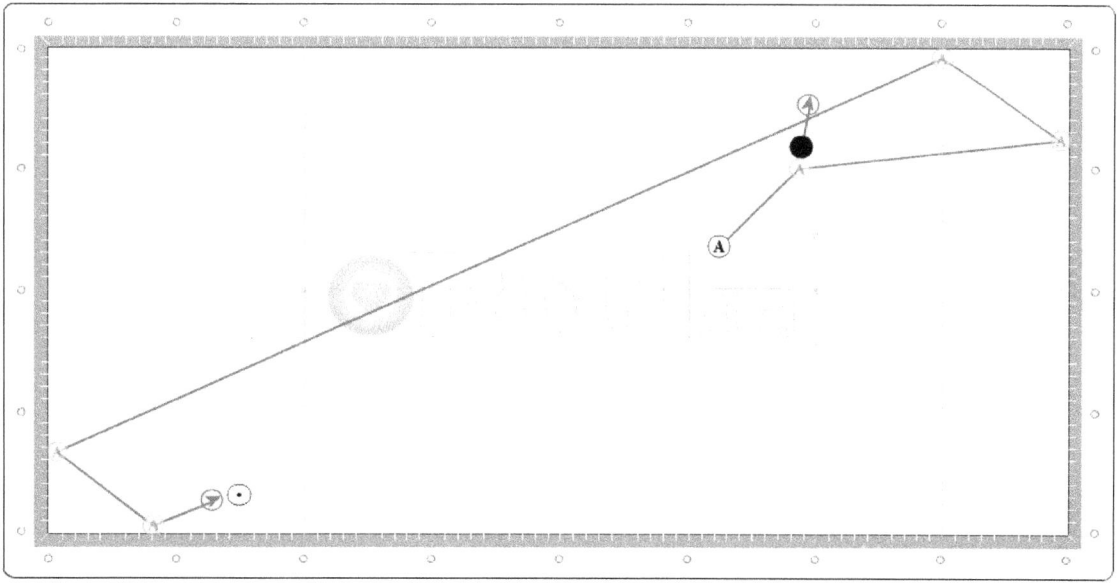

A:2b – Setup

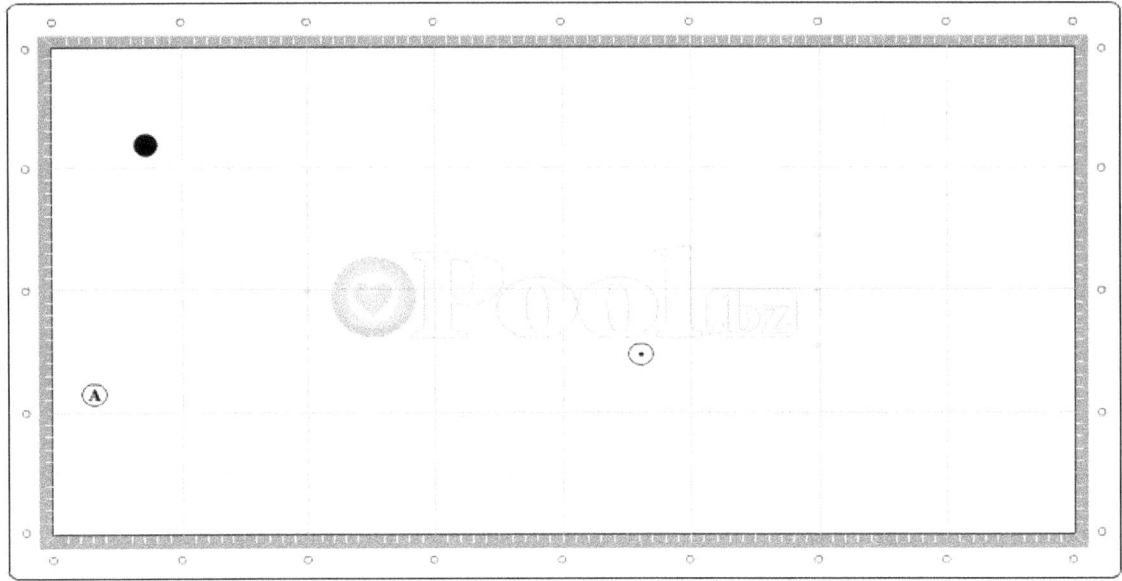

Shot Pattern

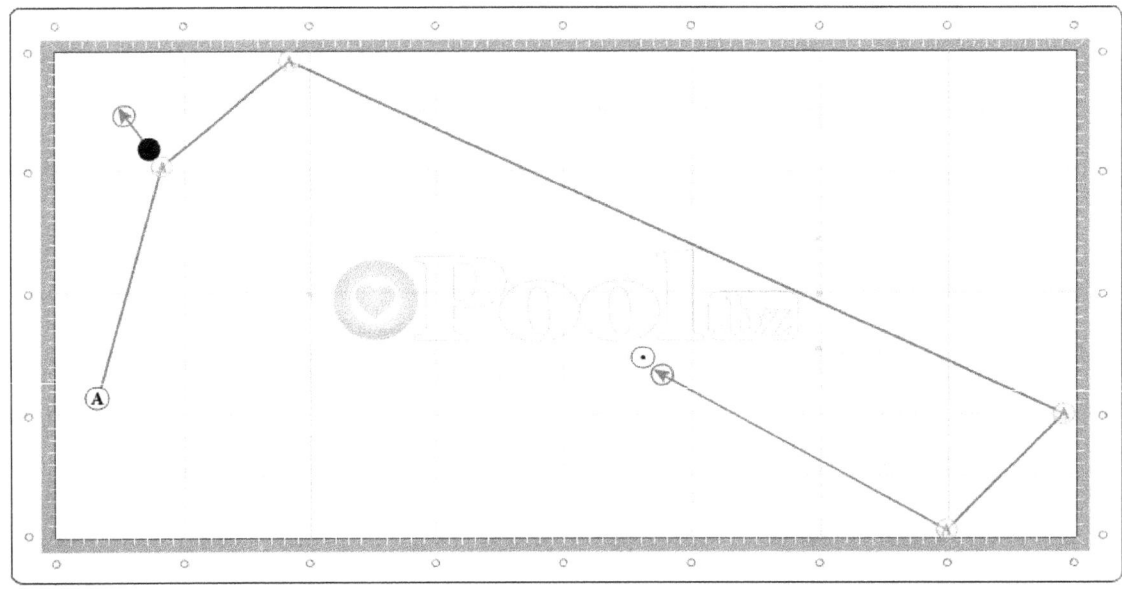

A:2c – Setup

Shot Pattern

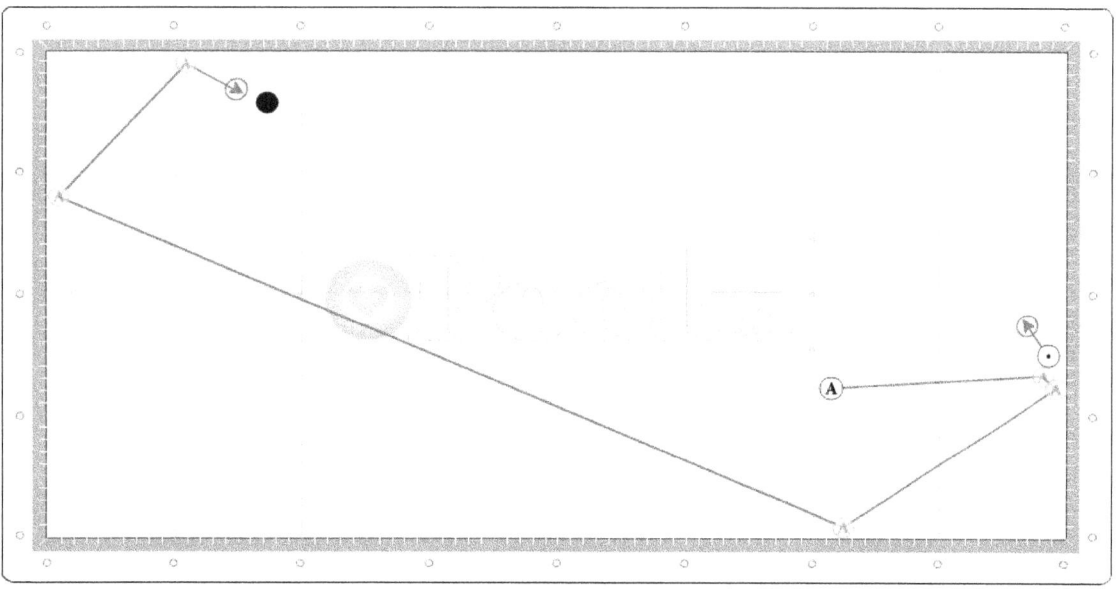

A:2d – Setup

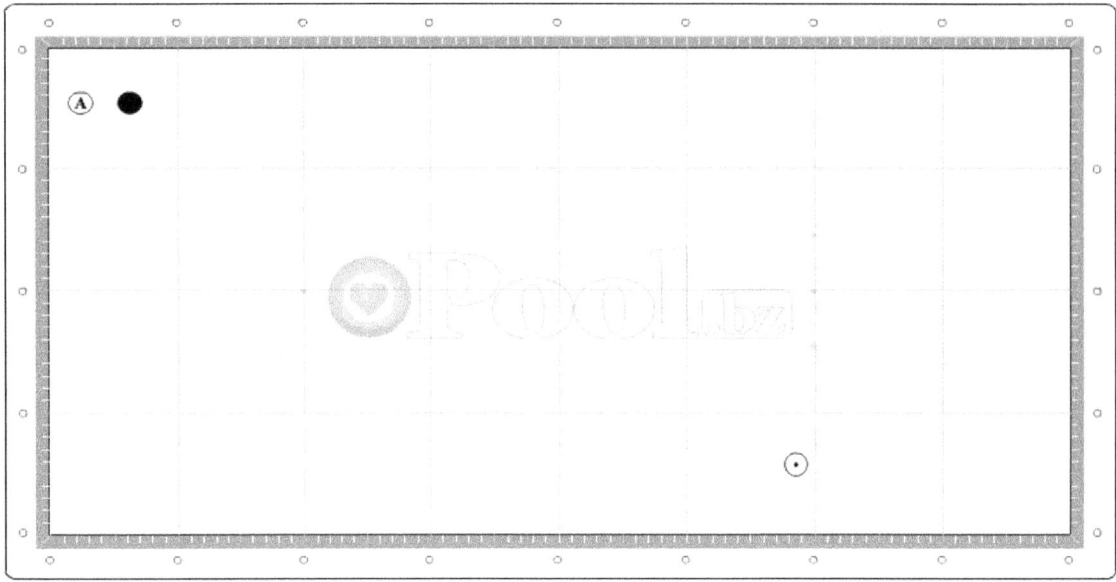

Shot Pattern

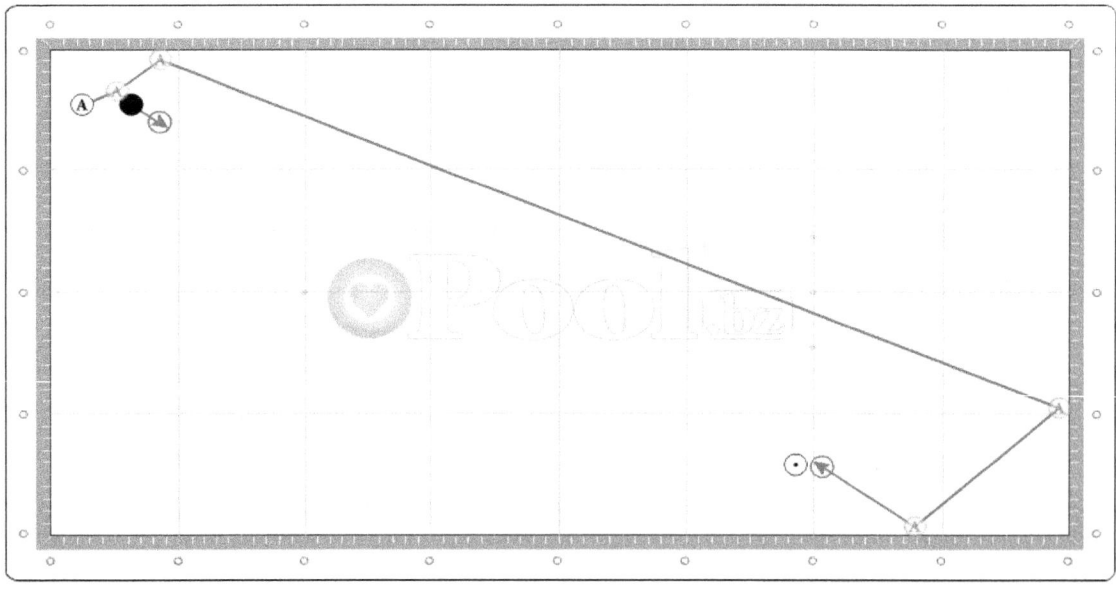

A: Group 3

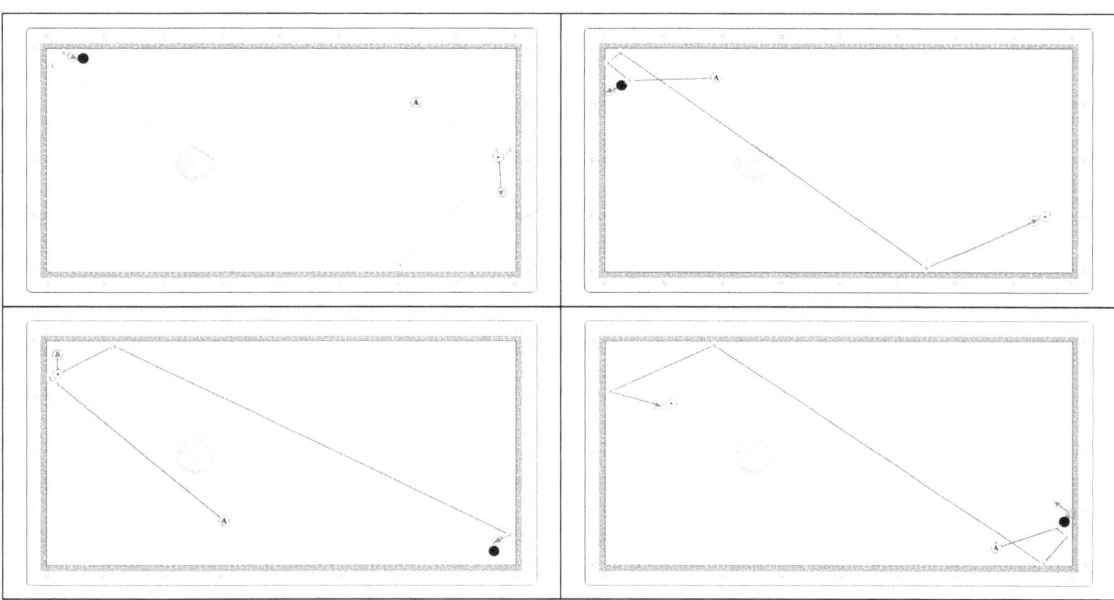

Analysis:

A:3a. _____

A:3b. _____

A:3c. _____

A:3d. _____

A:3a – Setup

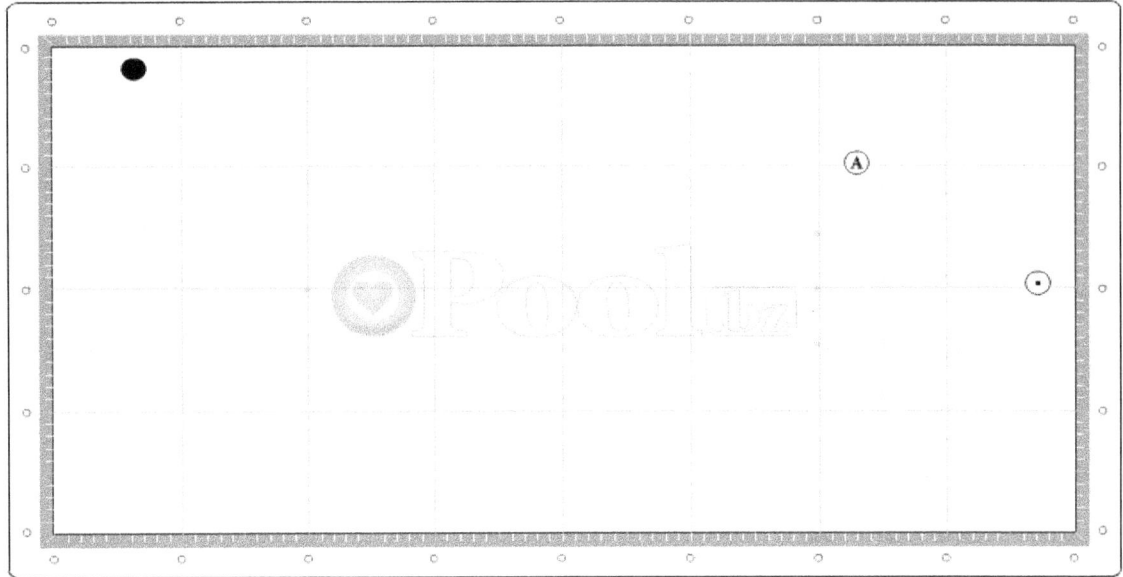

Shot Pattern

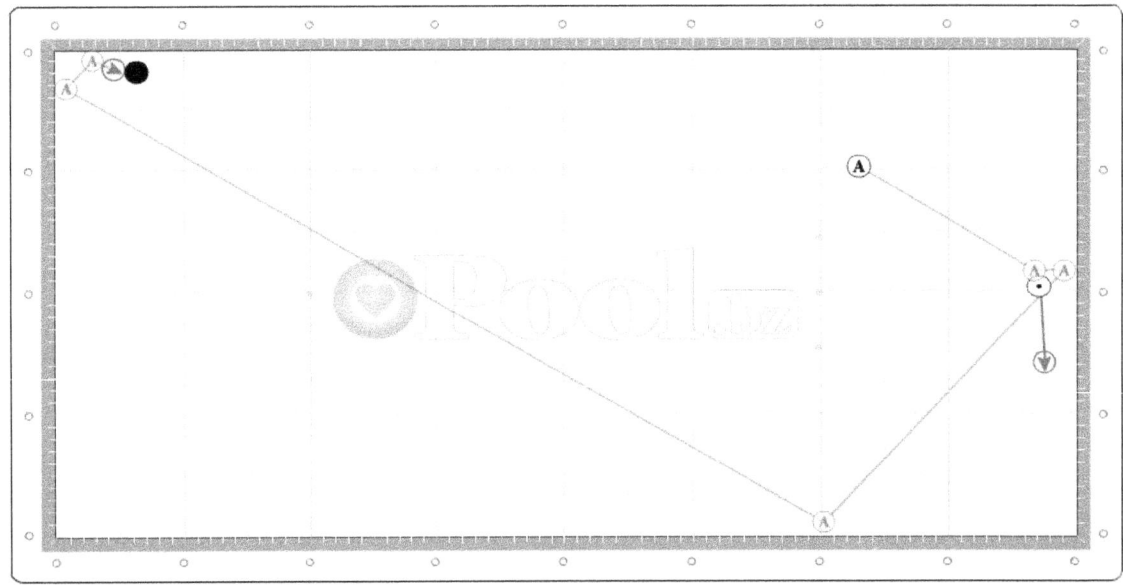

A:3b – Setup

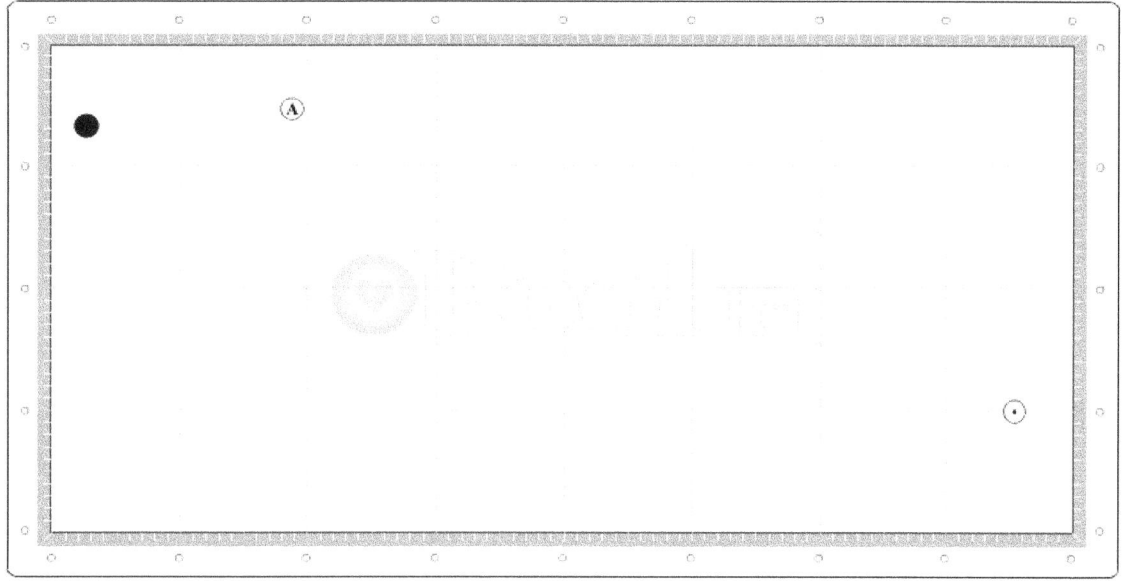

Shot Pattern

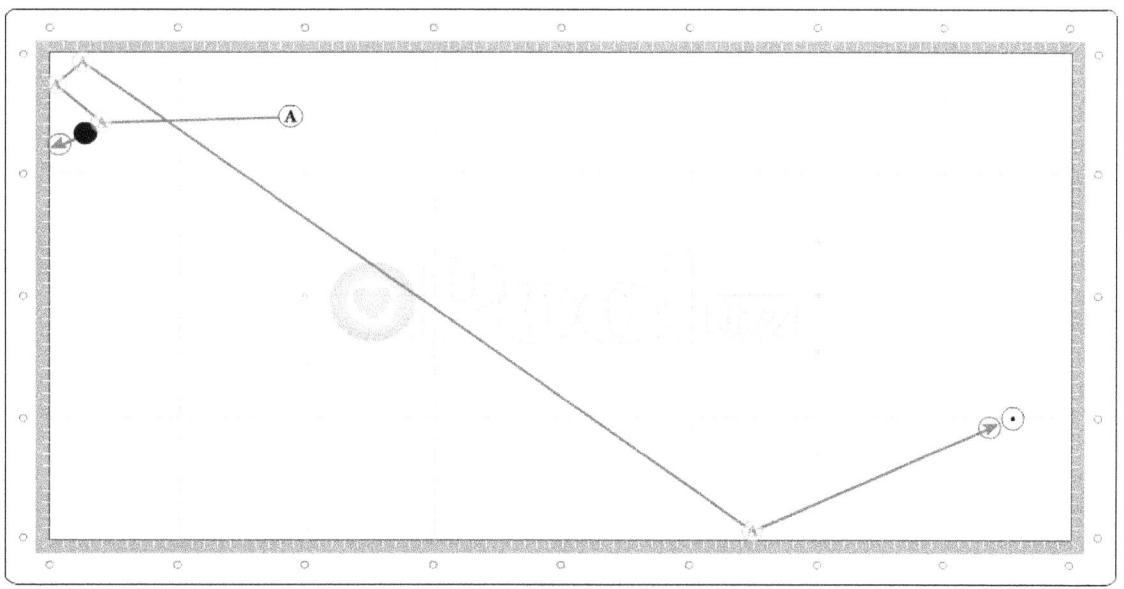

A:3c – Setup

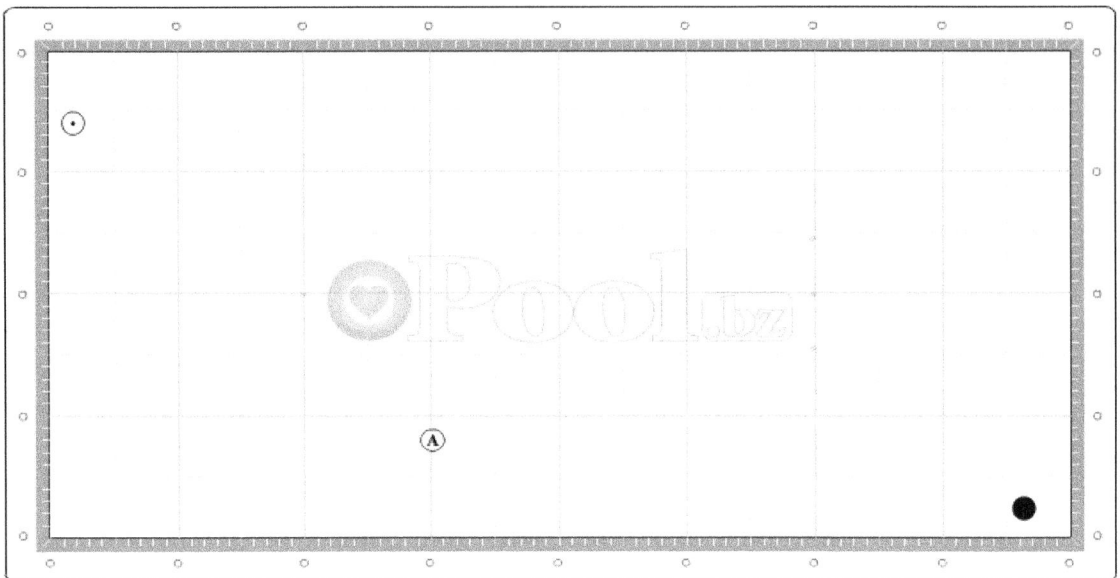

Shot Pattern

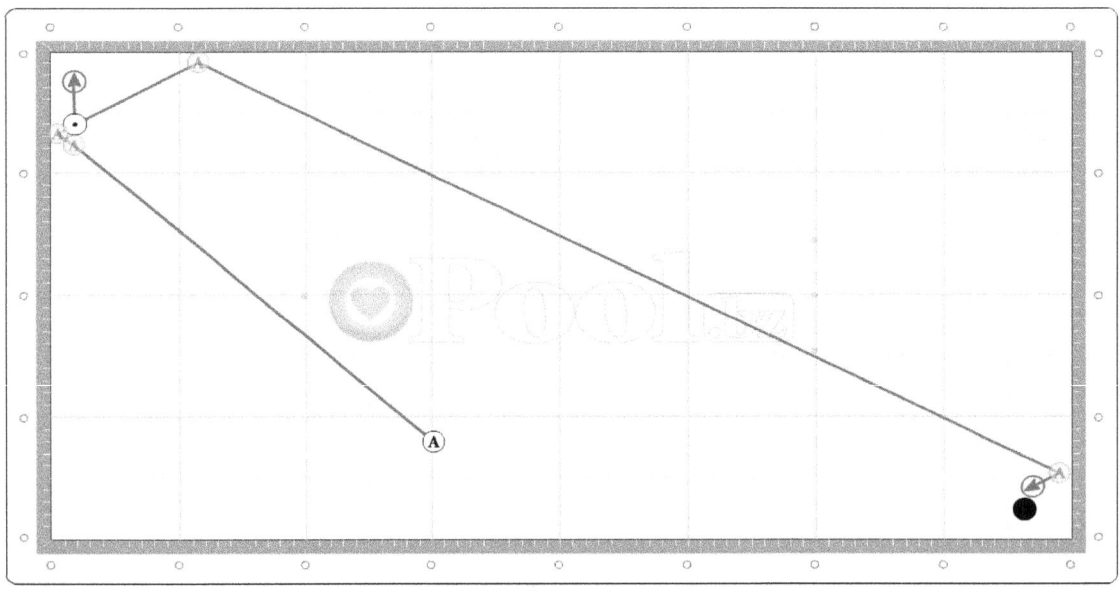

A:3d – Setup

Shot Pattern

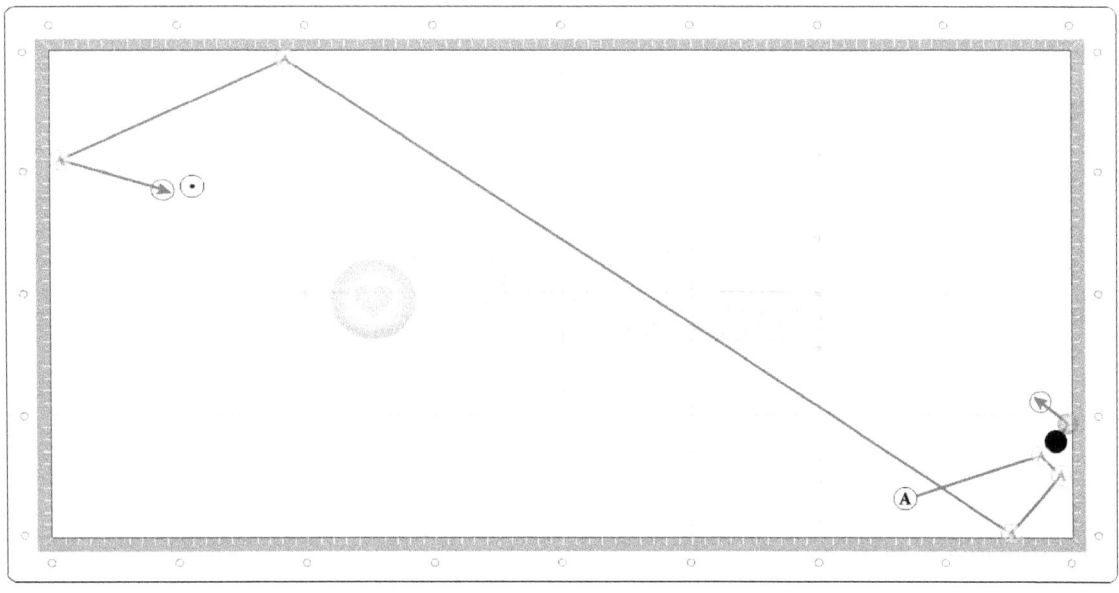

A: Group 4

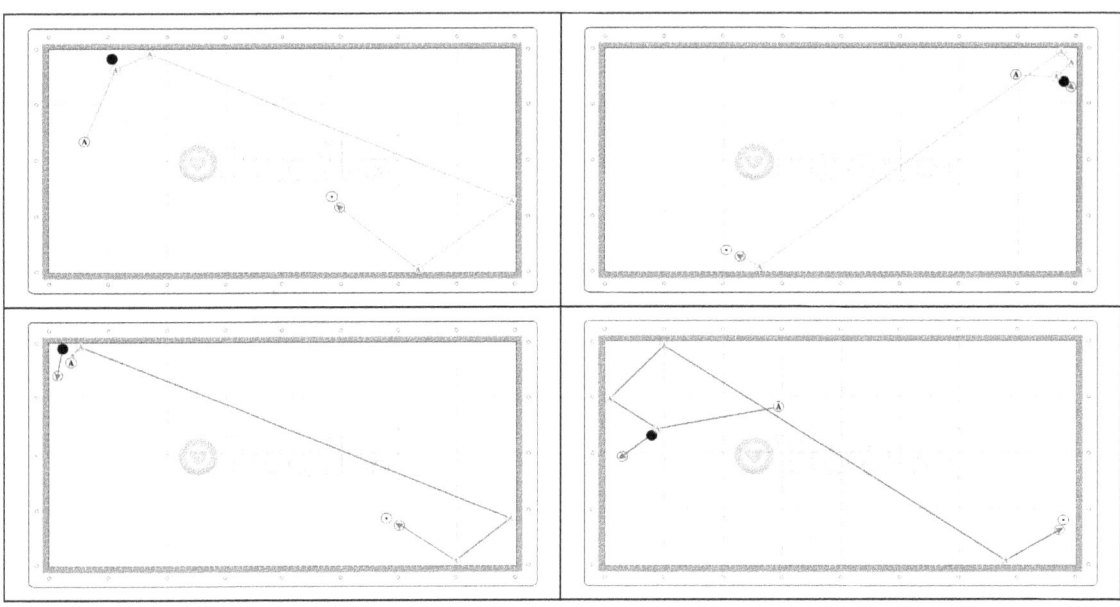

Analysis:

A:4a. _____

A:4b. _____

A:4c. _____

A:4d. _____

A:4a – Setup

Shot Pattern

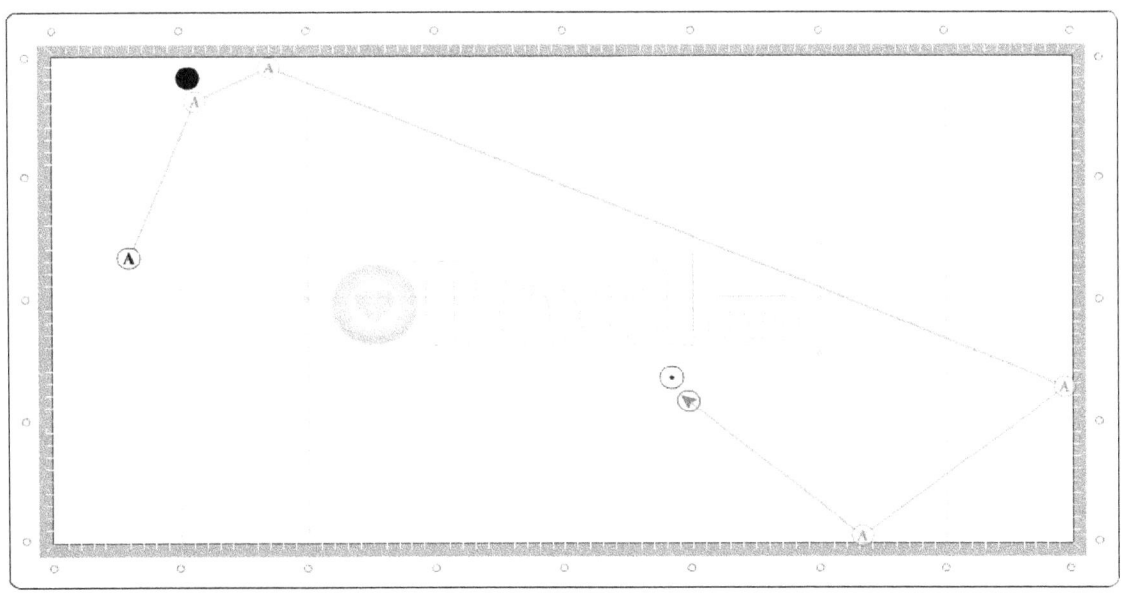

A:4b – Setup

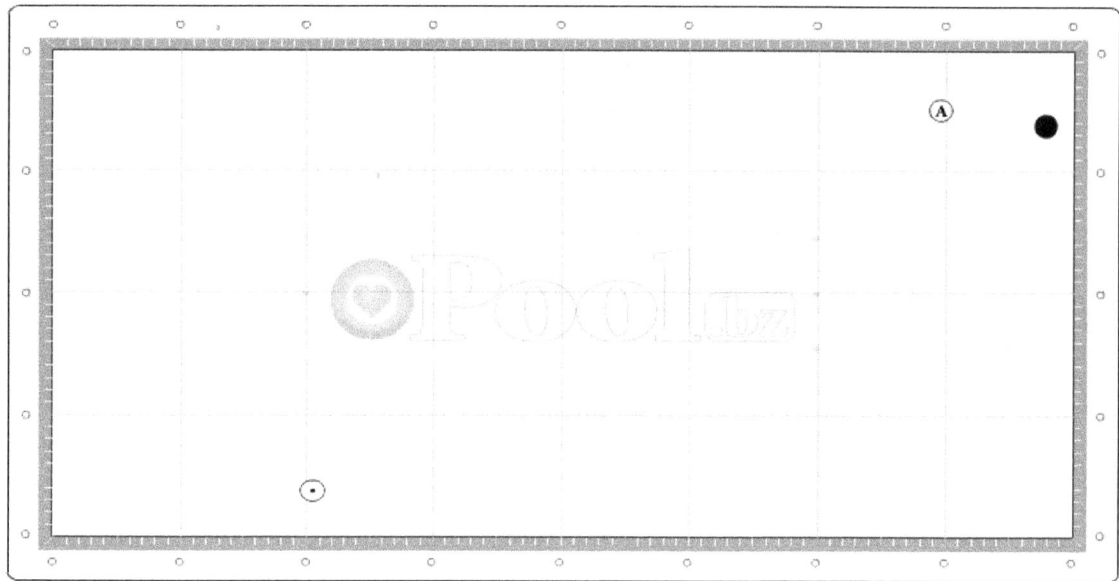

Shot Pattern

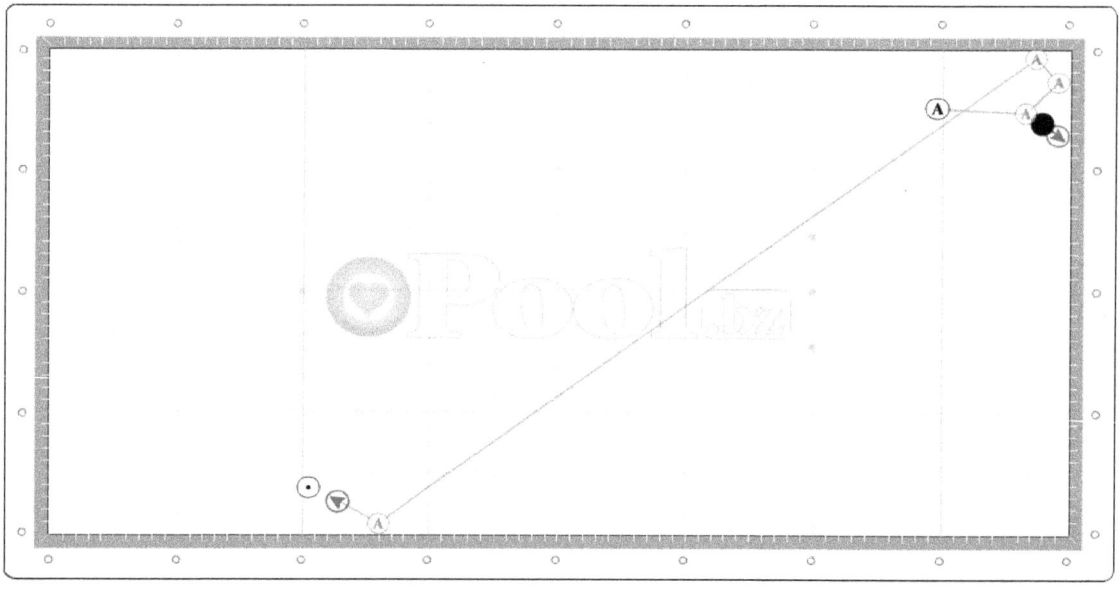

A:4c – Setup

Shot Pattern

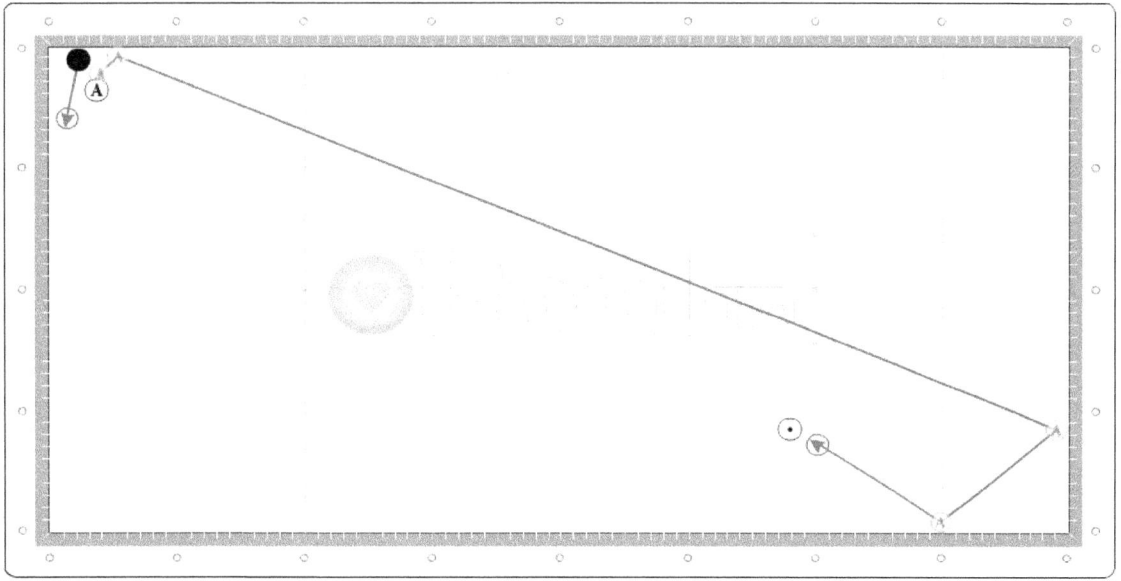

A:4d – Setup

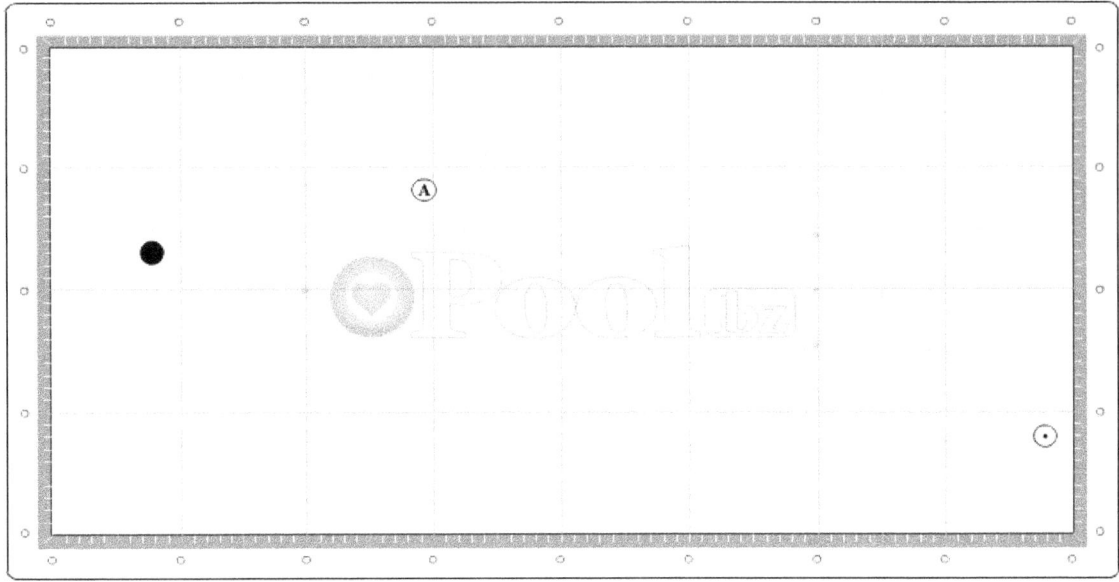

Shot Pattern

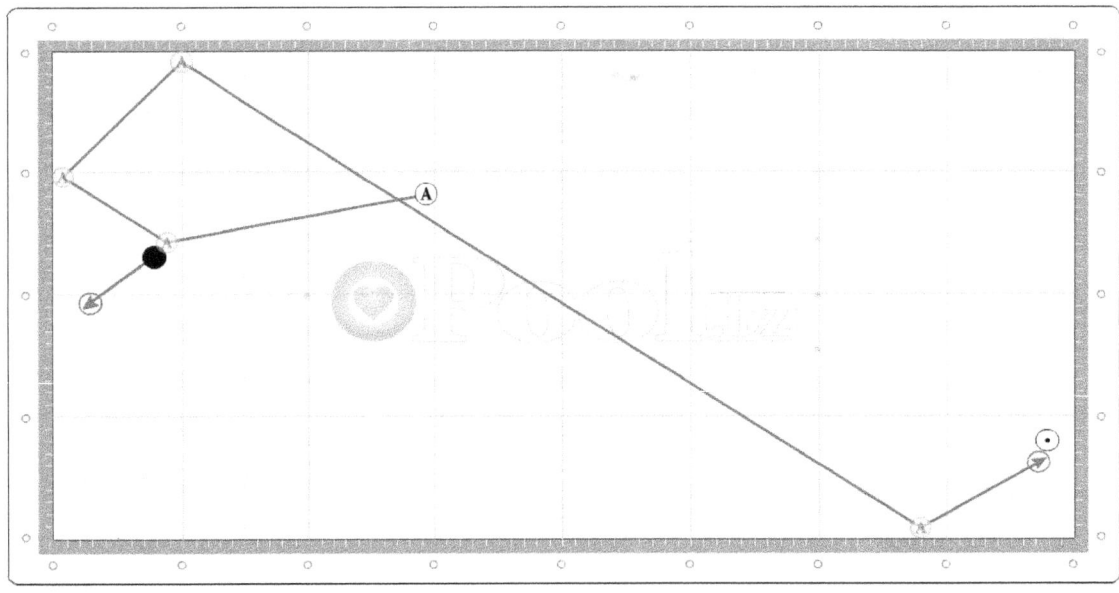

A: Group 5

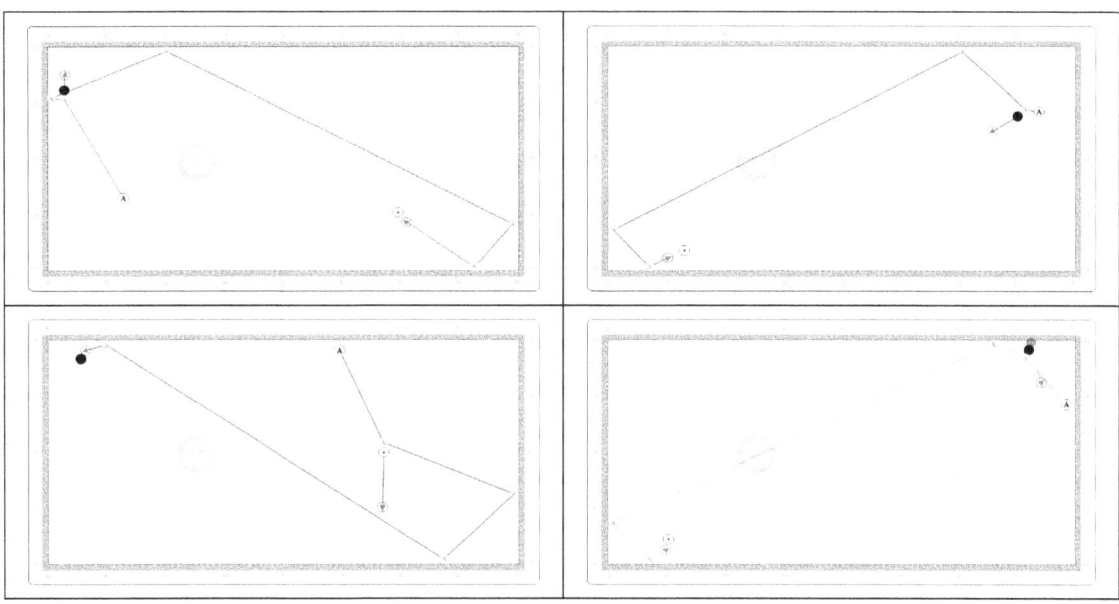

Analysis:

A:5a. _____

A:5b. _____

A:5c. _____

A:5d. _____

A:5a – Setup

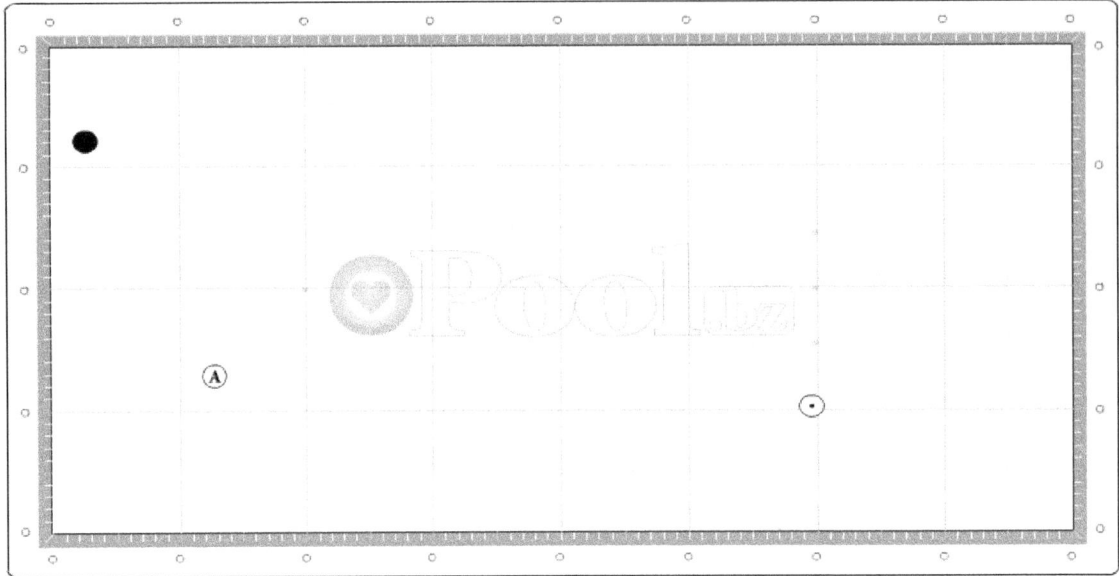

Shot Pattern

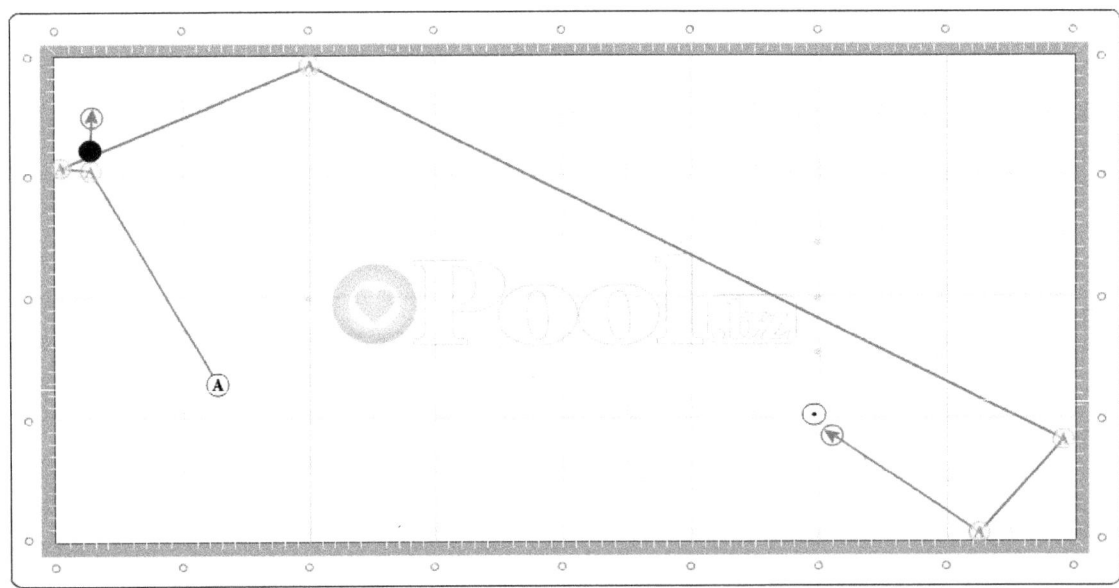

A:5b – Setup

Shot Pattern

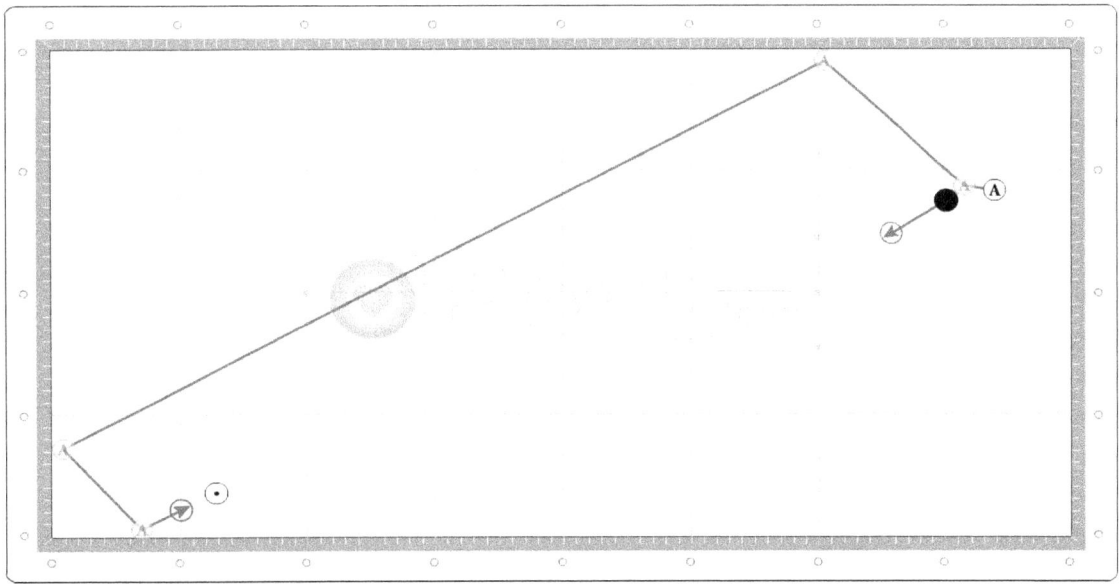

A:5c – Setup

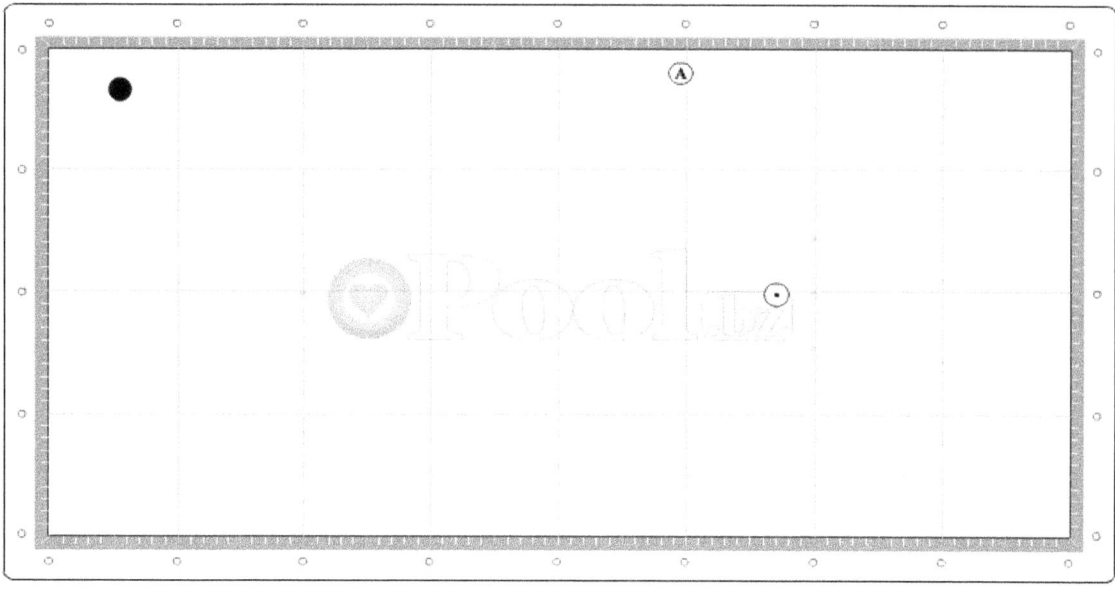

Shot Pattern

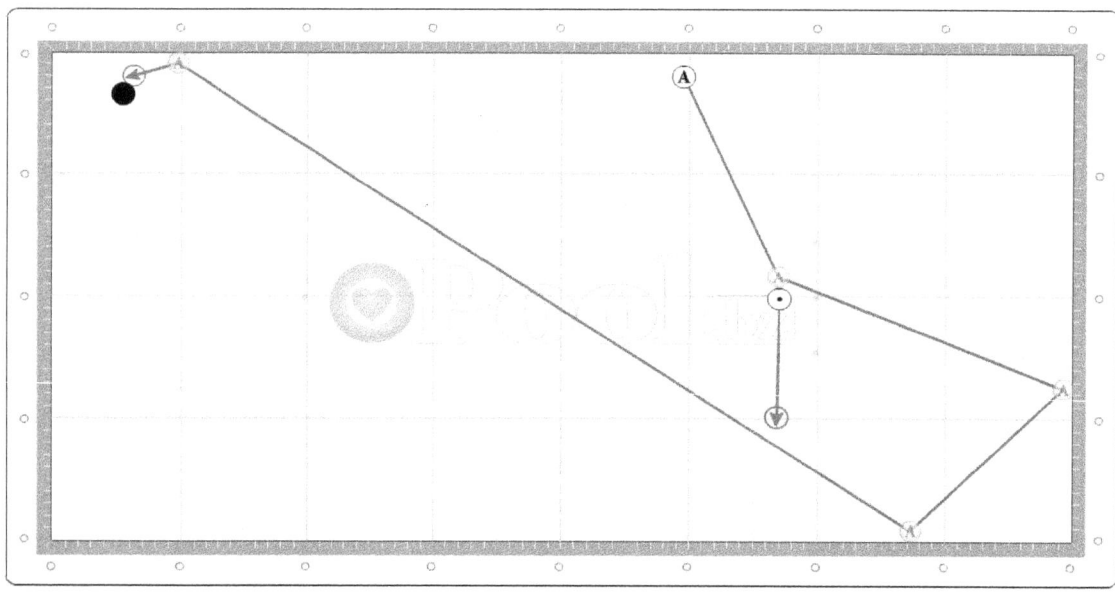

A:5d – Setup

Shot Pattern

A: Group 6

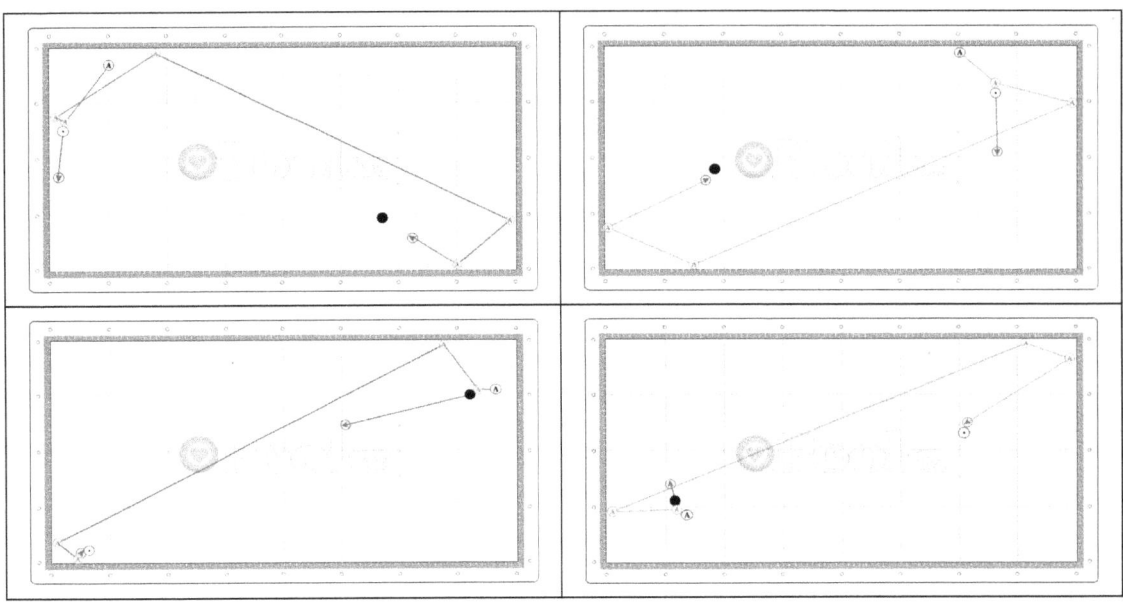

Analysis:

A:6a. _____

A:6b. _____

A:6c. _____

A:6d. _____

A:6a – Setup

Shot Pattern

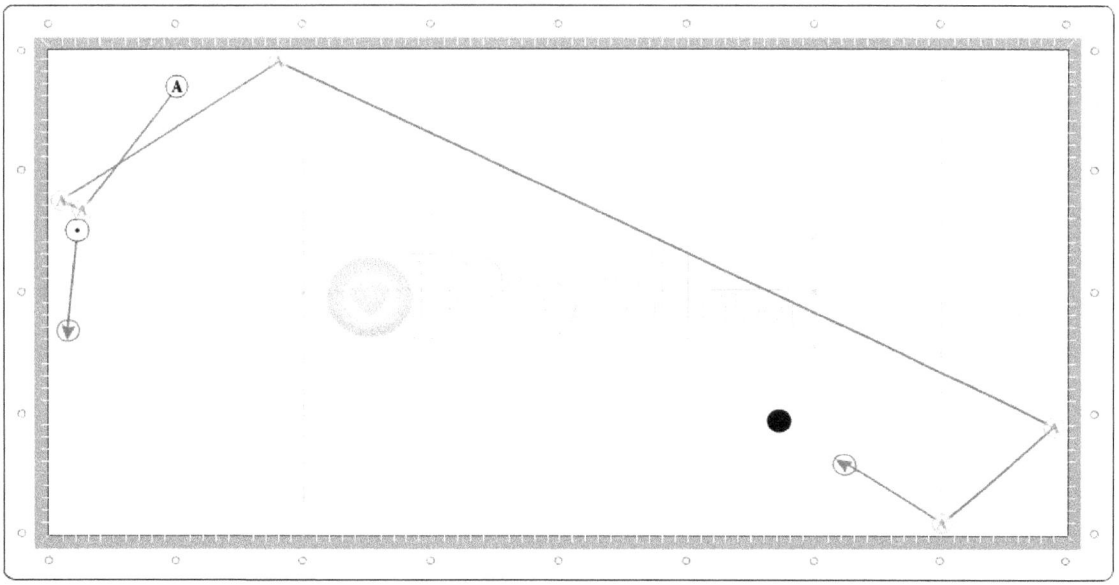

A:6b – Setup

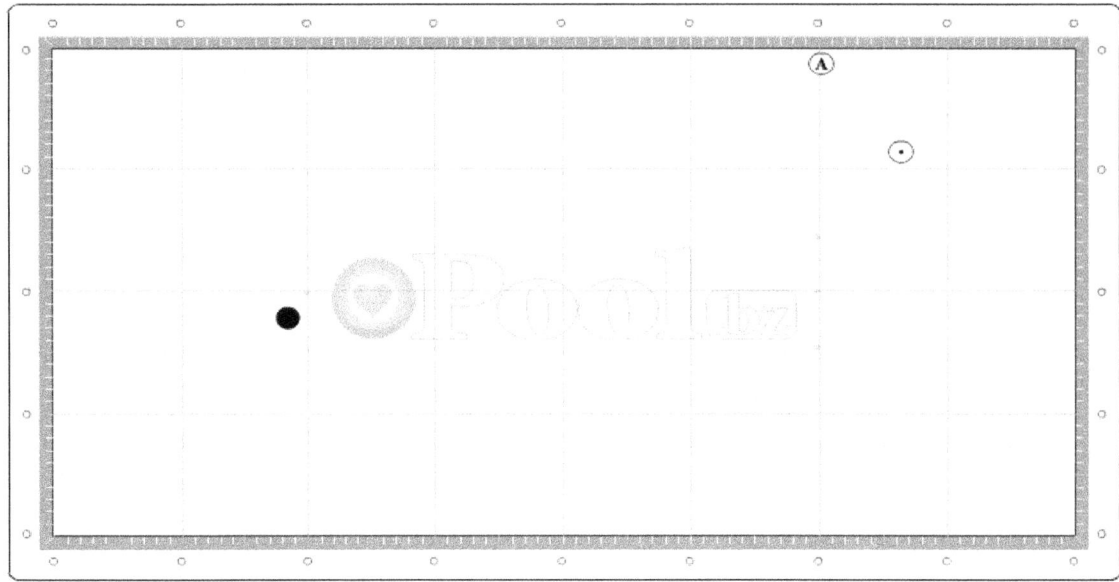

Shot Pattern

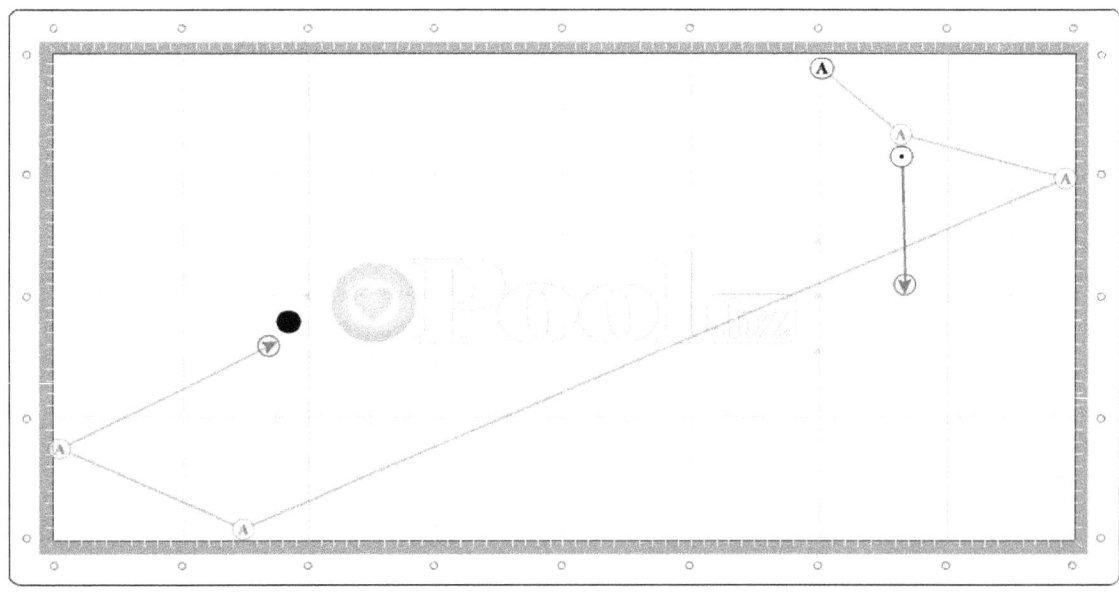

A:6c – Setup

Shot Pattern

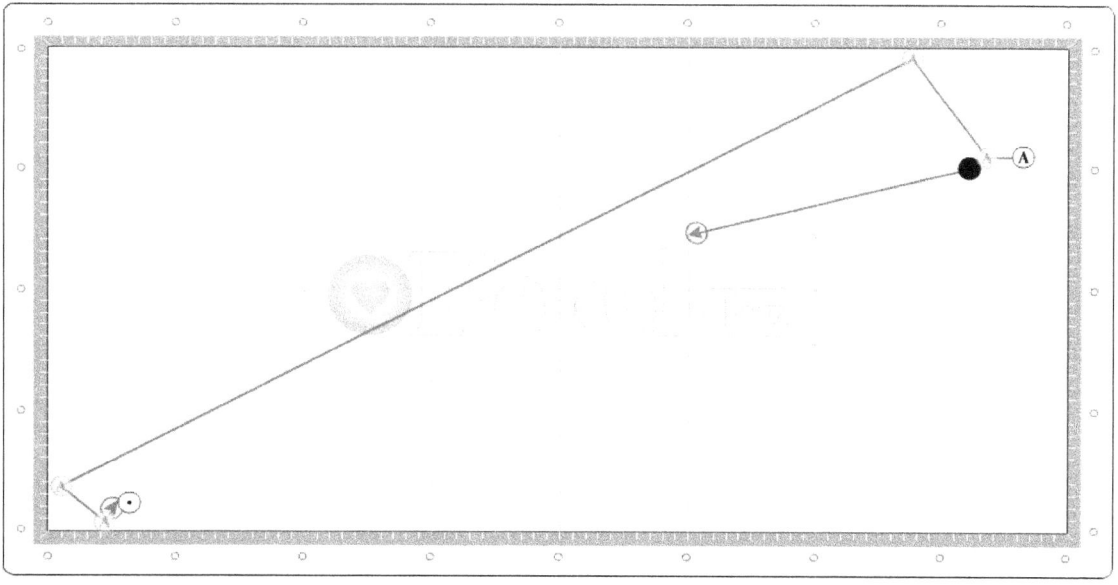

A:6d – Setup

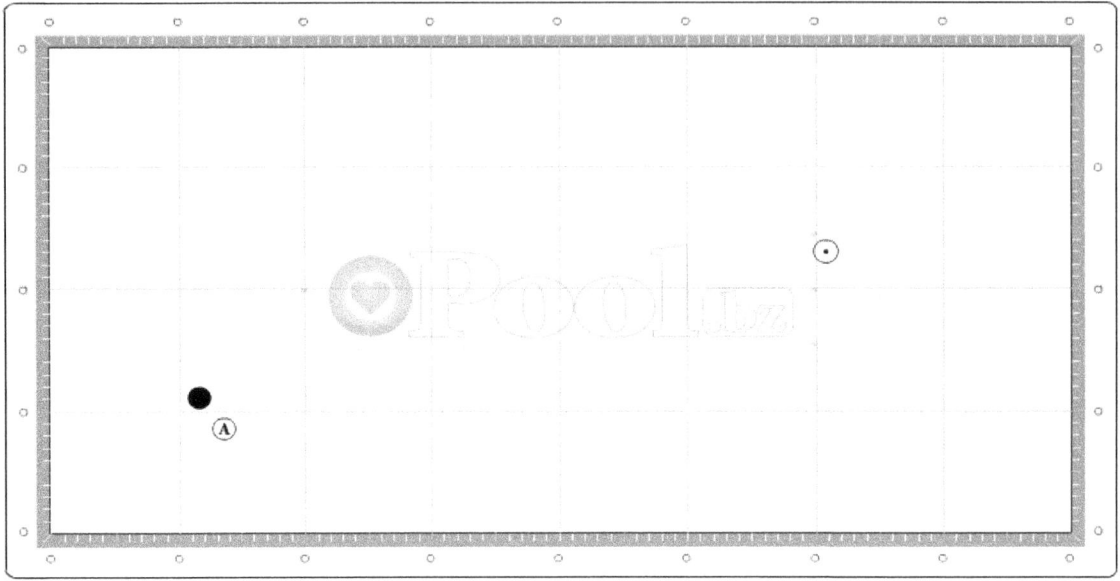

Shot Pattern

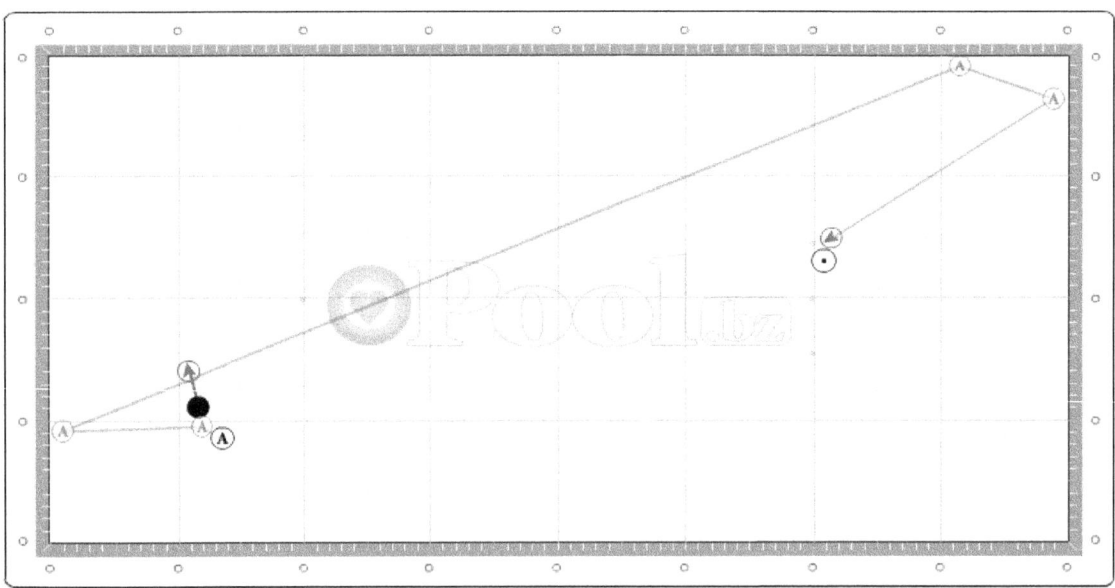

B: Simple Modified Diagonals

These corner to corner shots are slightly modified from the basic cross corner pattern. The shot requires a return hook to make point.

B: Group 1

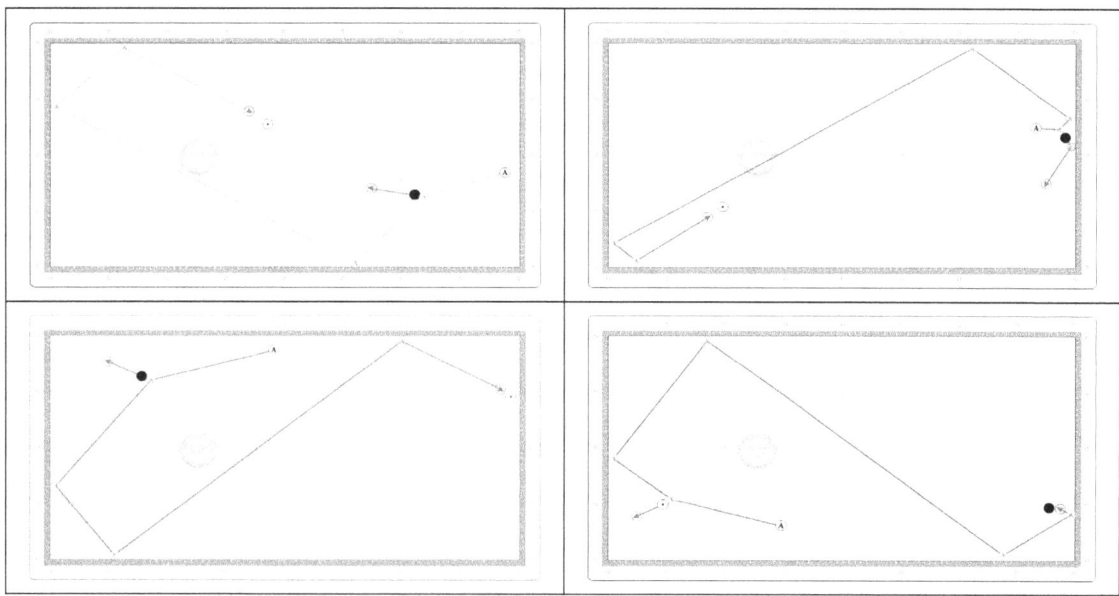

Analysis:

B:1a. _____

B:1b. _____

B:1c. _____

B:1d. _____

B:1a – Setup

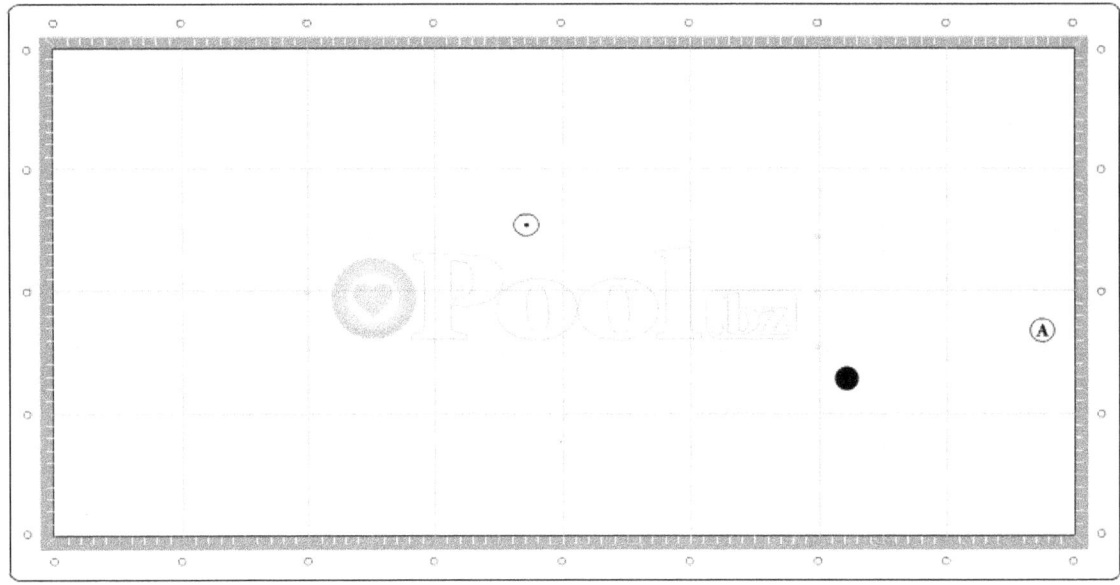

Shot Pattern

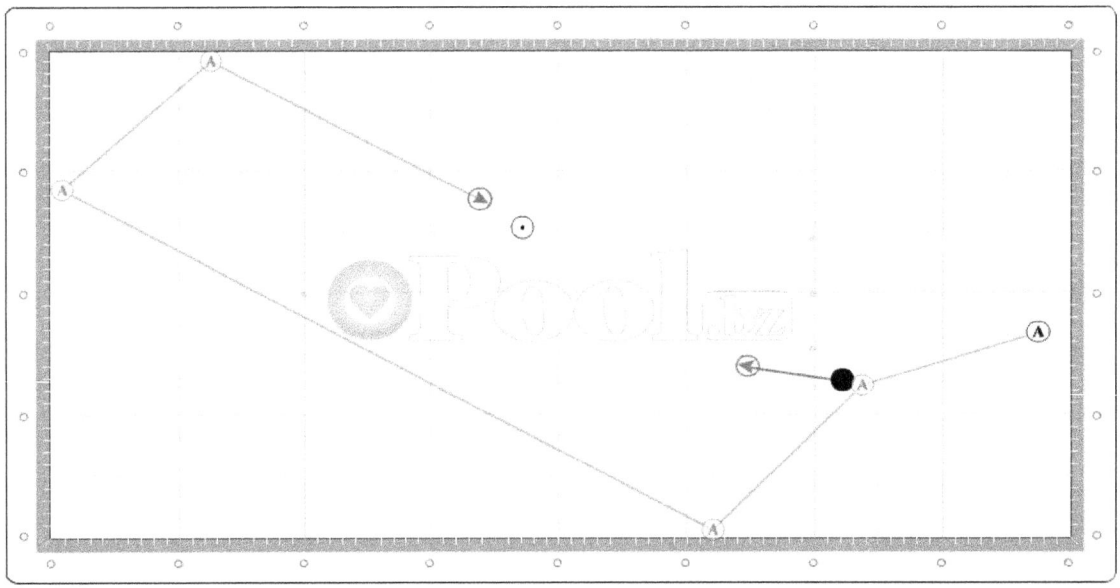

B:1b – Setup

Shot Pattern

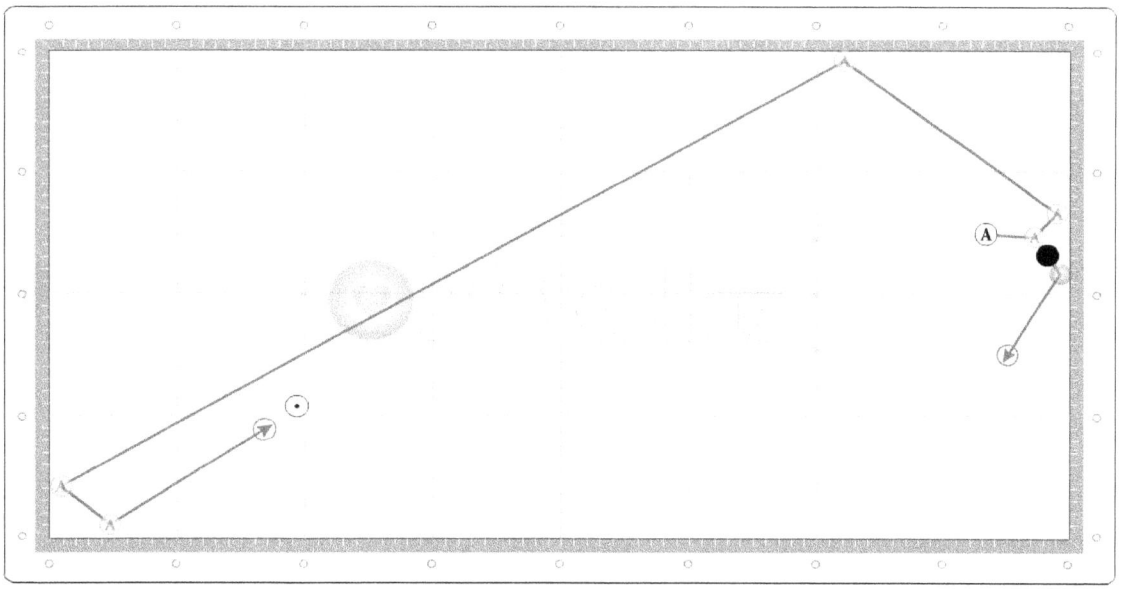

B:1c – Setup

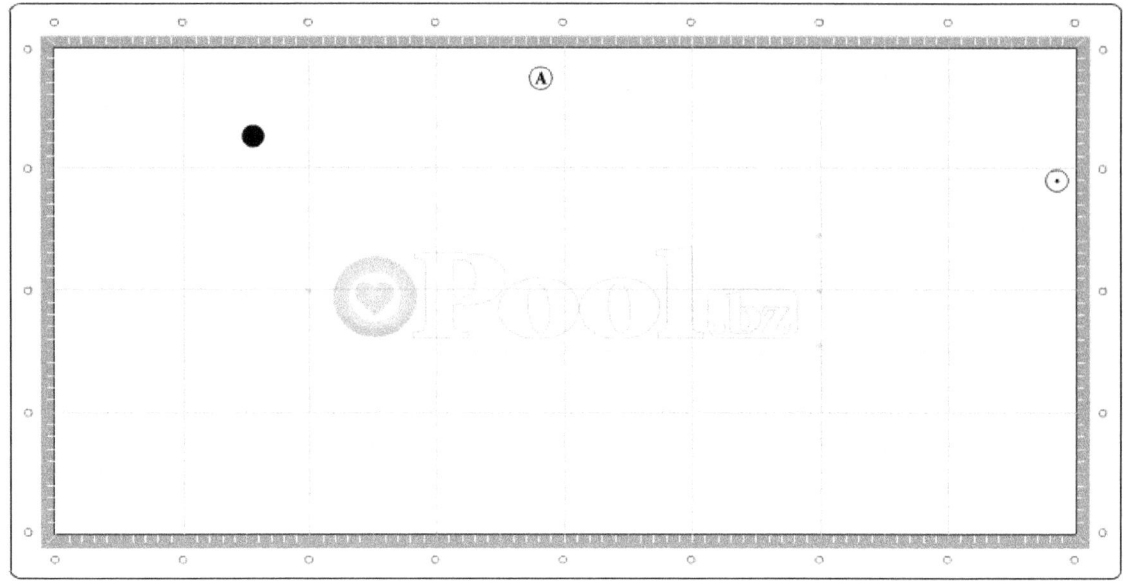

Shot Pattern

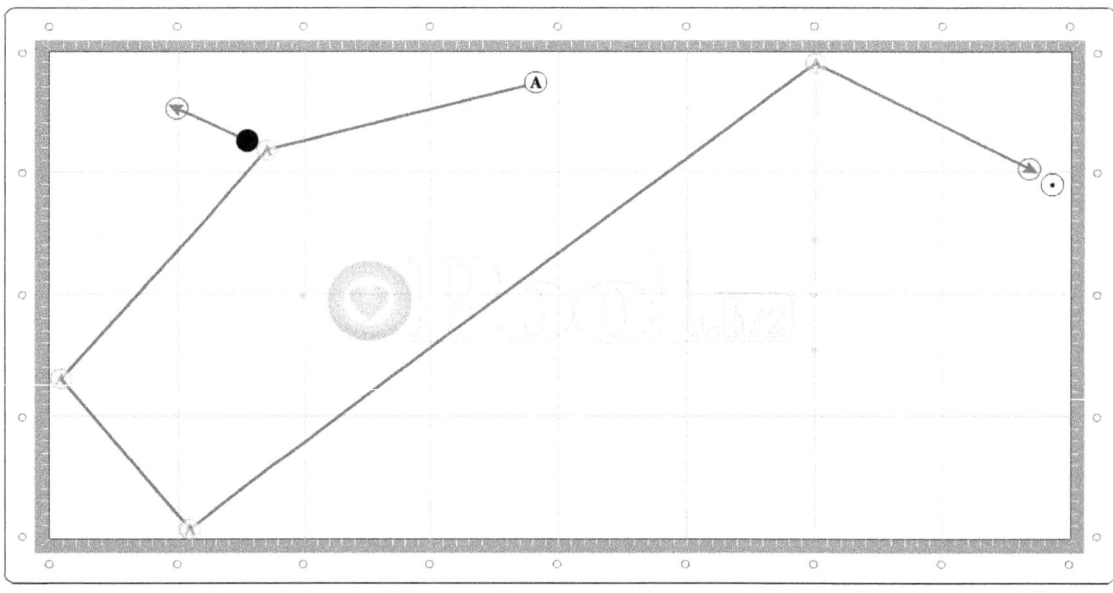

B:1d – Setup

Shot Pattern

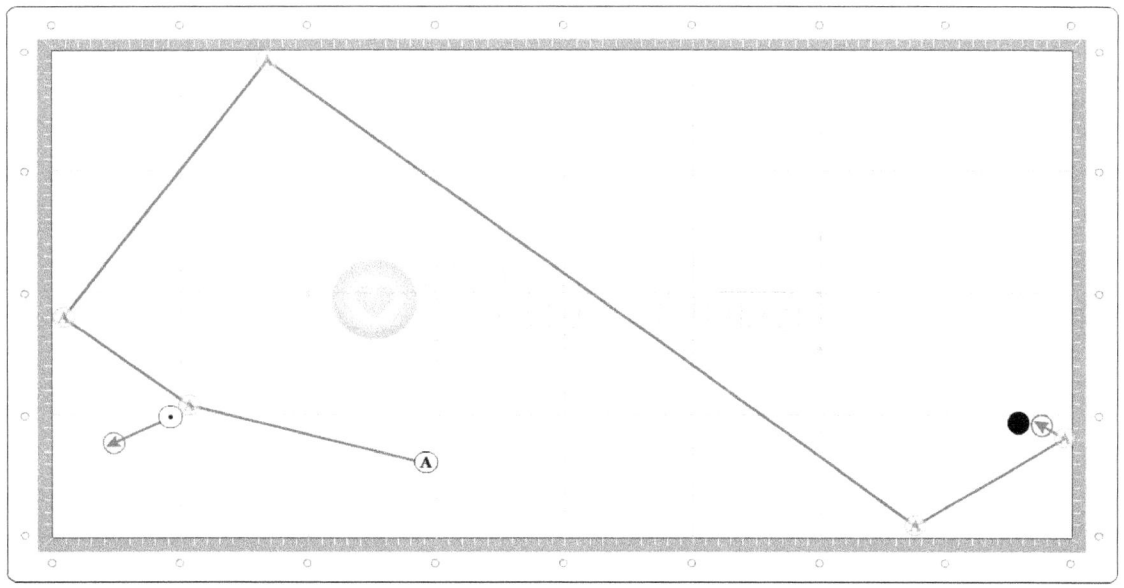

B: Group 2

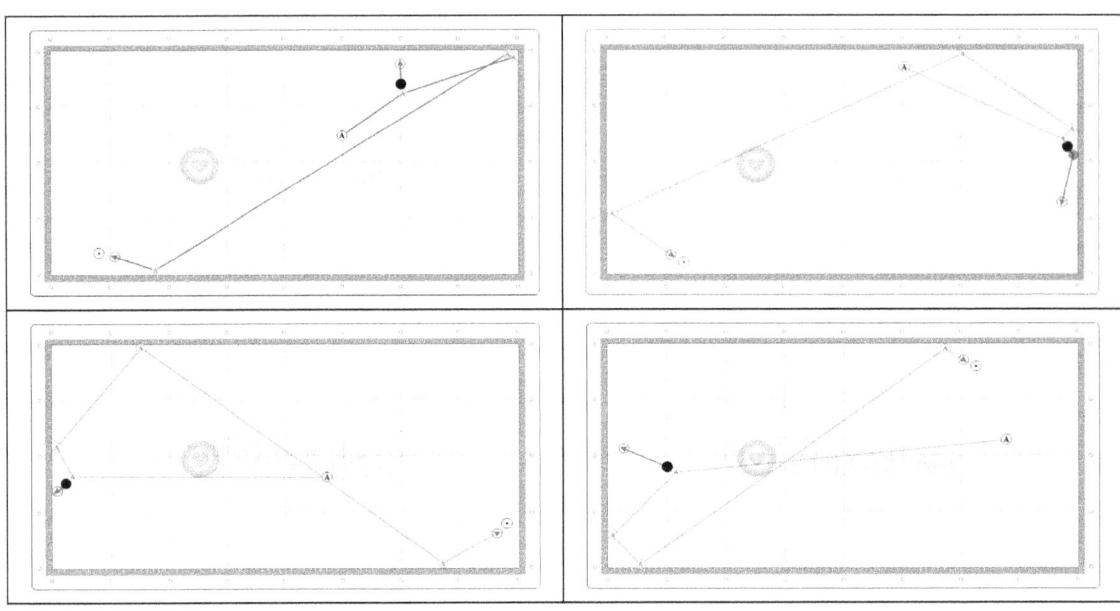

Analysis:

B:2a. _____

B:2b. _____

B:2c. _____

B:2d. _____

B:2a – Setup

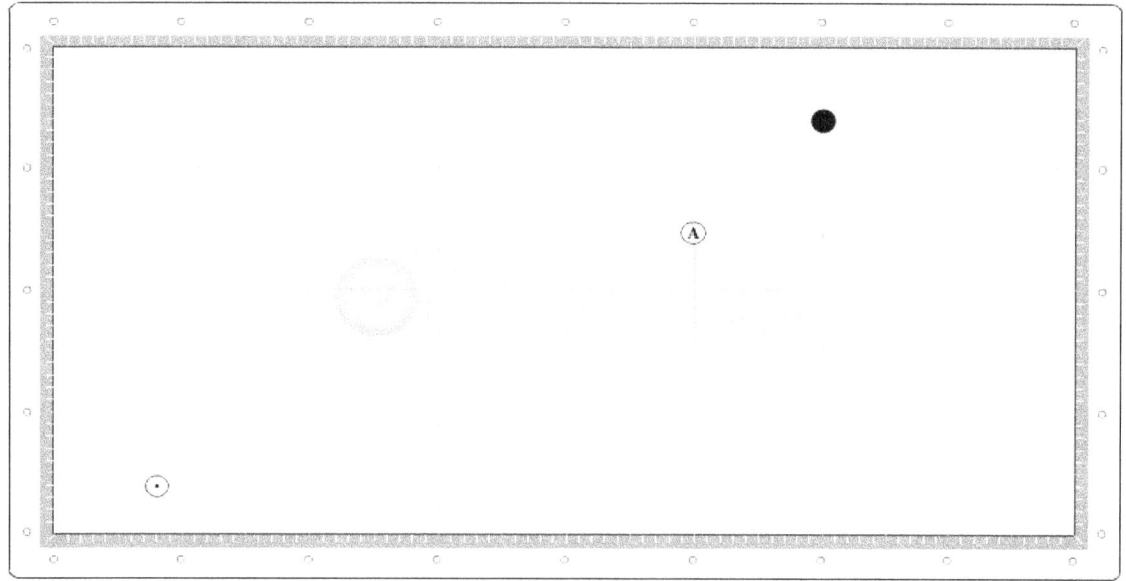

Shot Pattern

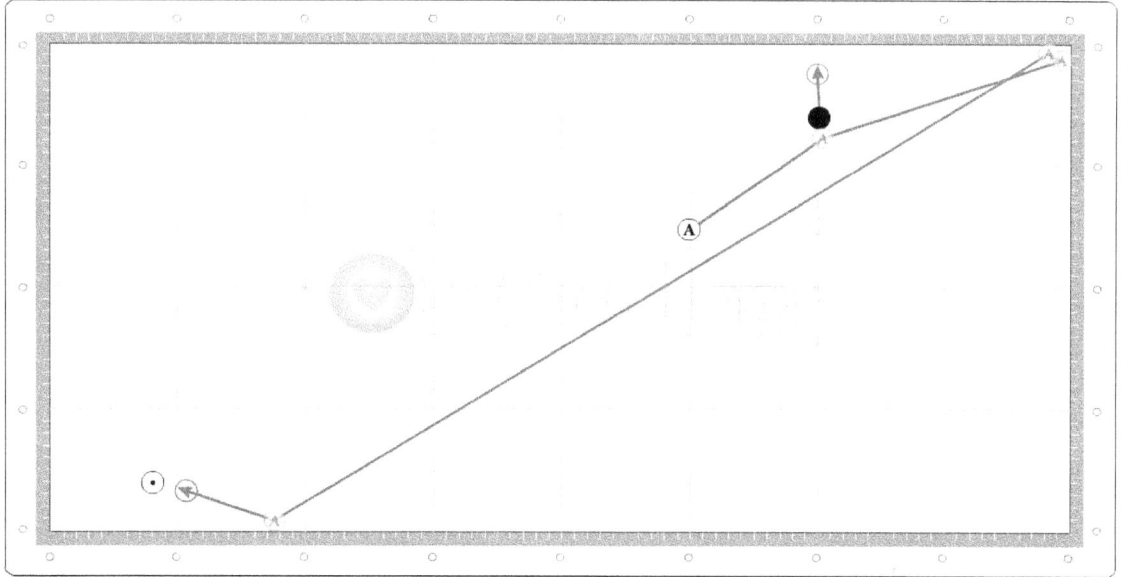

B:2b – Setup

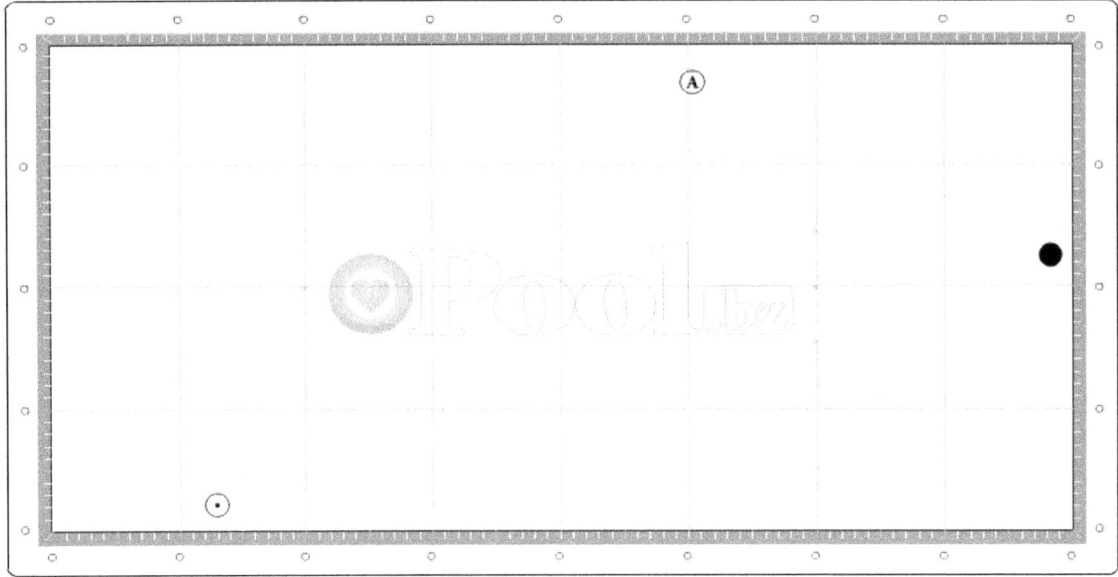

Shot Pattern

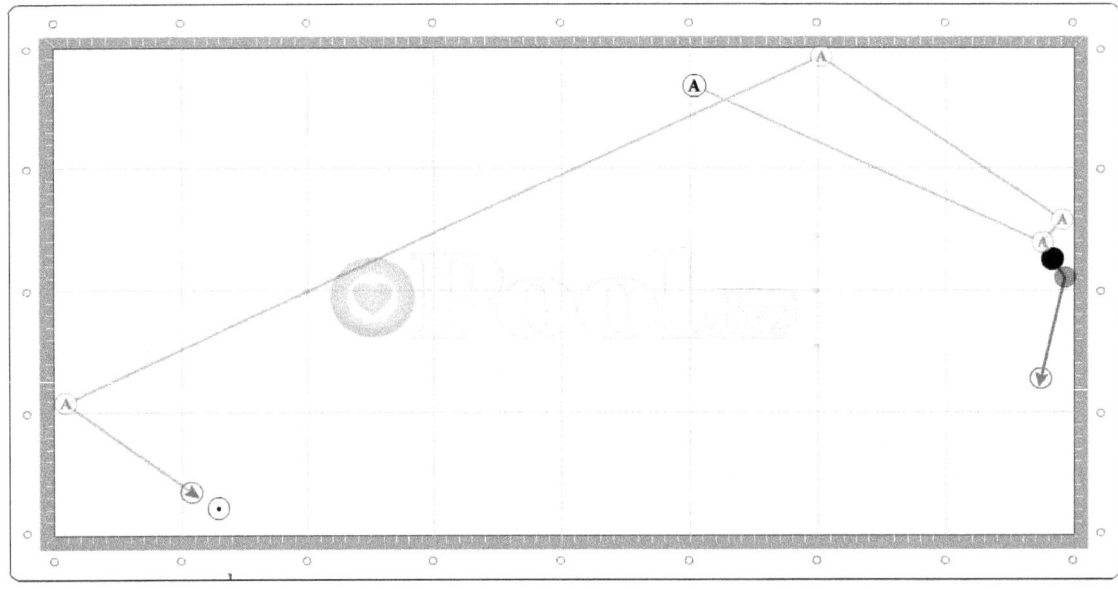

B:2c – Setup

Shot Pattern

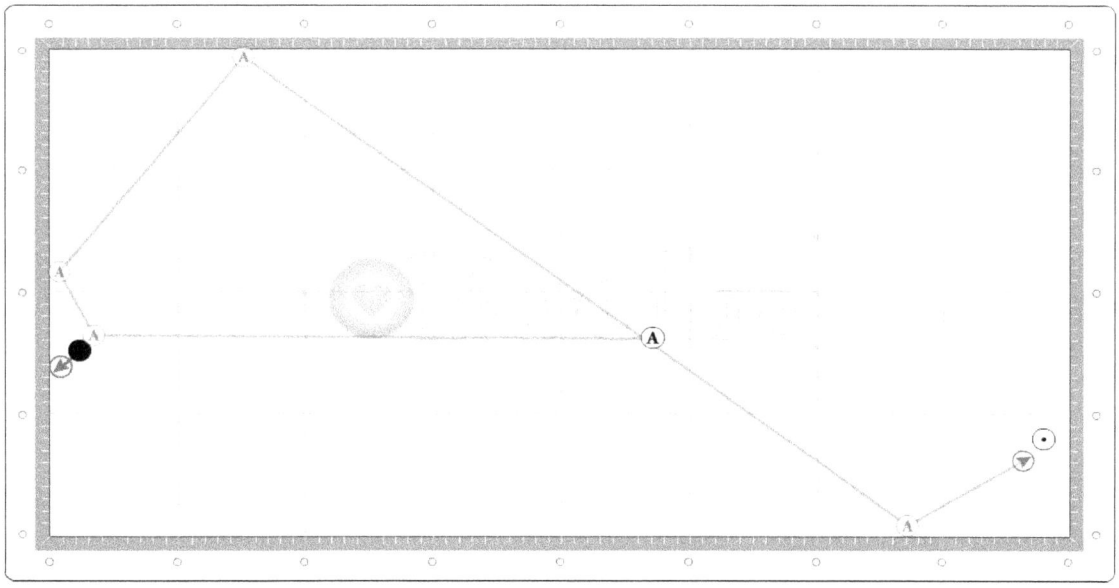

B:2d – Setup

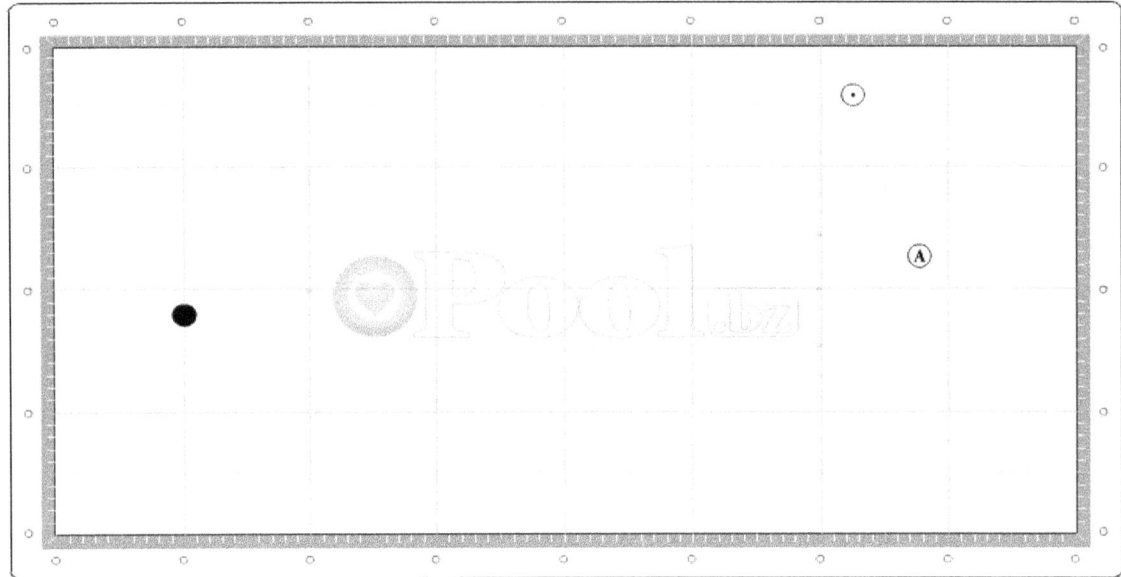

Shot Pattern

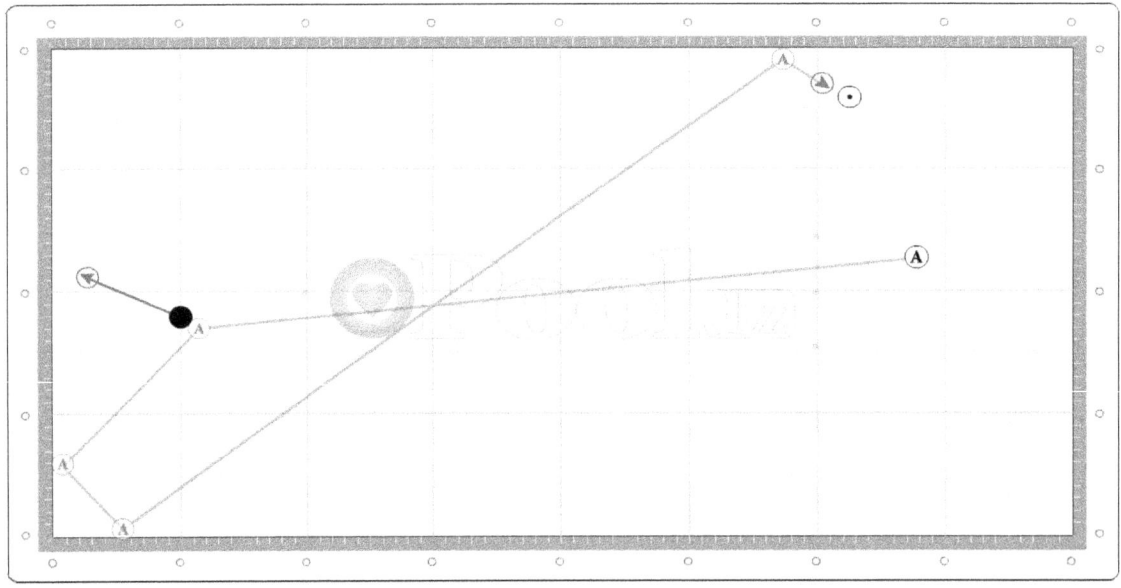

B: Group 3

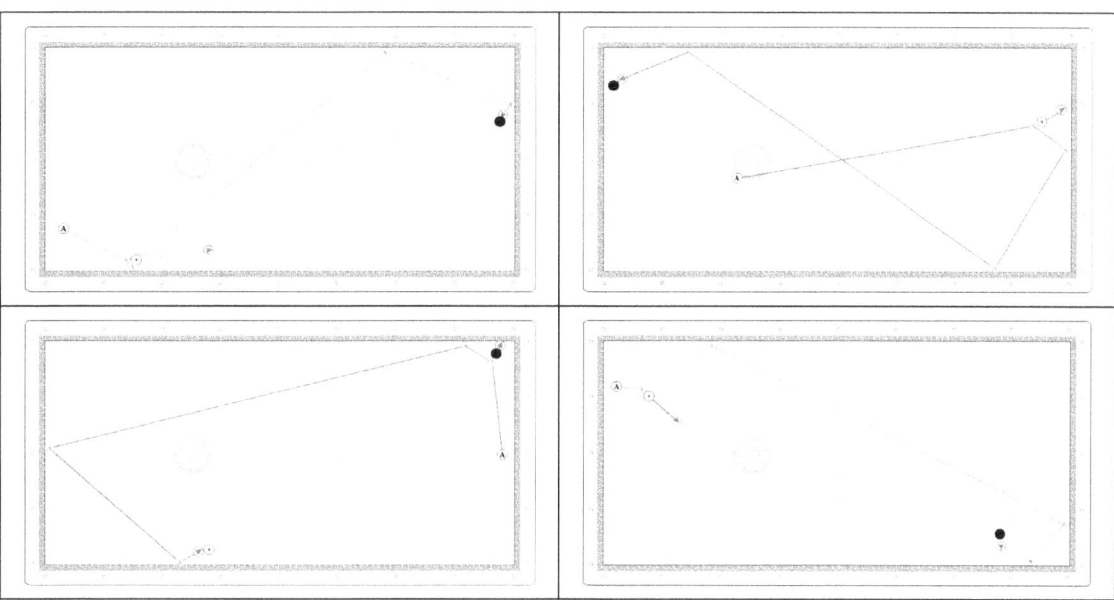

Analysis:

B:3a. _____

B:3b. _____

B:3c. _____

B:3d. _____

B:3a – Setup

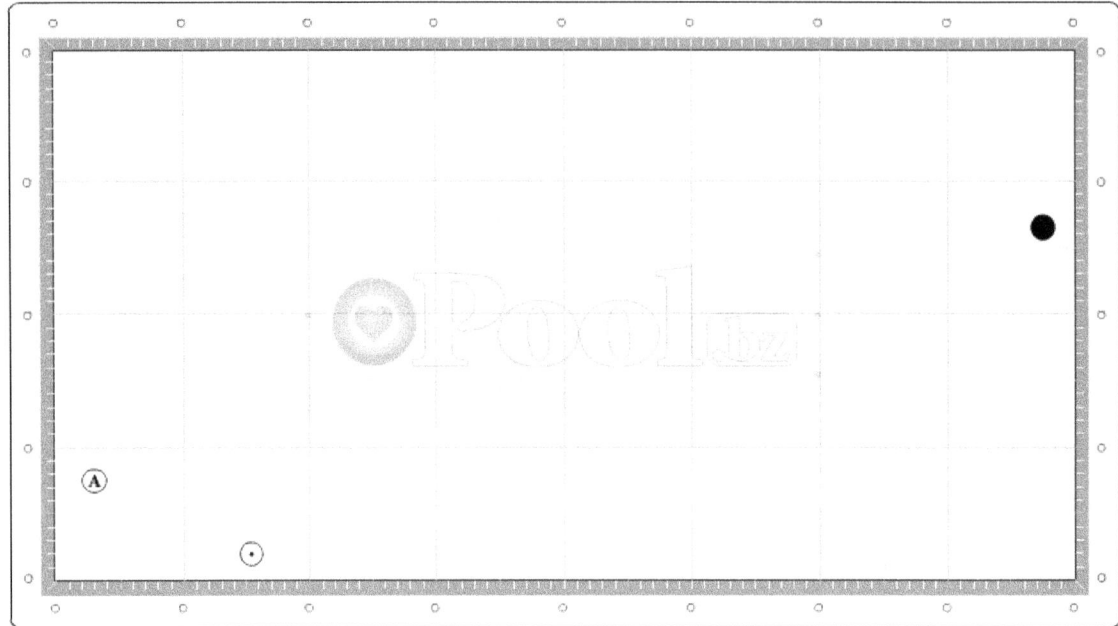

Shot Pattern

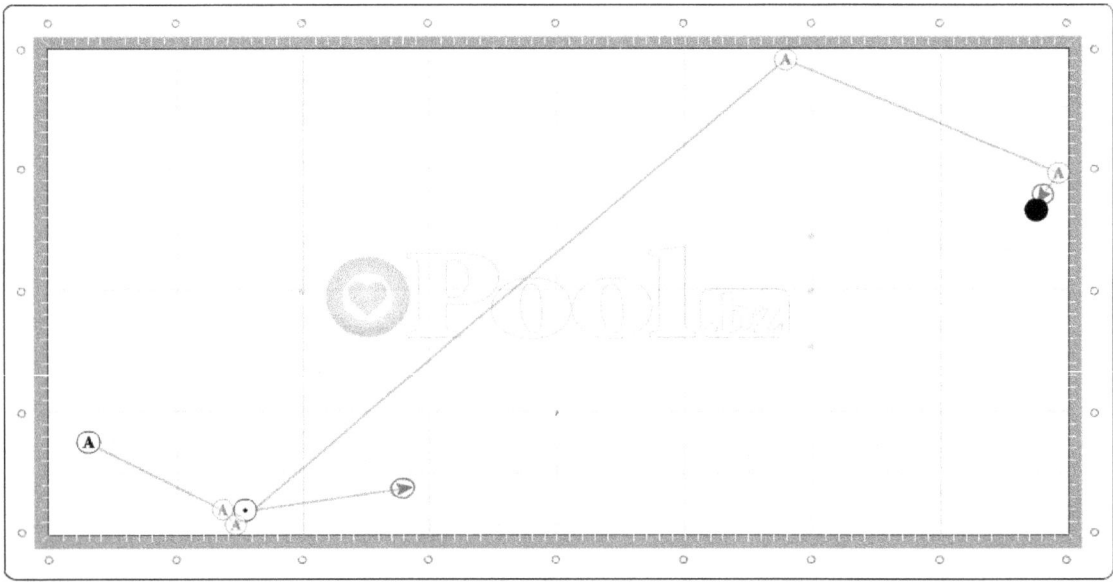

B:3b – Setup

Shot Pattern

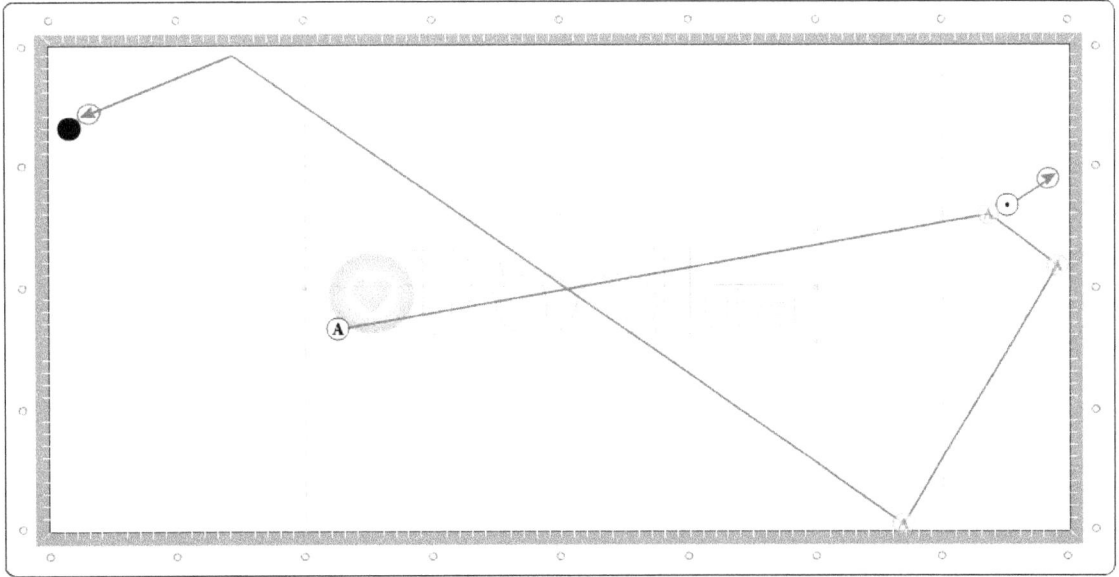

B:3c – Setup

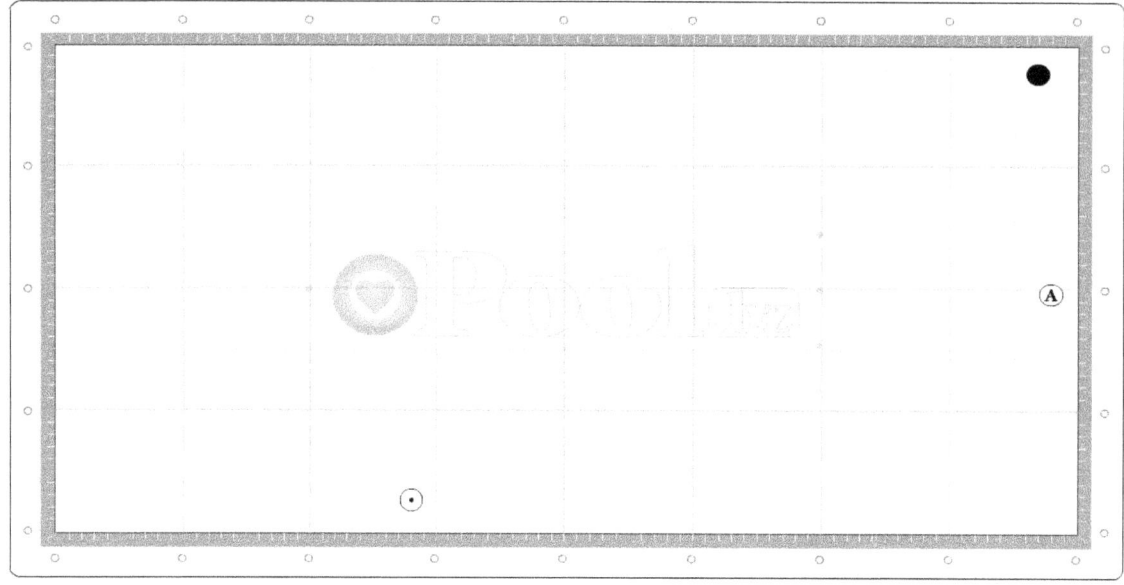

Shot Pattern

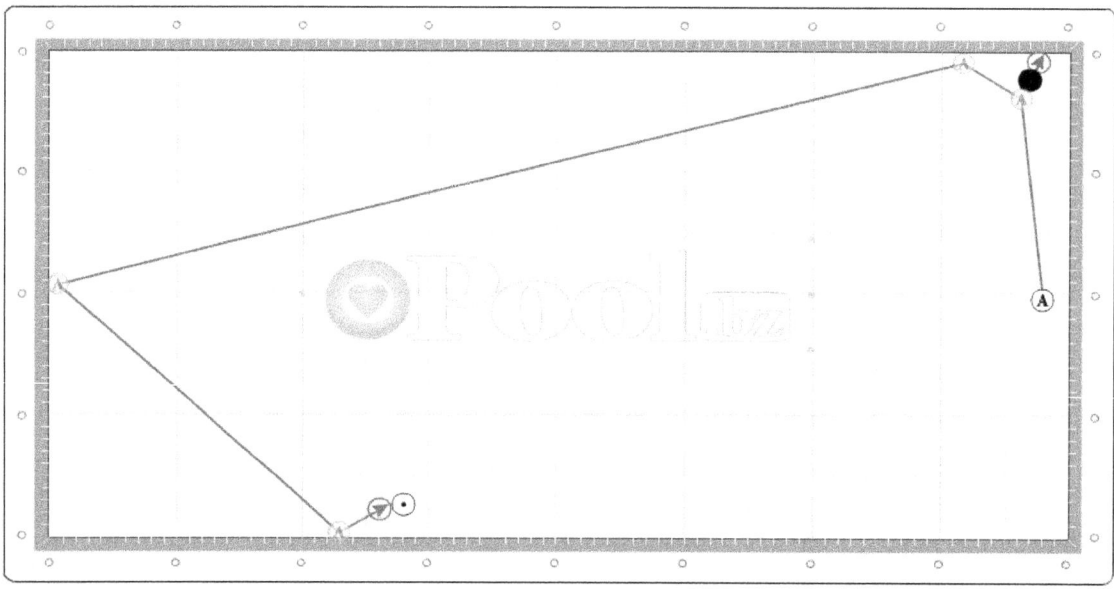

B:3d – Setup

Shot Pattern

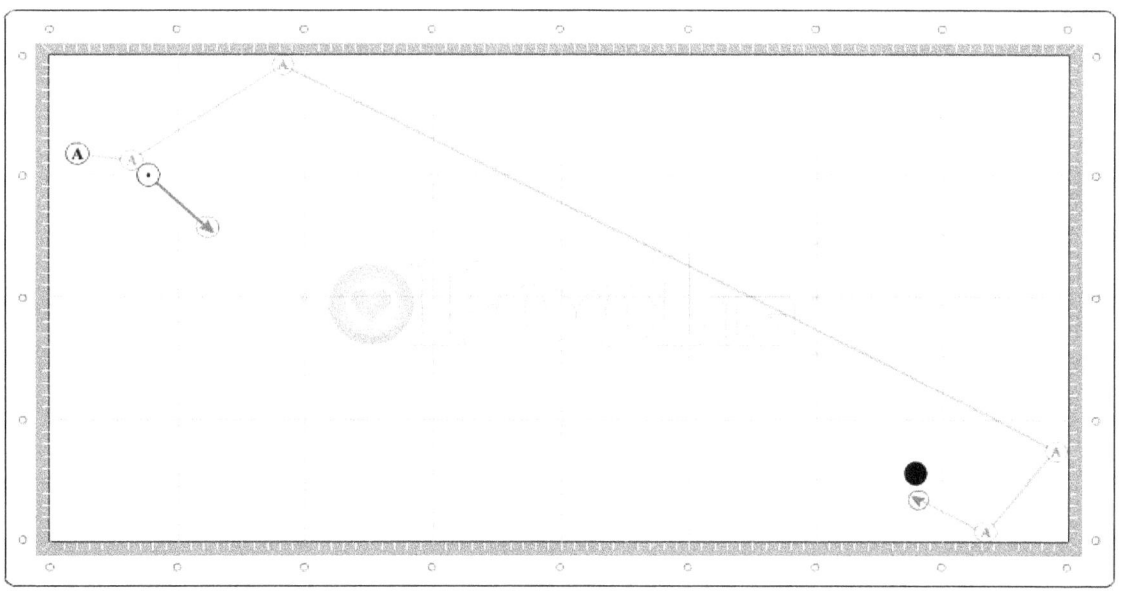

C: Parallel Diagonals

On these shots, the CB comes off the first OB and travels to the opposite cross corner and then comes back in a parallel path back to make contact with the second OB and a point.

C: Group 1

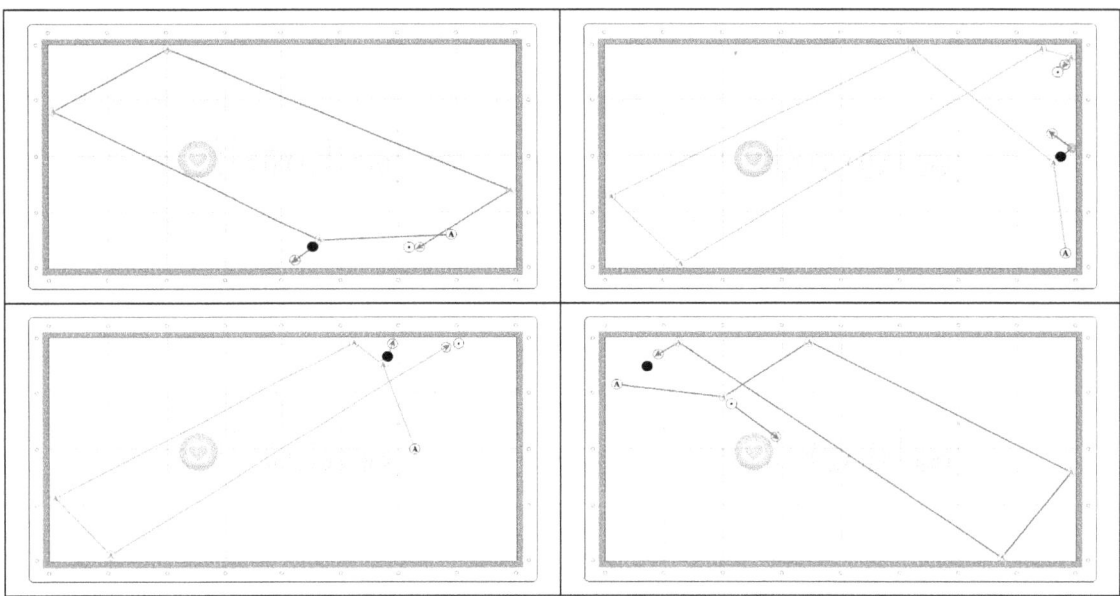

Analysis:

C:1a. _____

C:1b. _____

C:1c. _____

C:1d. _____

C:1a – Setup

Shot Pattern

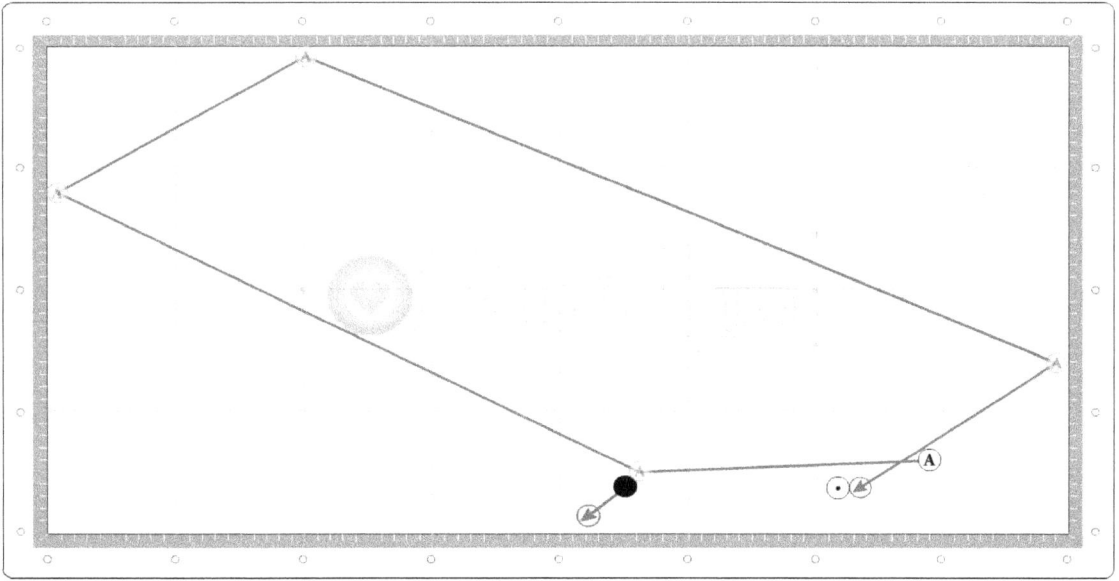

C:1b – Setup

Shot Pattern

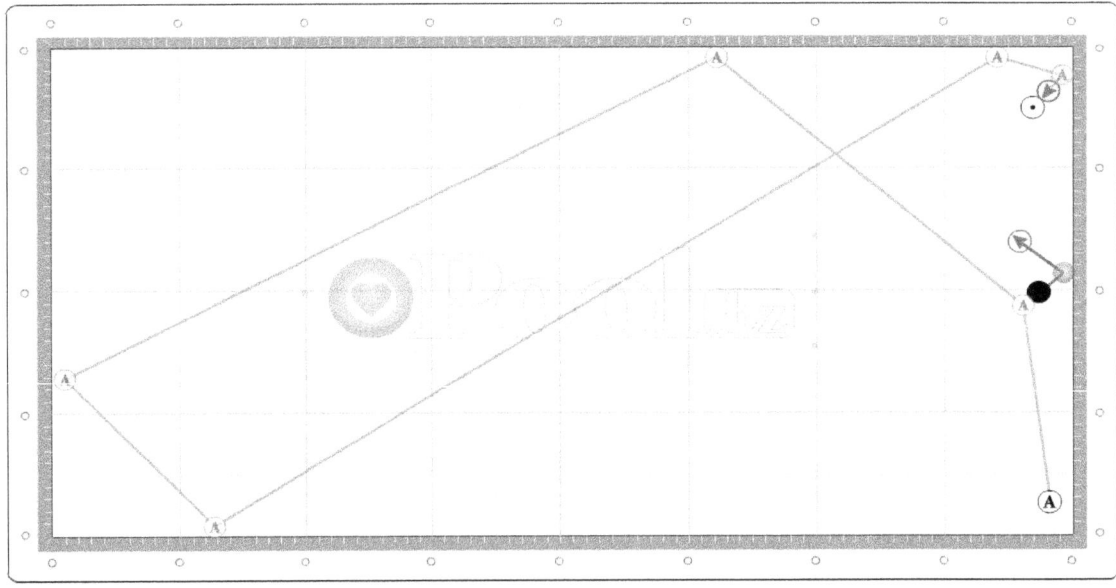

C:1c – Setup

Shot Pattern

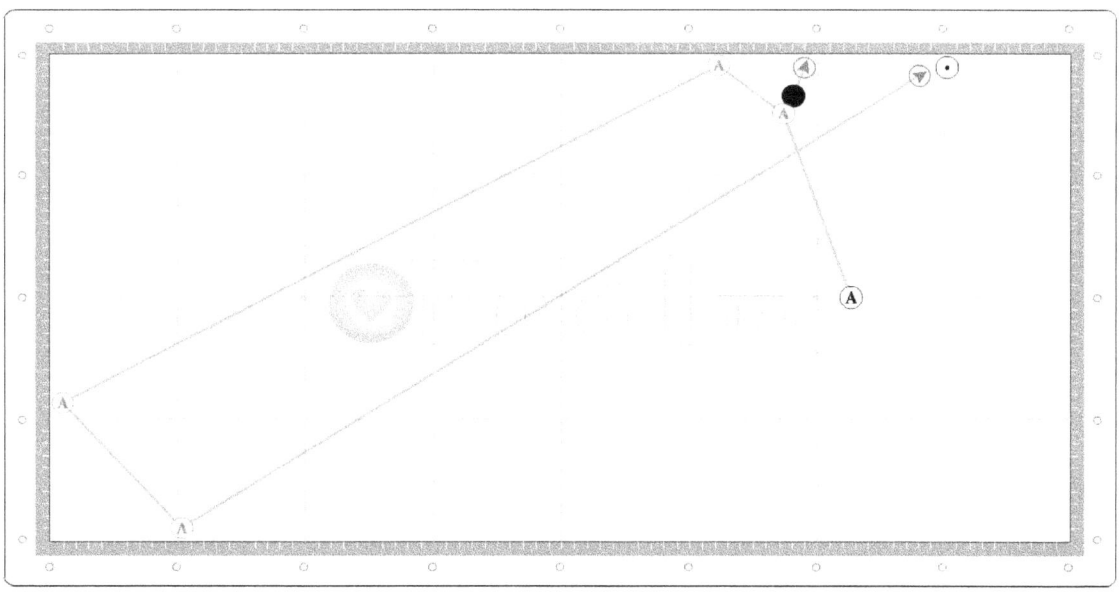

C:1d – Setup

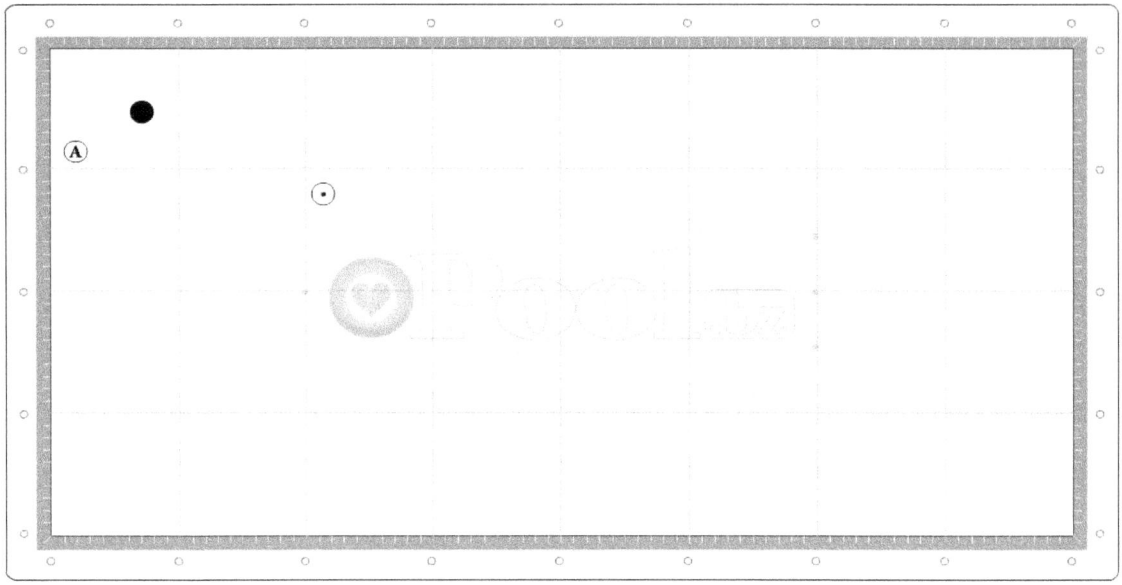

Shot Pattern

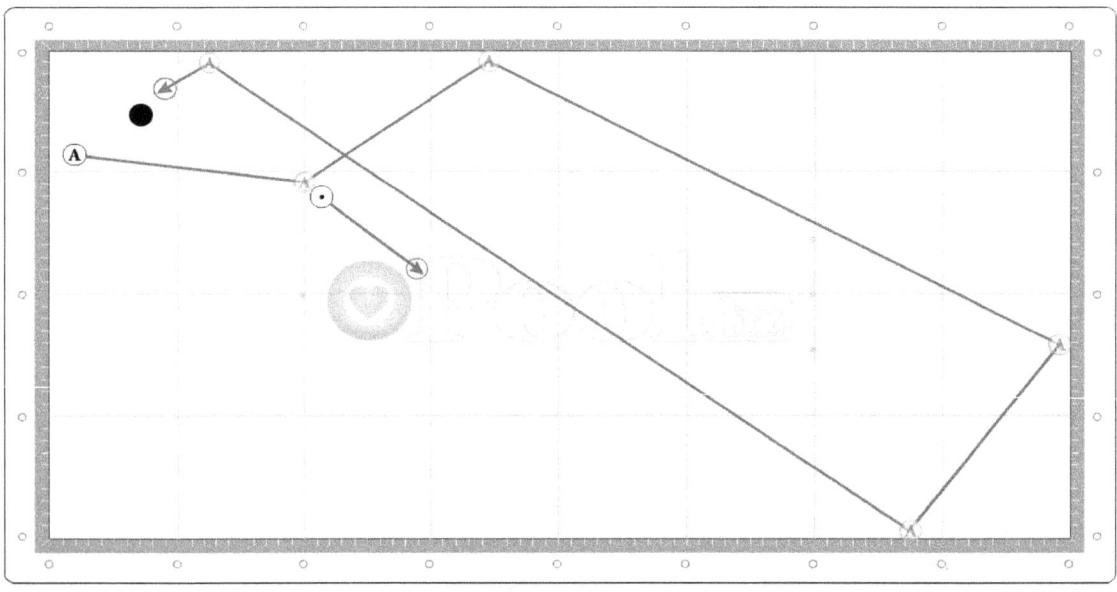

C: Group 2

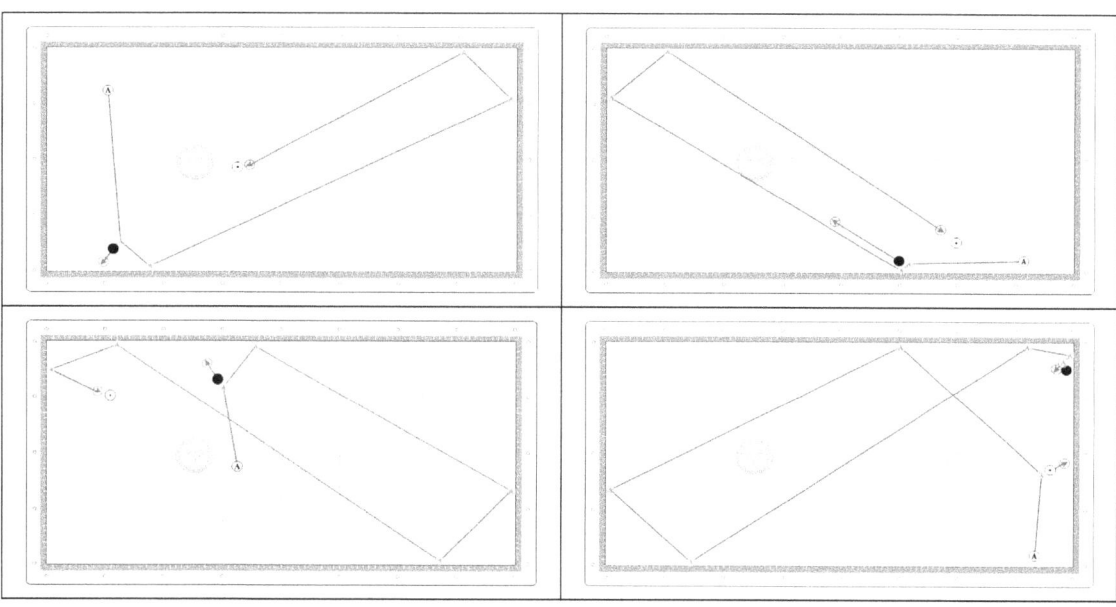

Analysis:

C:2a. _____

C:2b. _____

C:2c. _____

C:2d. _____

C:2a – Setup

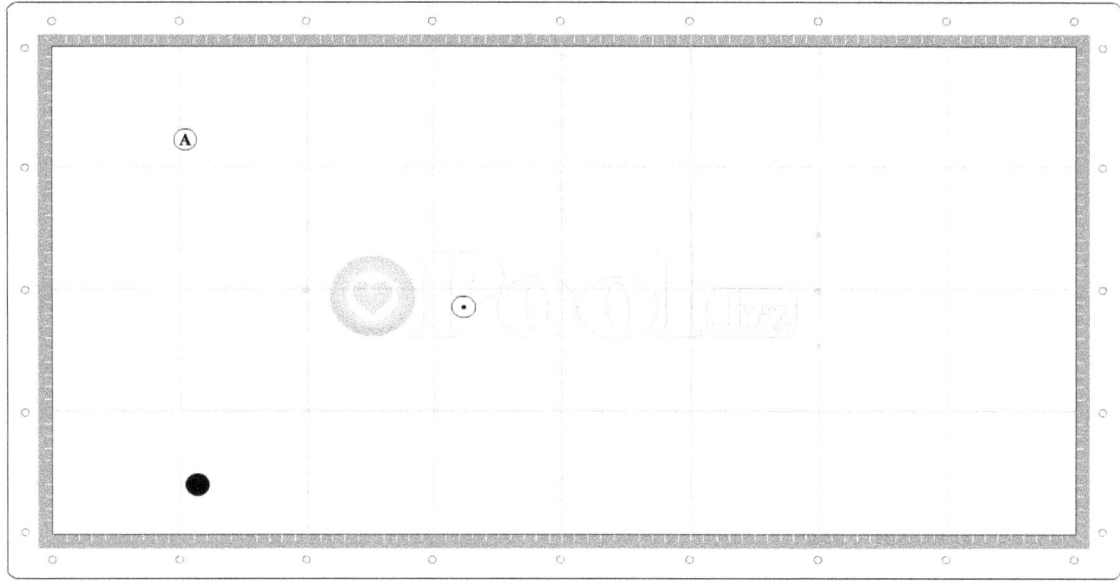

Shot Pattern

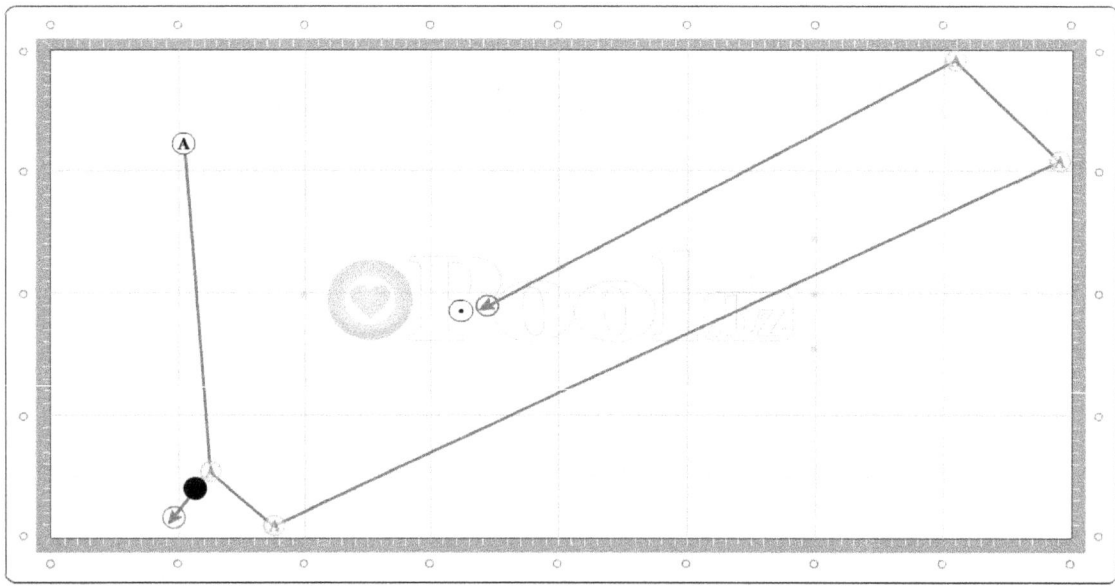

C:2b – Setup

Shot Pattern

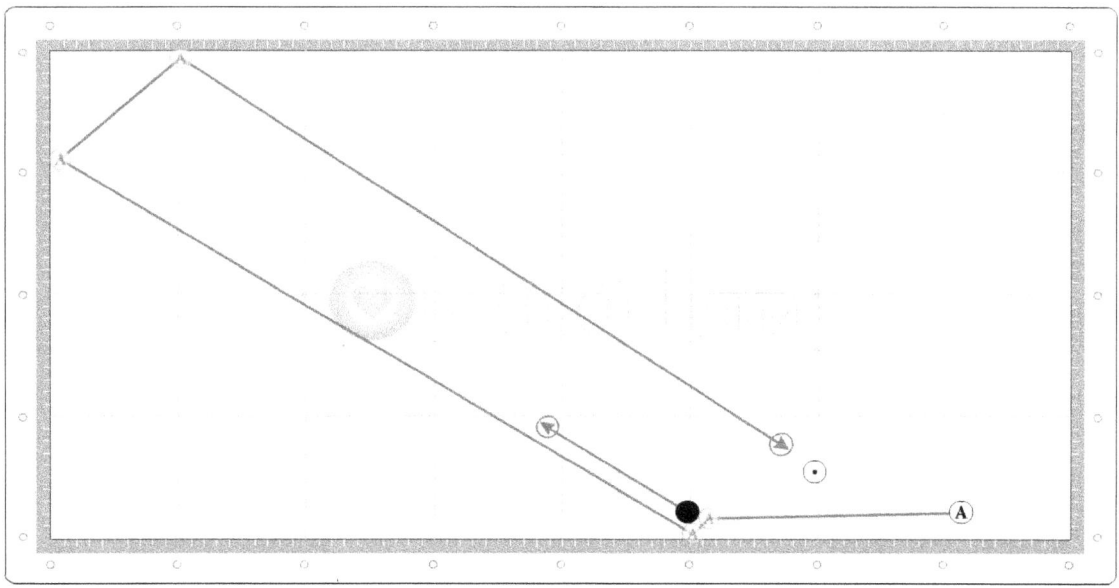

C:2c – Setup

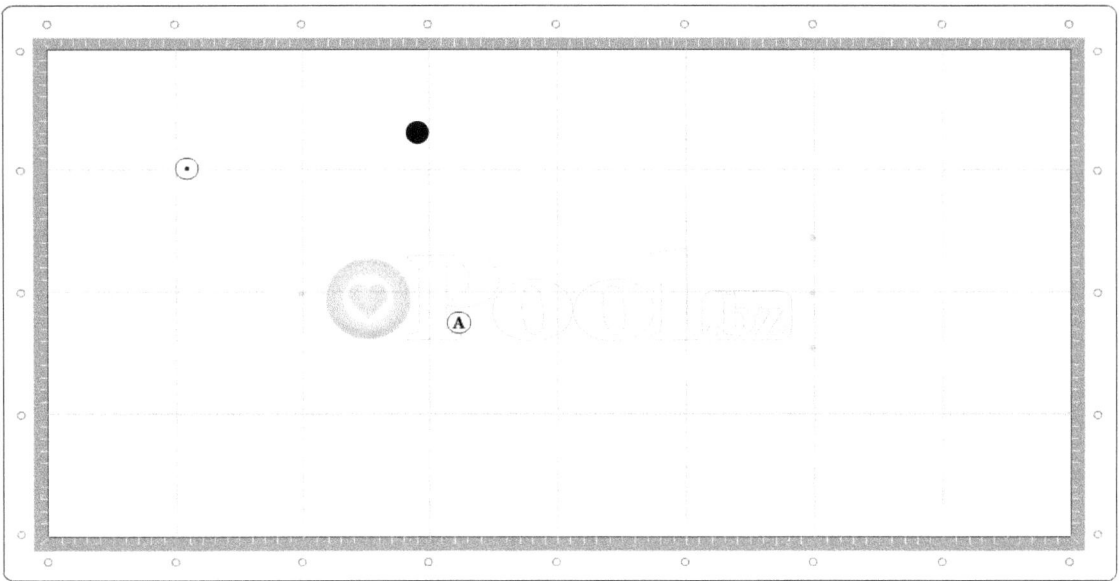

Shot Pattern

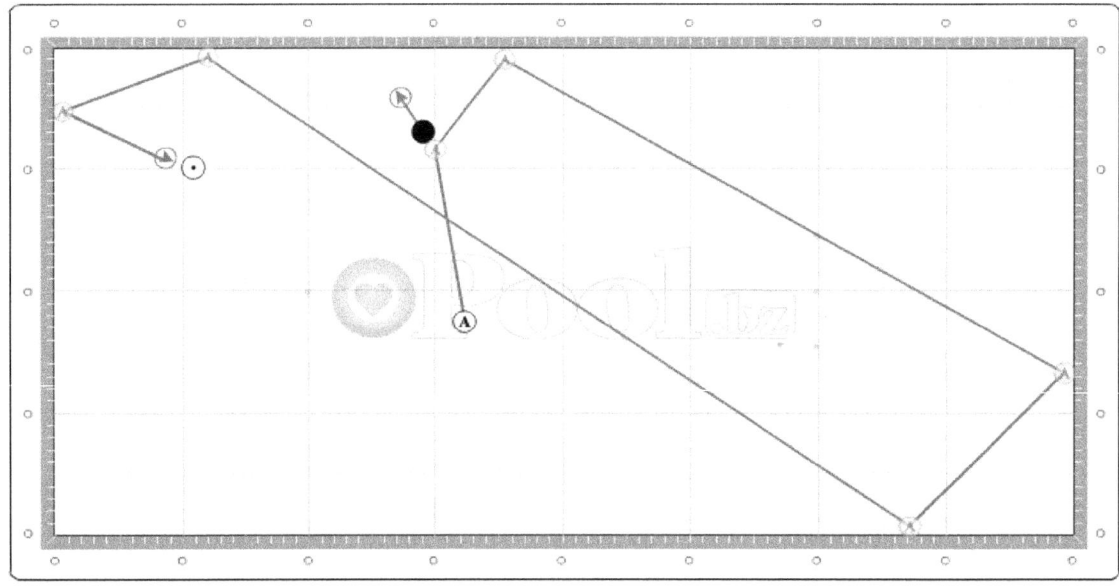

C:2d – Setup

Shot Pattern

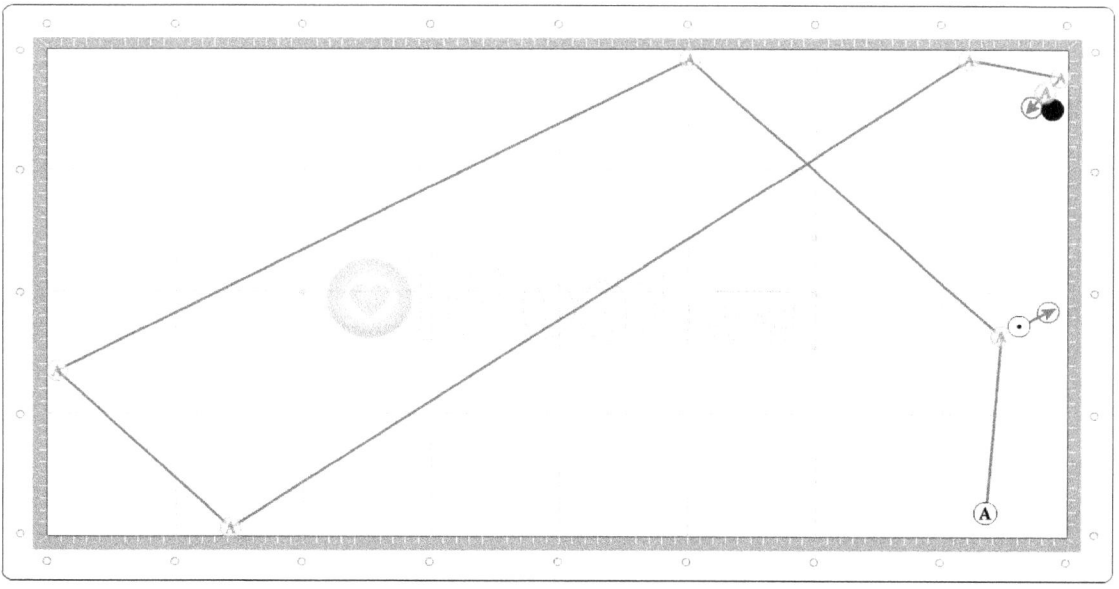

C: Group 3

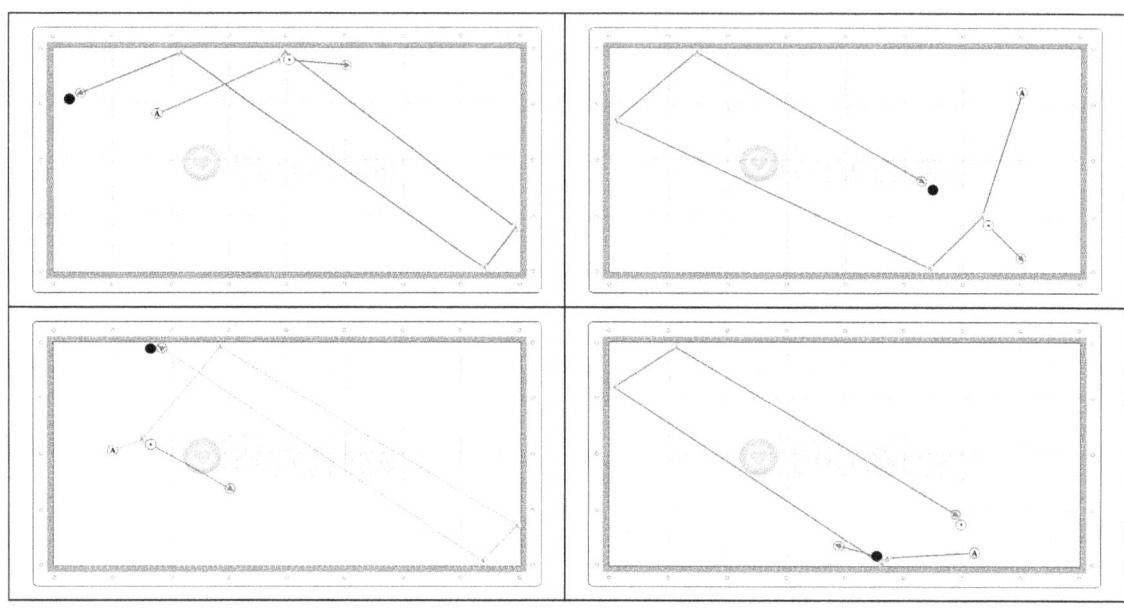

Analysis:

C:3a. _____

C:3b. _____

C:3c. _____

C:3d. _____

C:3a – Setup

Shot Pattern

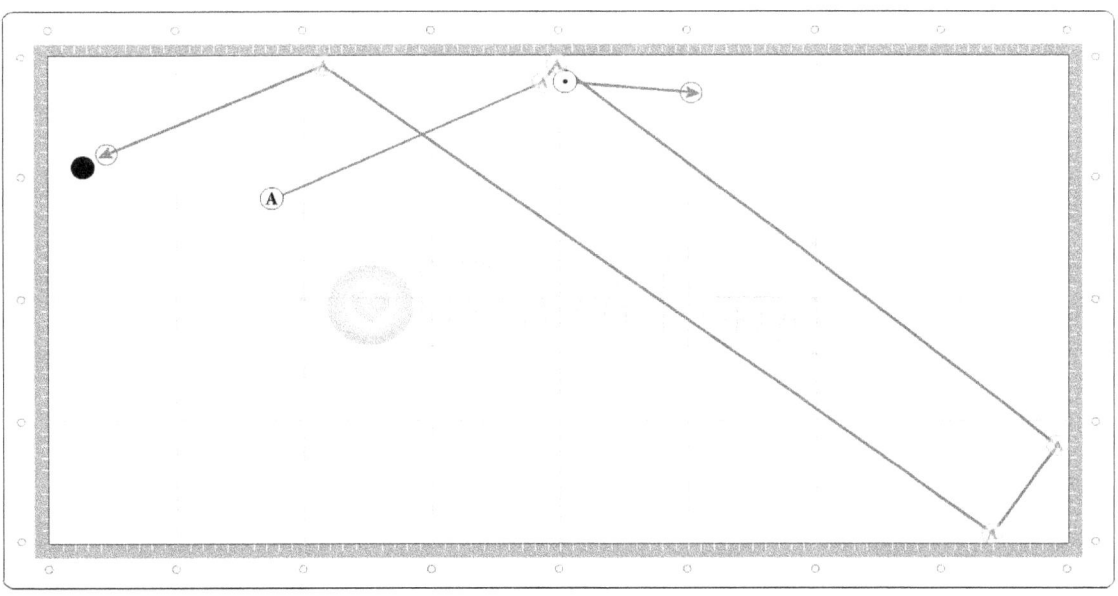

C:3b – Setup

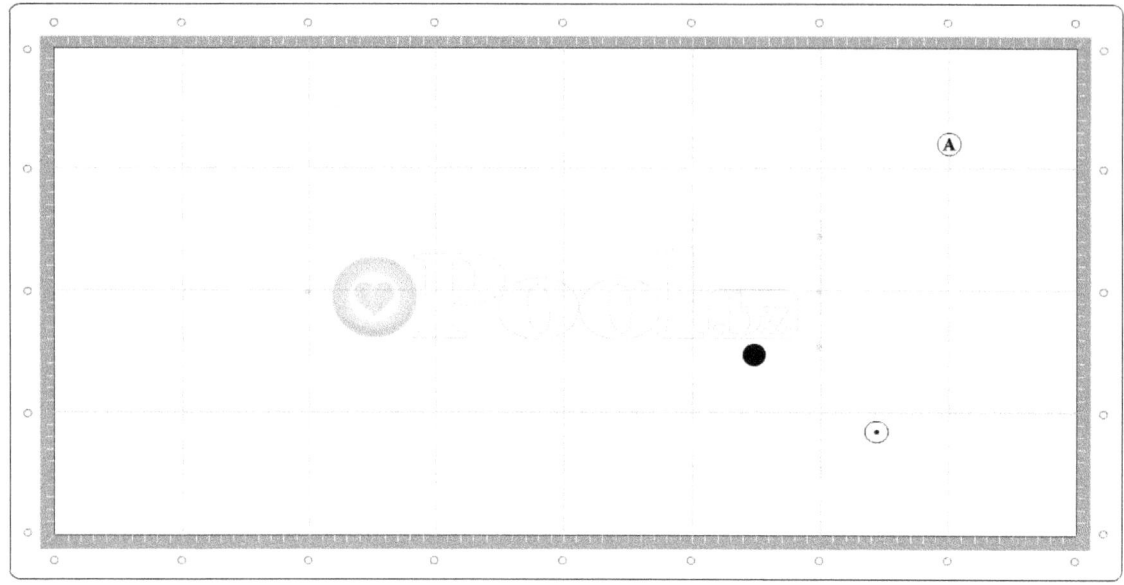

Shot Pattern

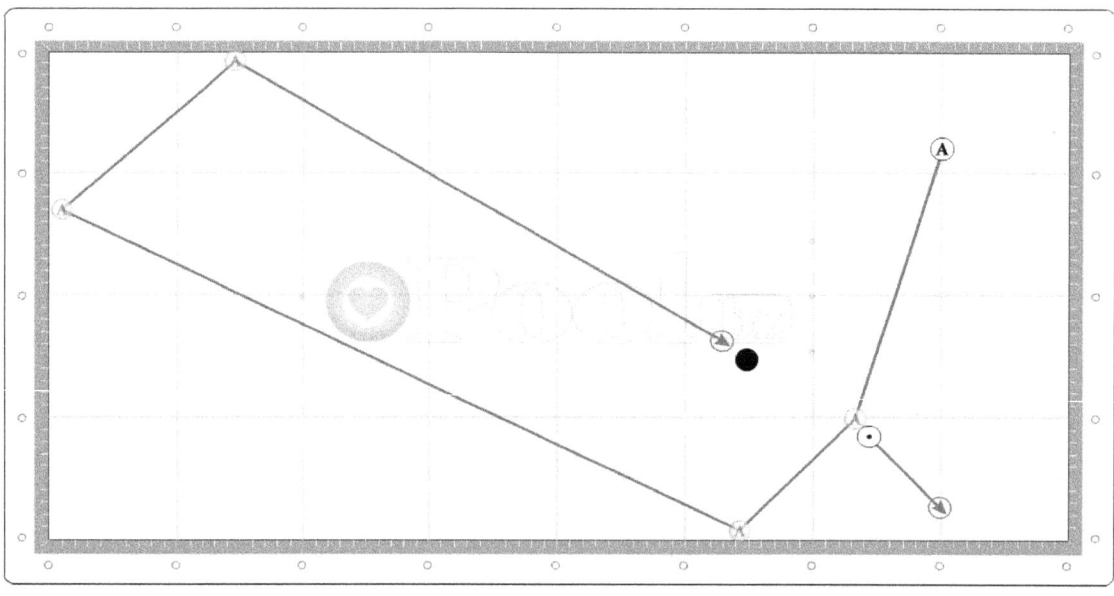

C:3c – Setup

Shot Pattern

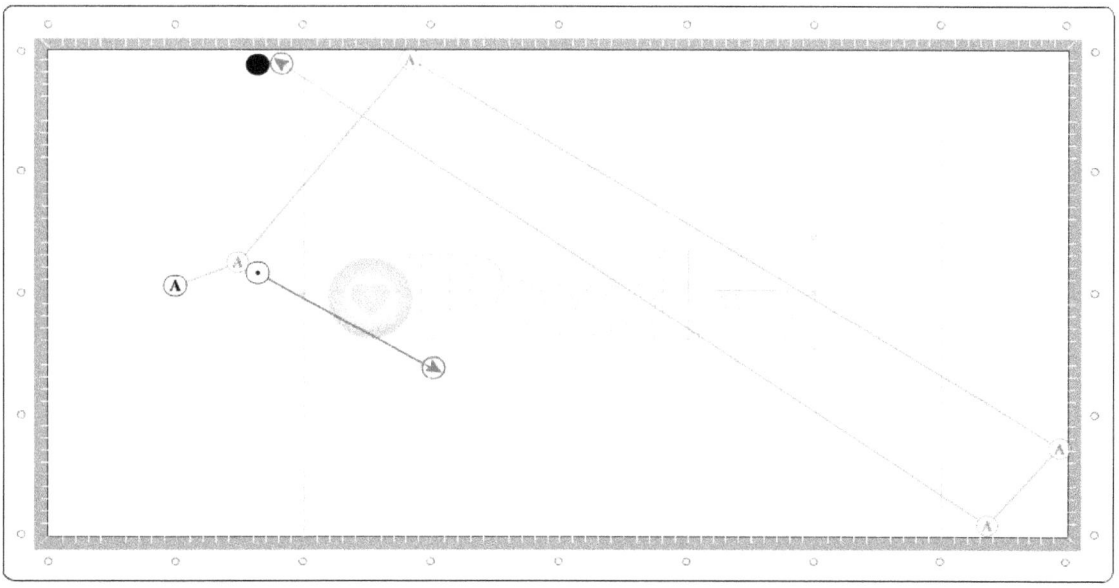

C:3d – Setup

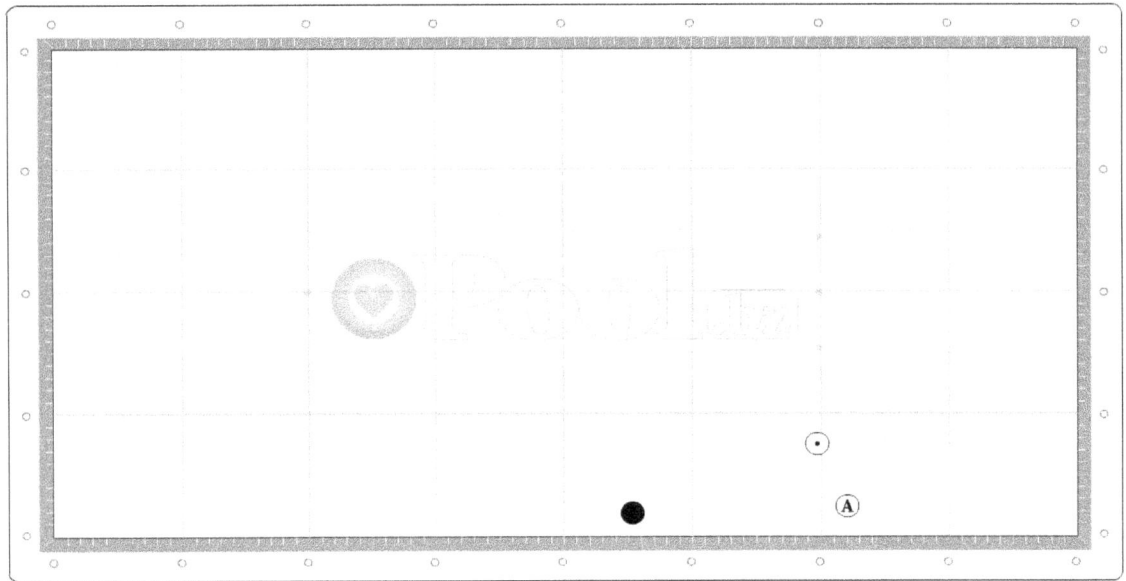

Shot Pattern

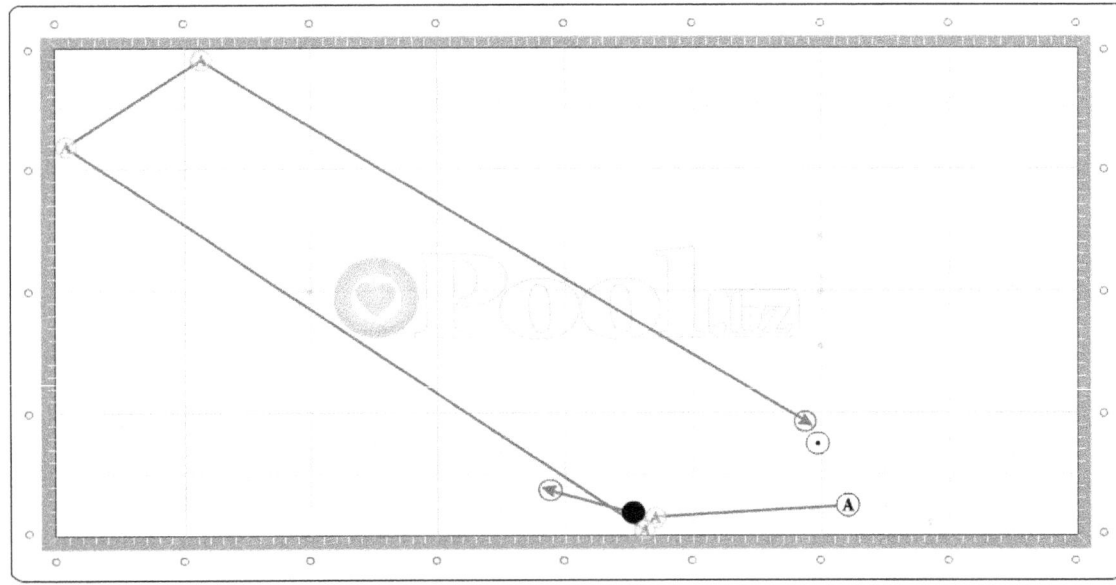

C: Group 4

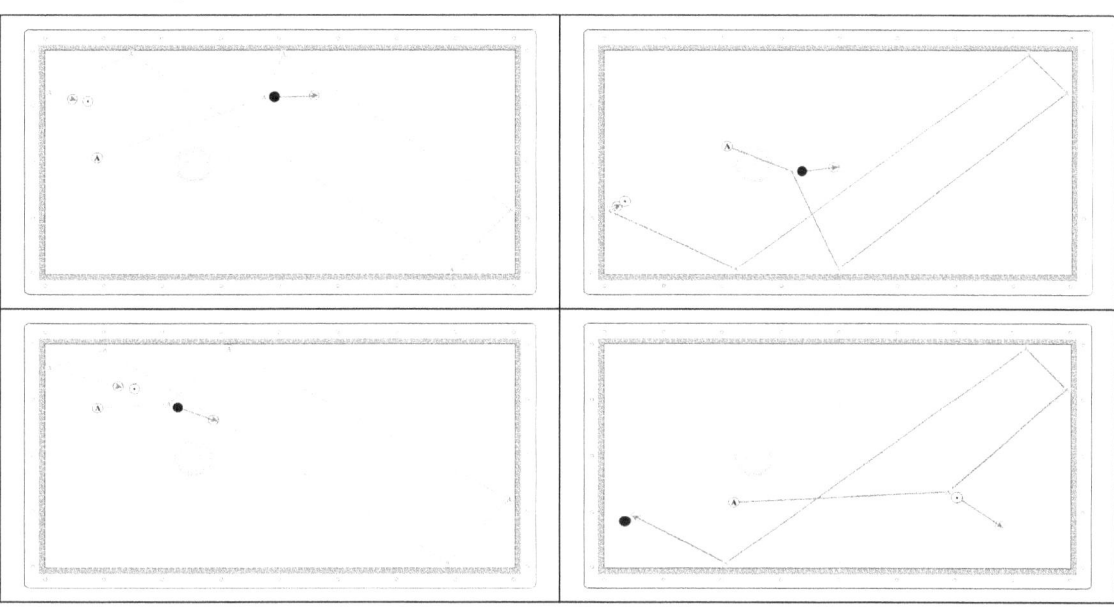

Analysis:

C:4a. _____

C:4b. _____

C:4c. _____

C:4d. _____

C:4a – Setup

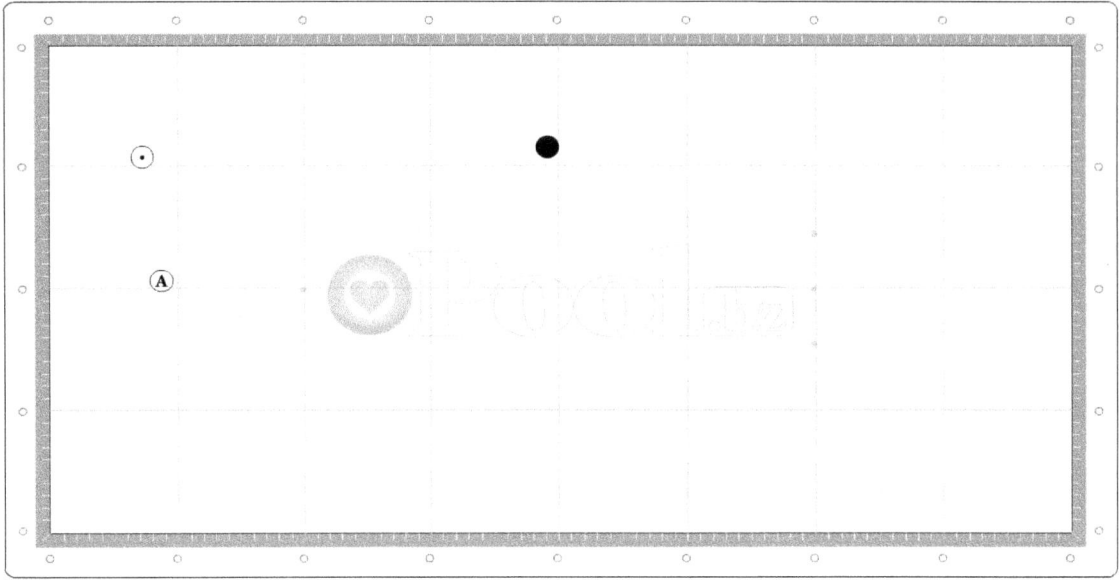

Shot Pattern

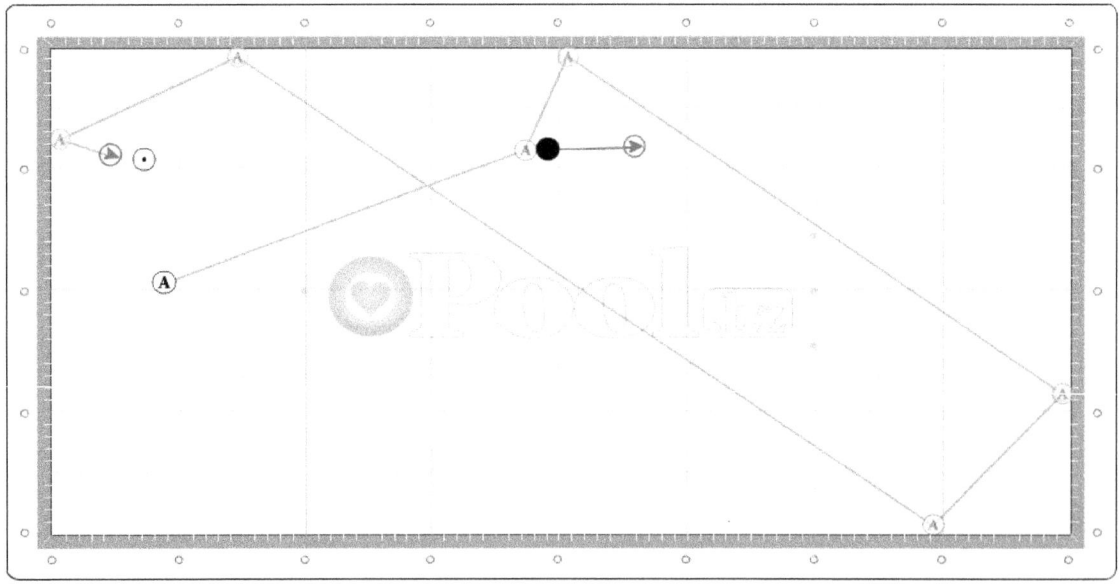

C:4b – Setup

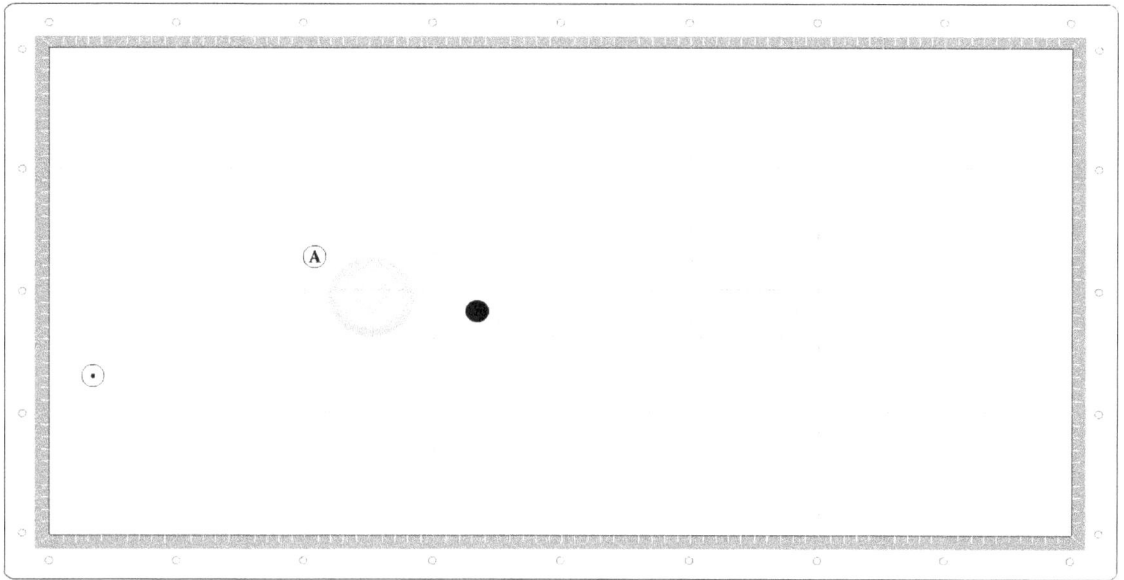

Shot Pattern

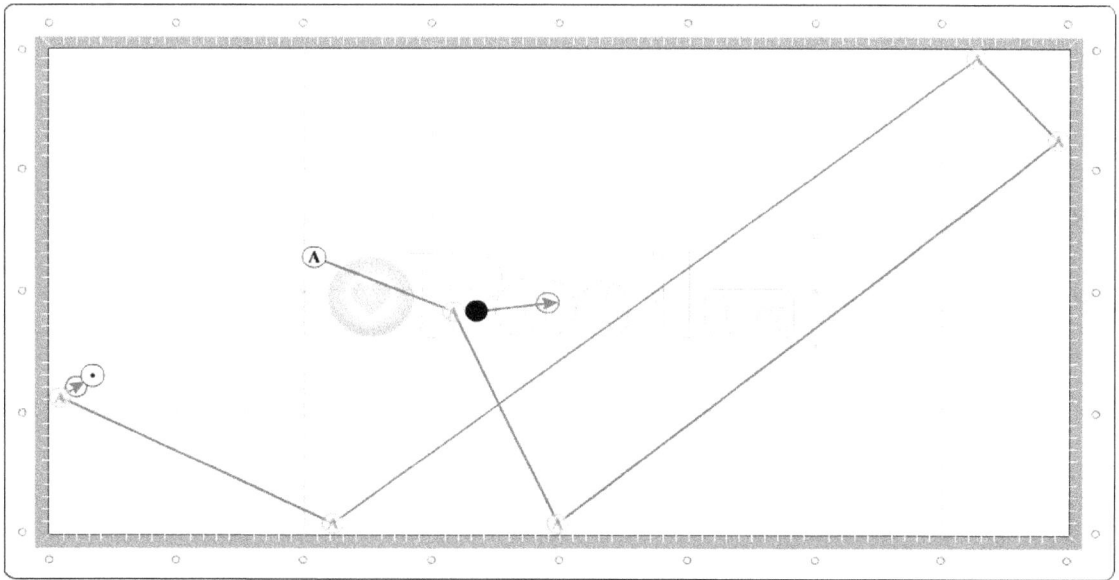

C:4c – Setup

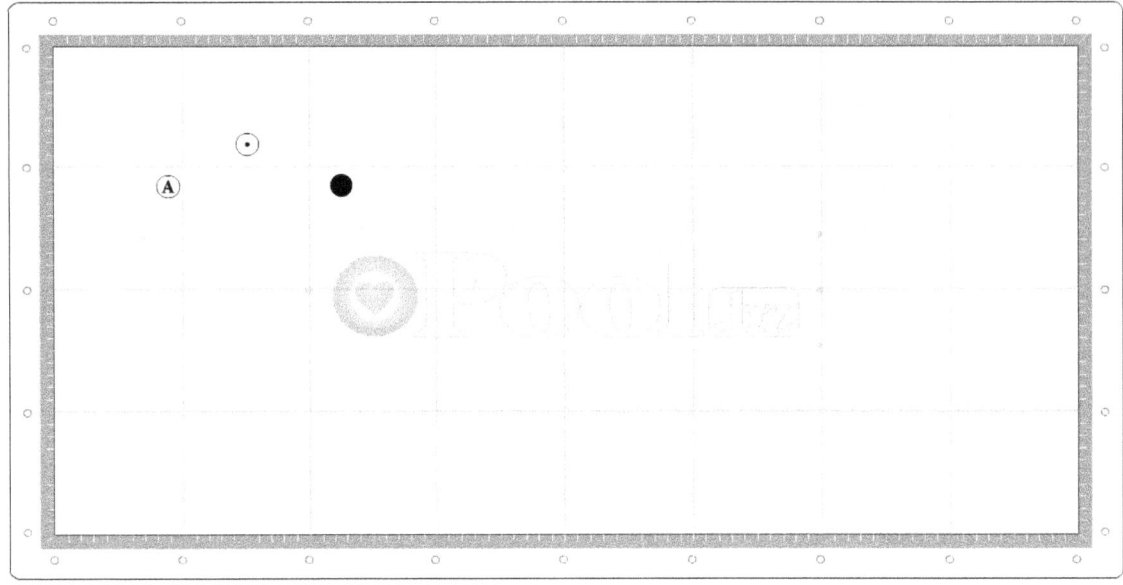

Shot Pattern

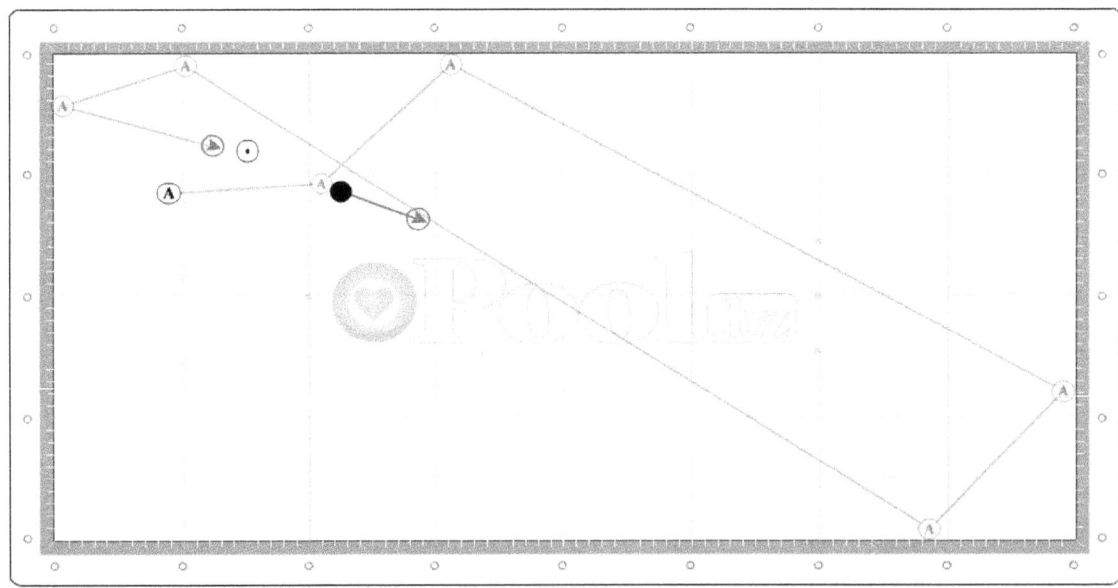

C:4d – Setup

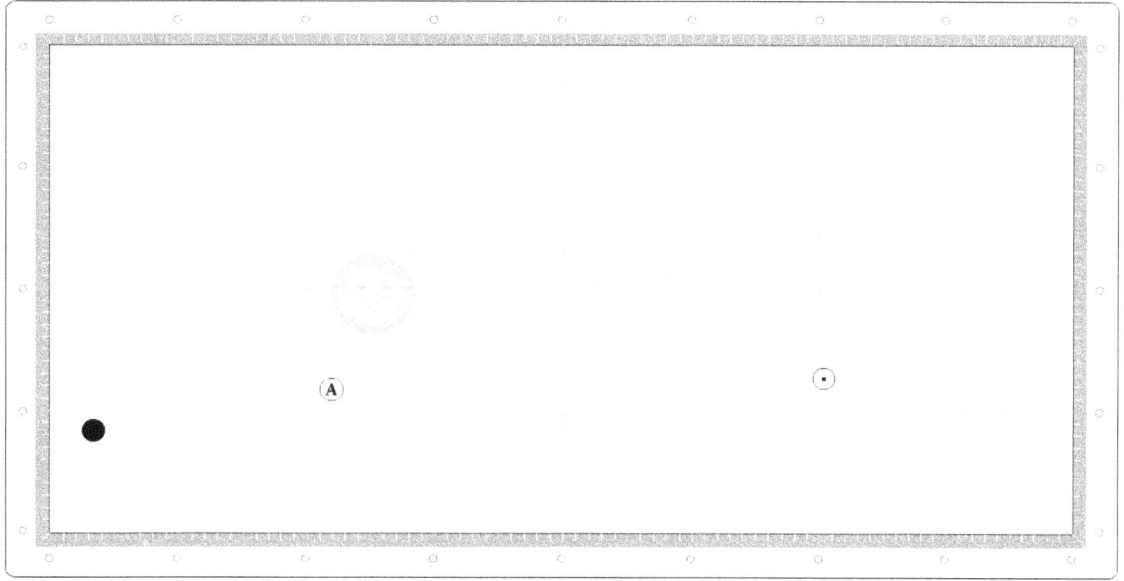

Shot Pattern

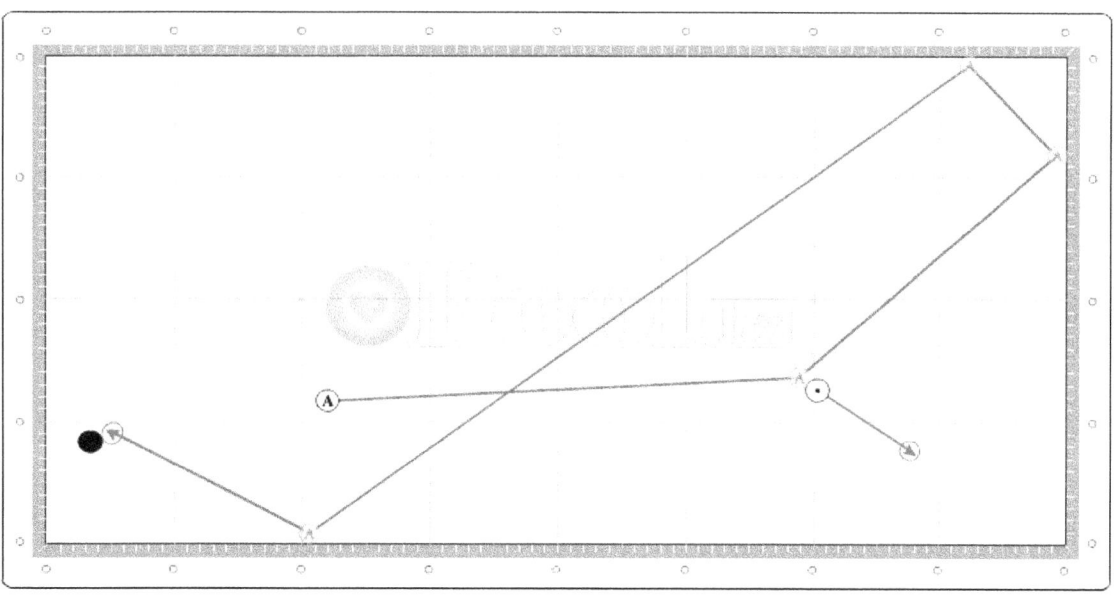

C: Group 5

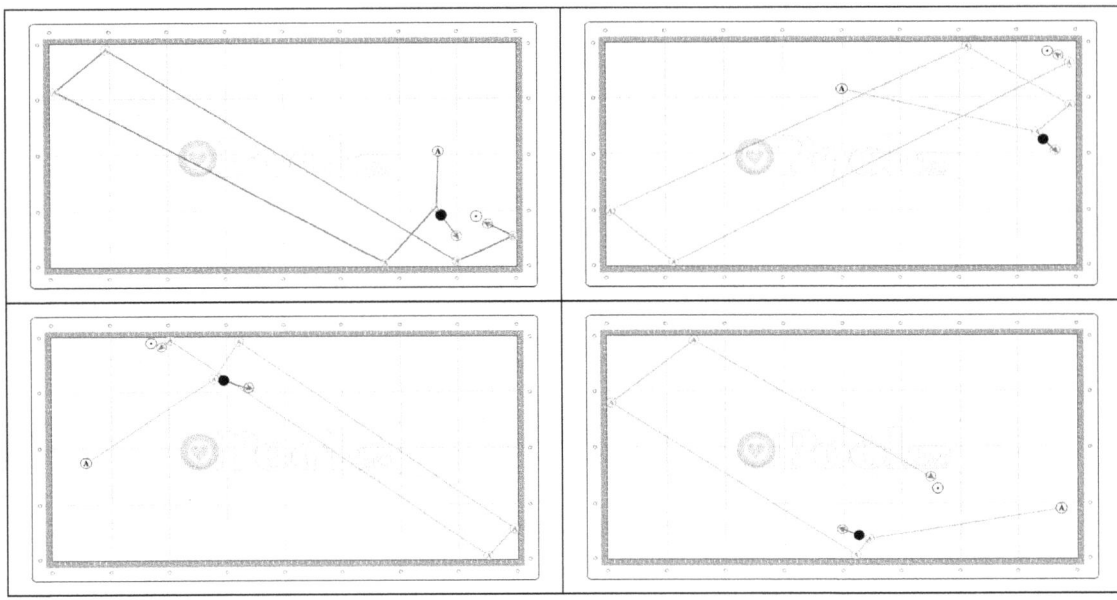

Analysis:

C:5a. _____

C:5b. _____

C:5c. _____

C:5d. _____

C:5a – Setup

Shot Pattern

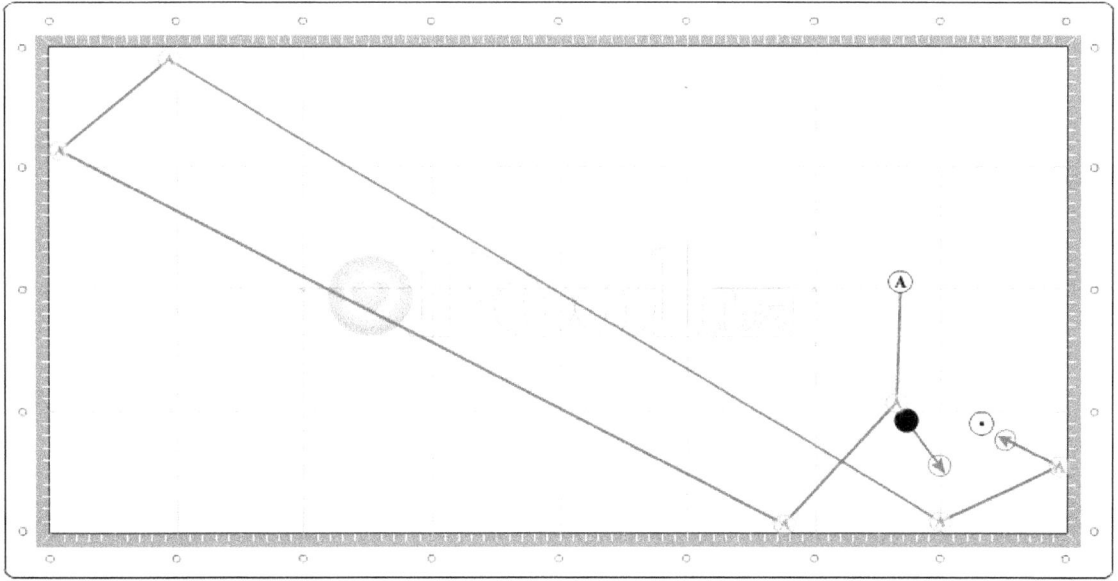

C:5b – Setup

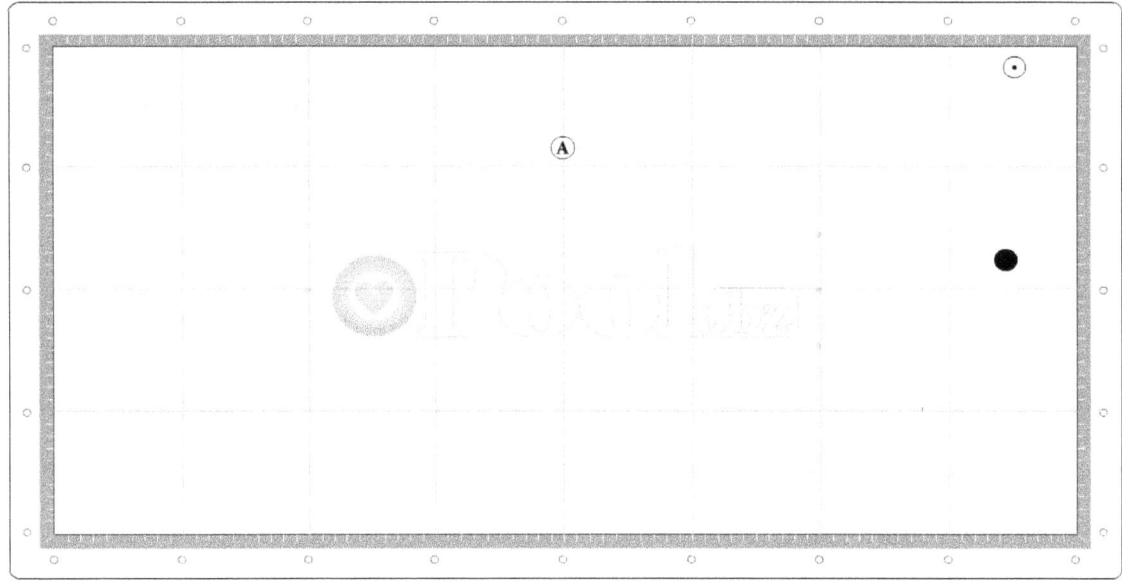

Shot Pattern

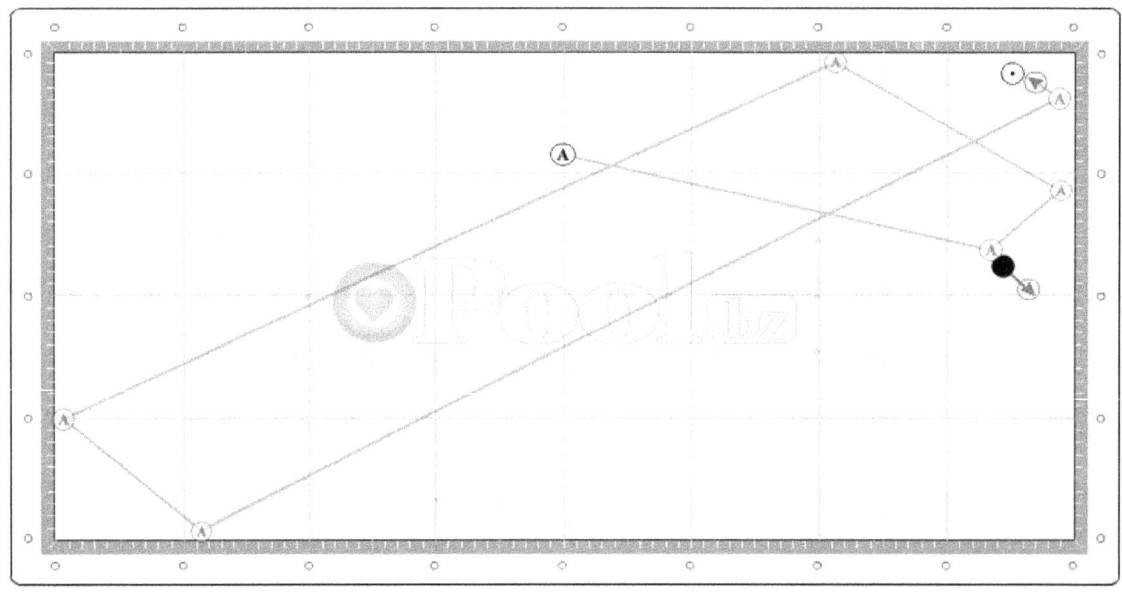

C:5c – Setup

Shot Pattern

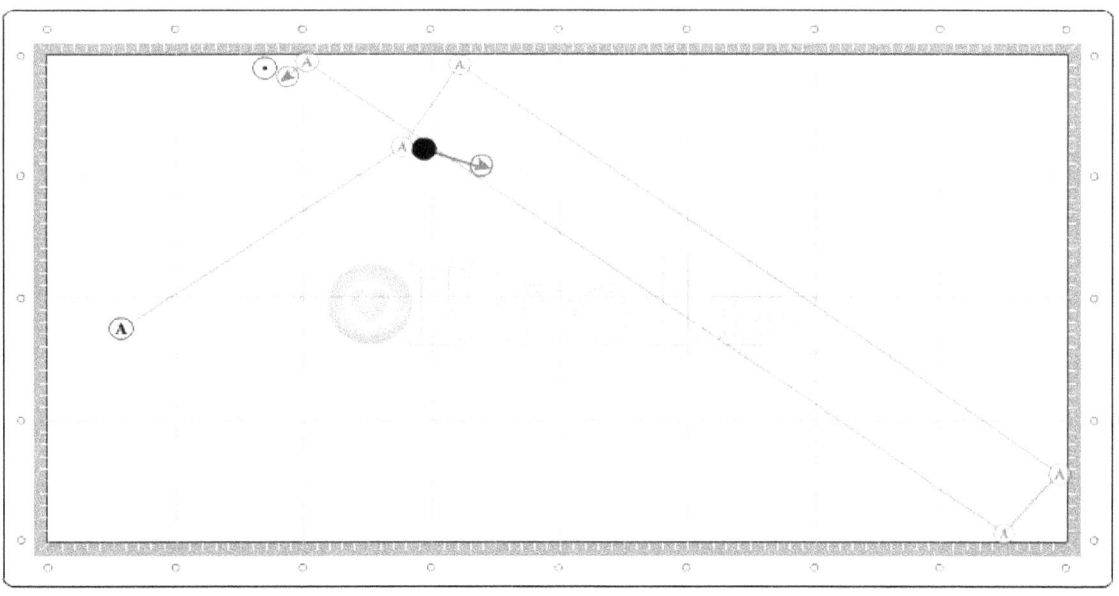

C:5d – Setup

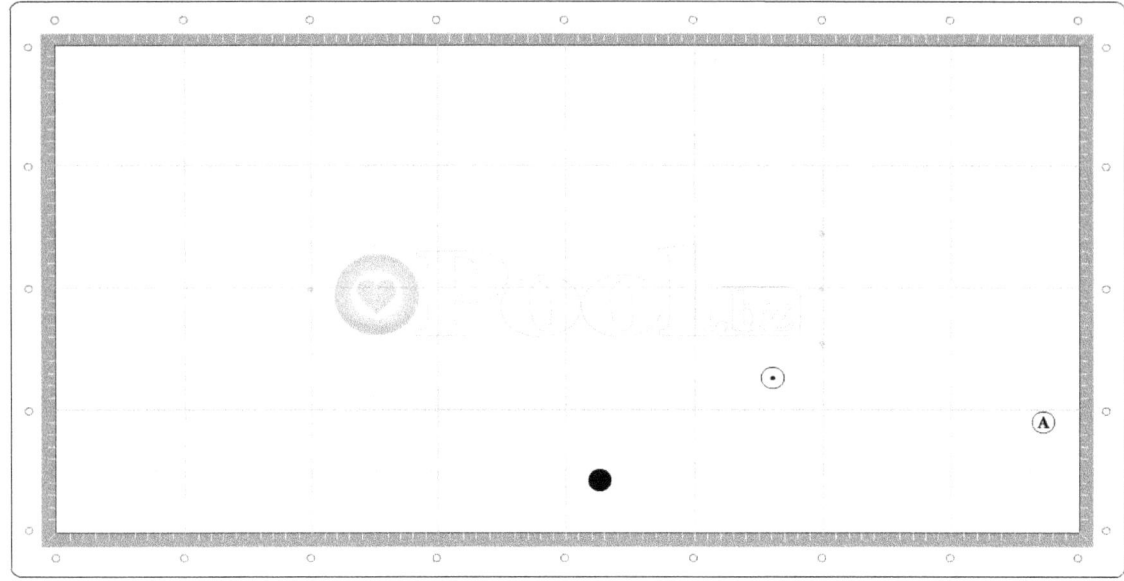

Shot Pattern

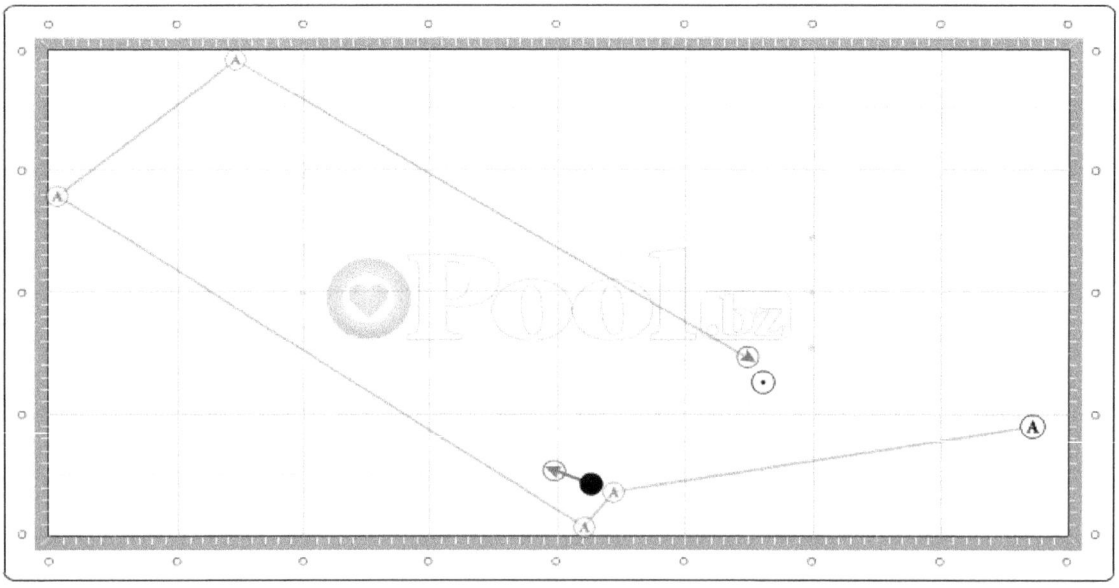

D: Double Diagonals

On these shots, the CB comes off the first OB into one of the corners. It comes out and heads to the opposite corner. These incoming and outgoing path are not parallel.

D: Group 1

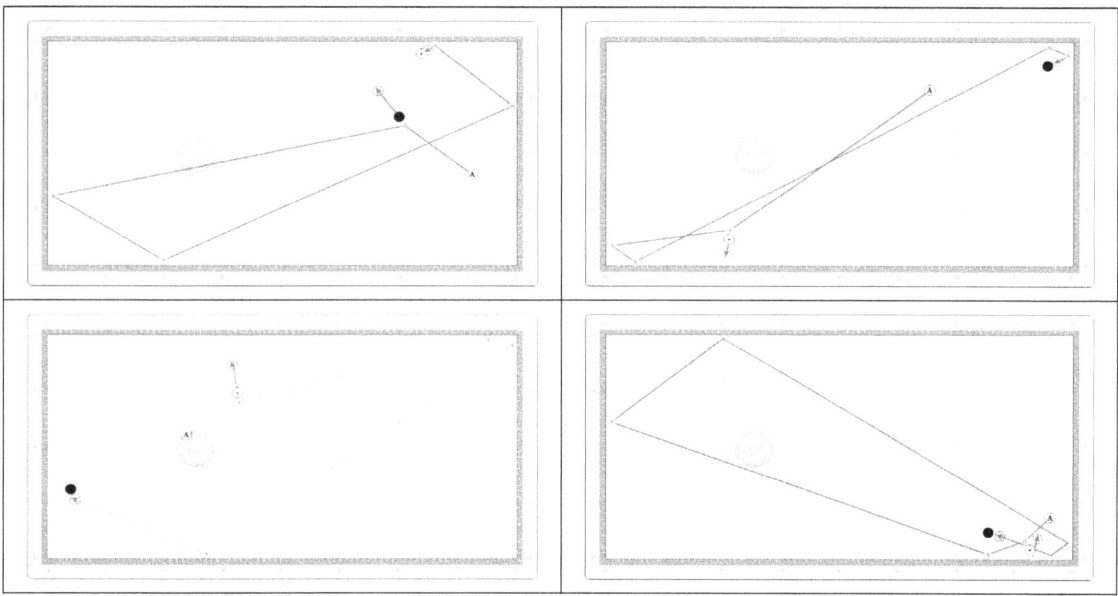

Analysis:

D:1a. _____

D:1b. _____

D:1c. _____

D:1d. _____

D:1a – Setup

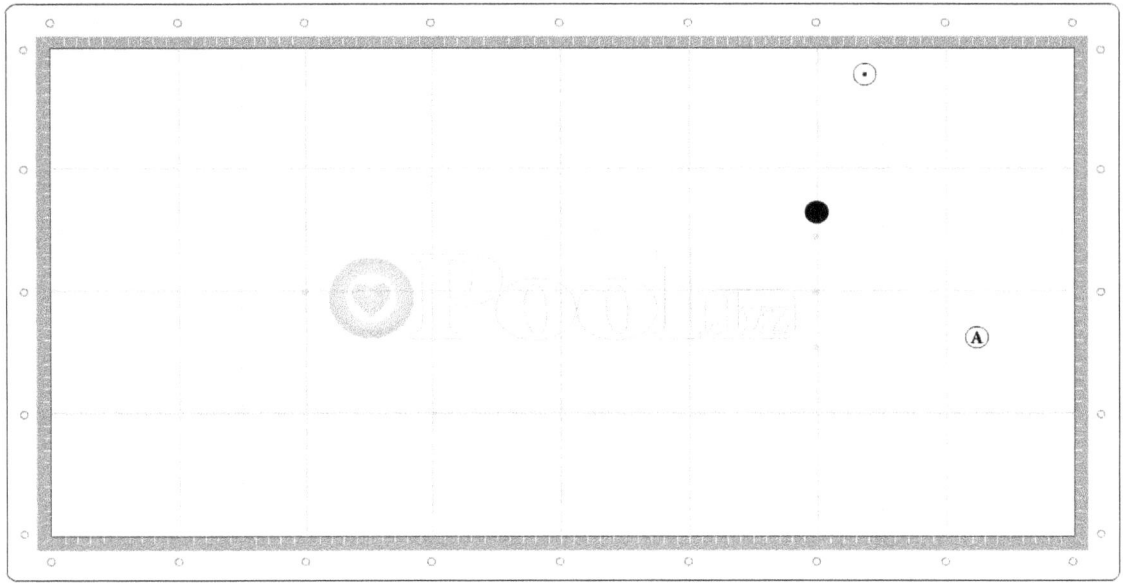

Shot Pattern

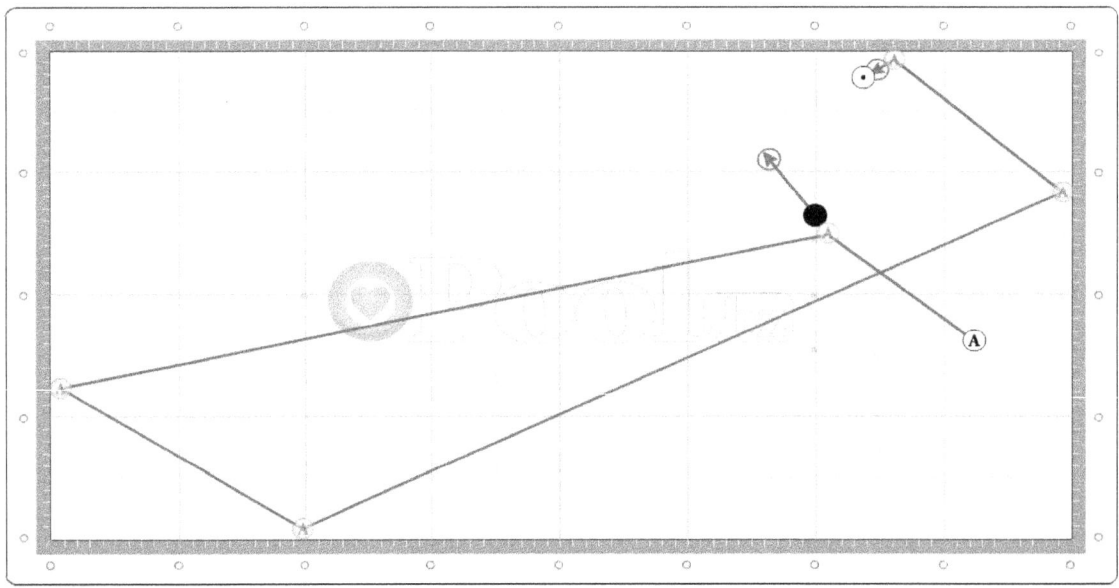

D:1b – Setup

Shot Pattern

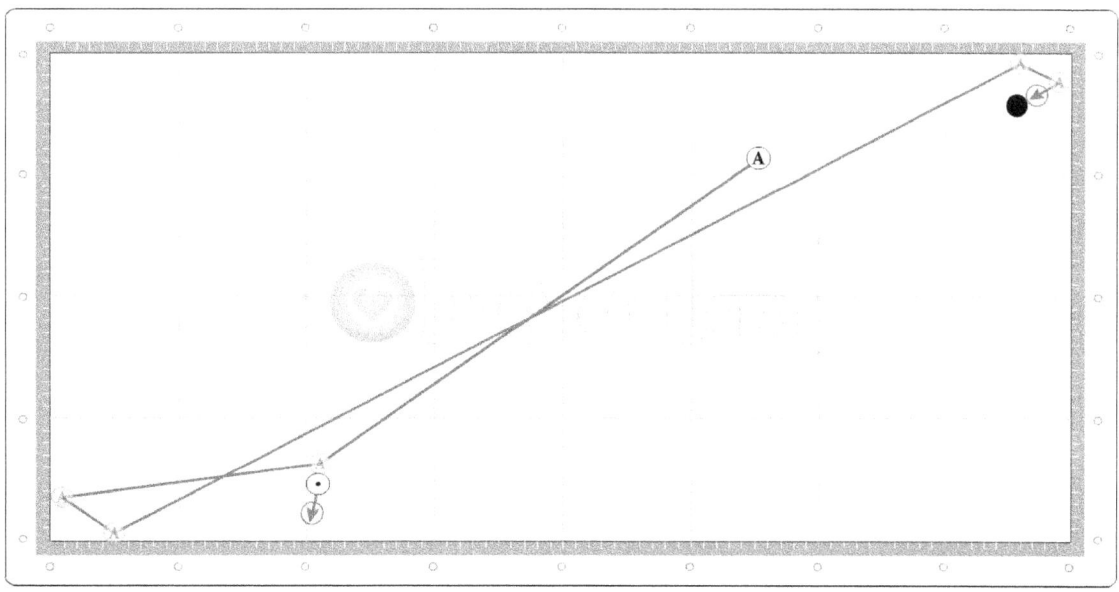

D:1c – Setup

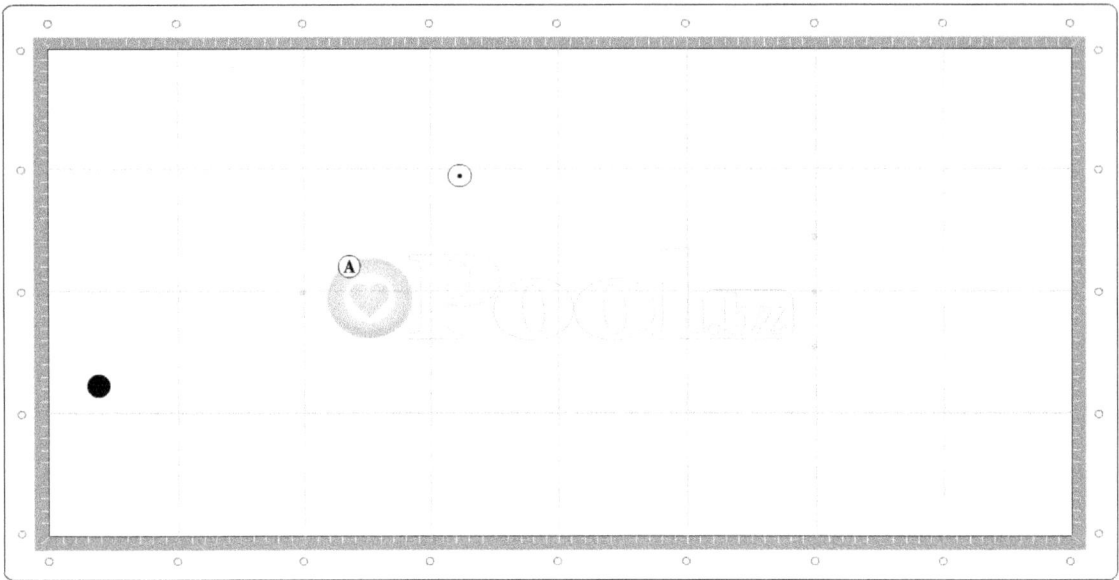

Shot Pattern

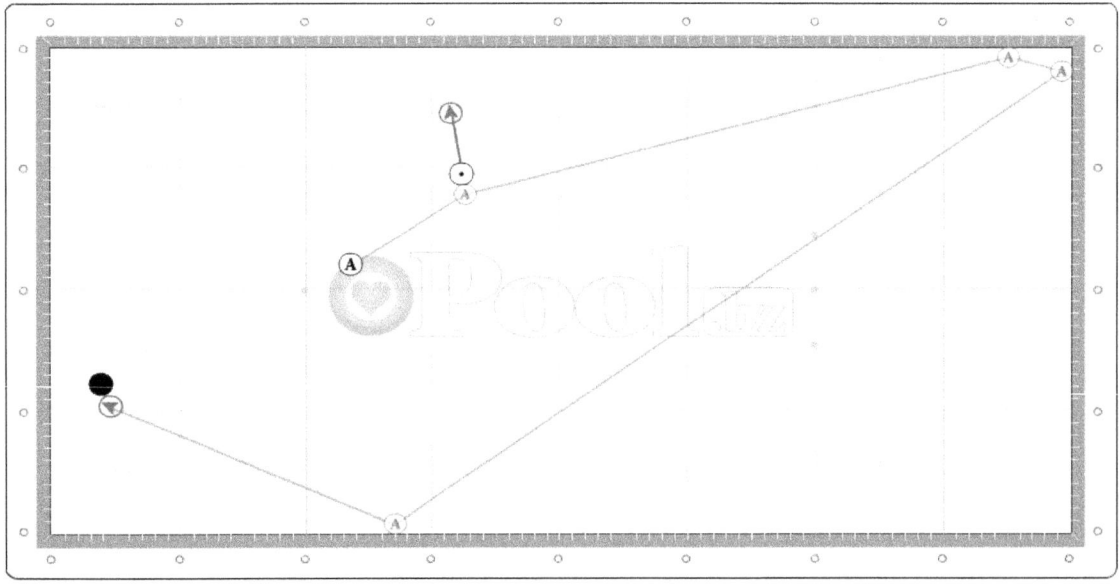

D:1d – Setup

Shot Pattern

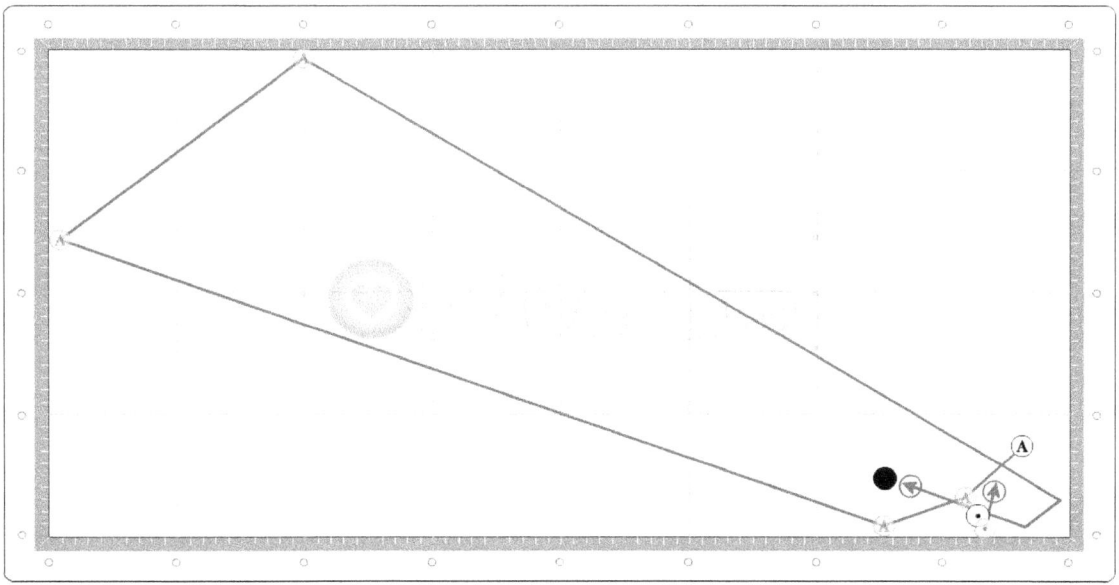

D: Group 2

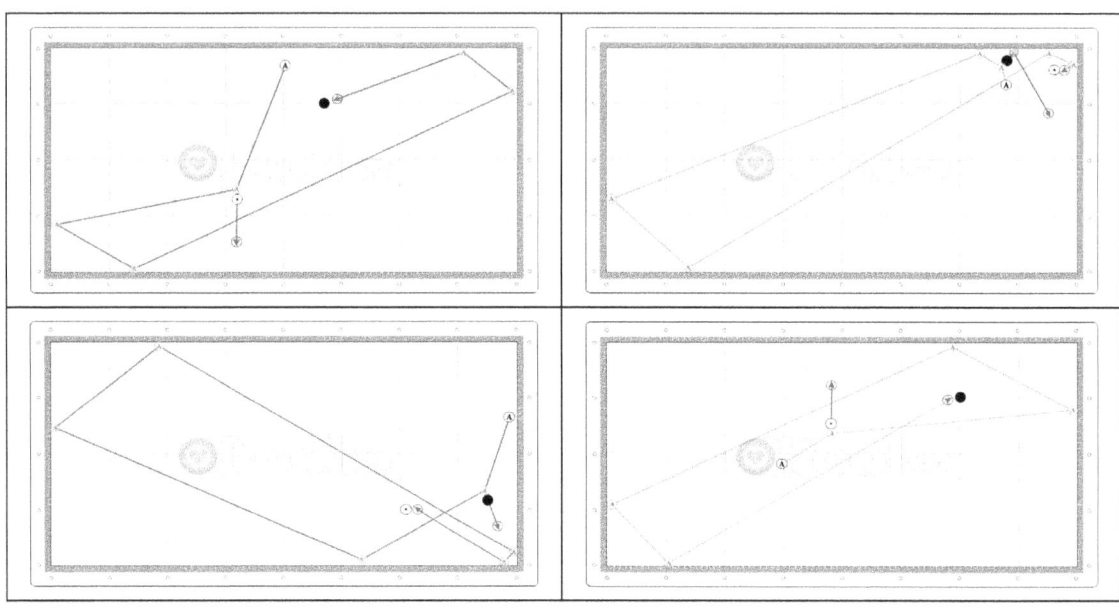

Analysis:

D:2a. _____

D:2b. _____

D:2c. _____

D:2d. _____

D:2a – Setup

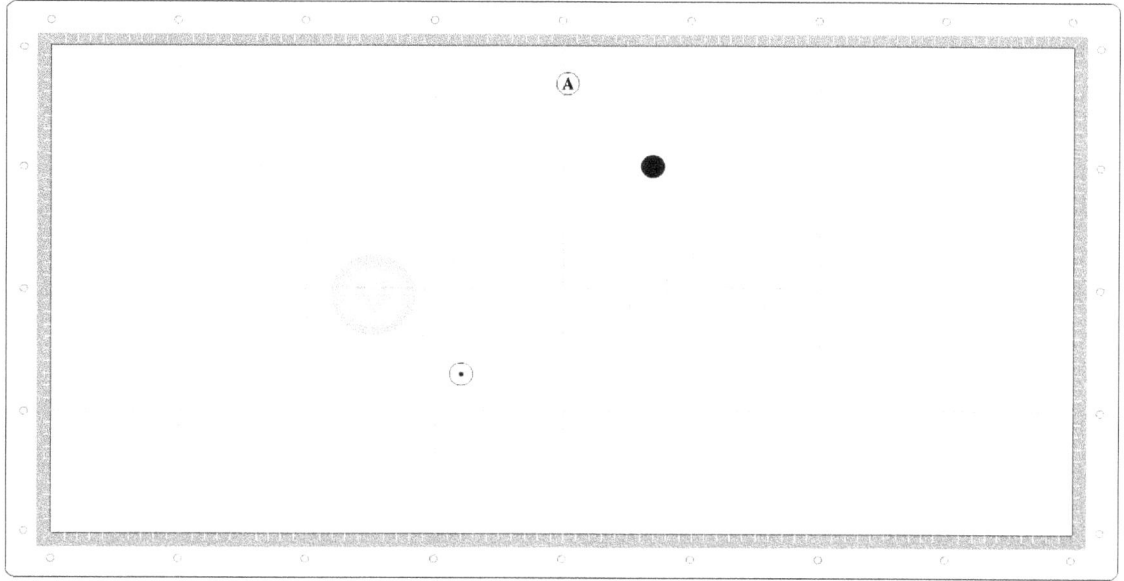

Shot Pattern

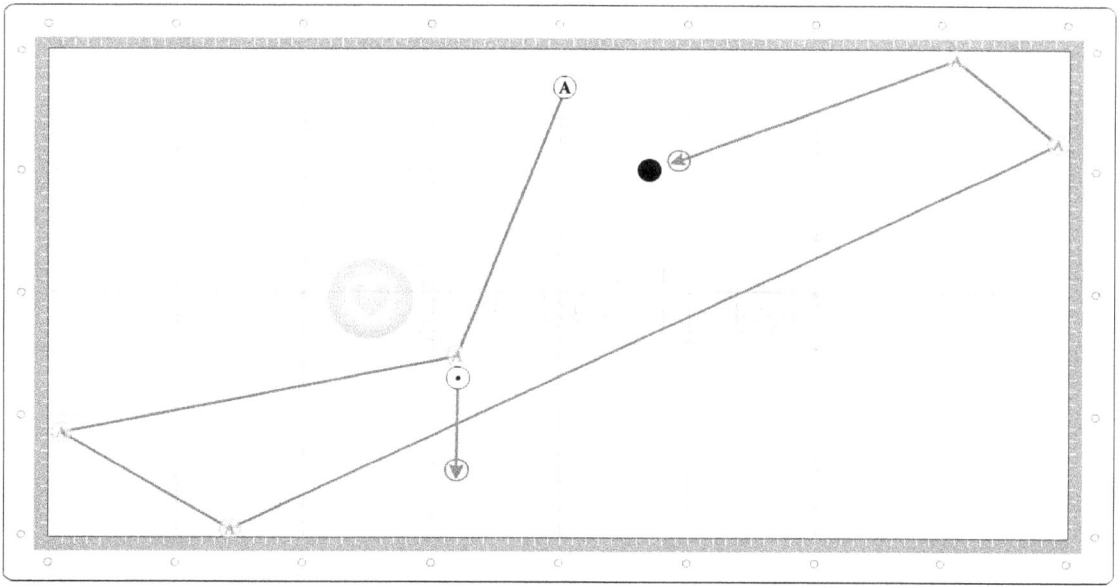

D:2b – Setup

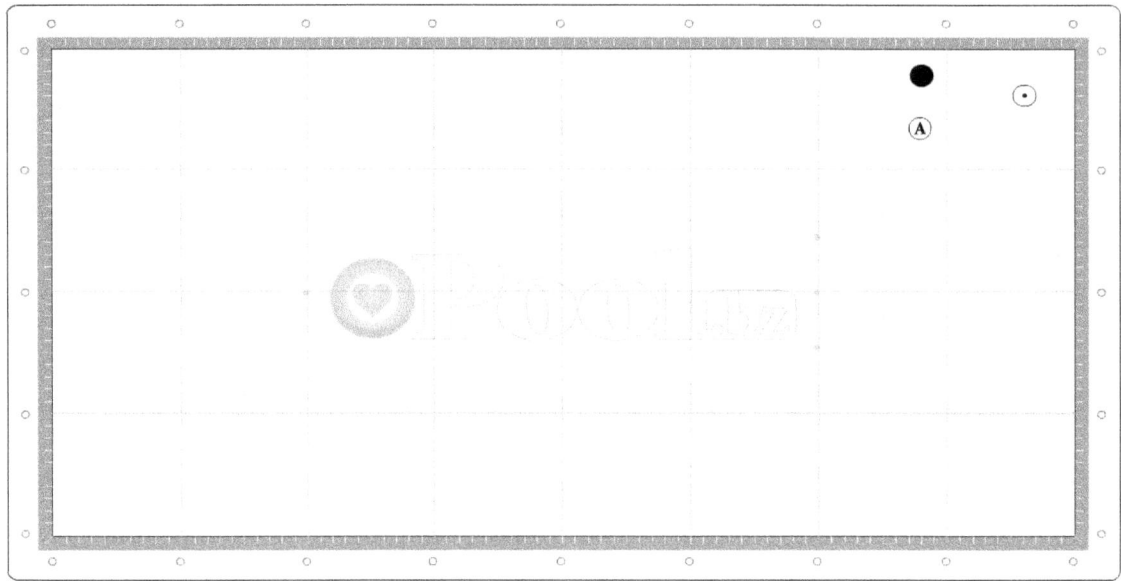

Shot Pattern

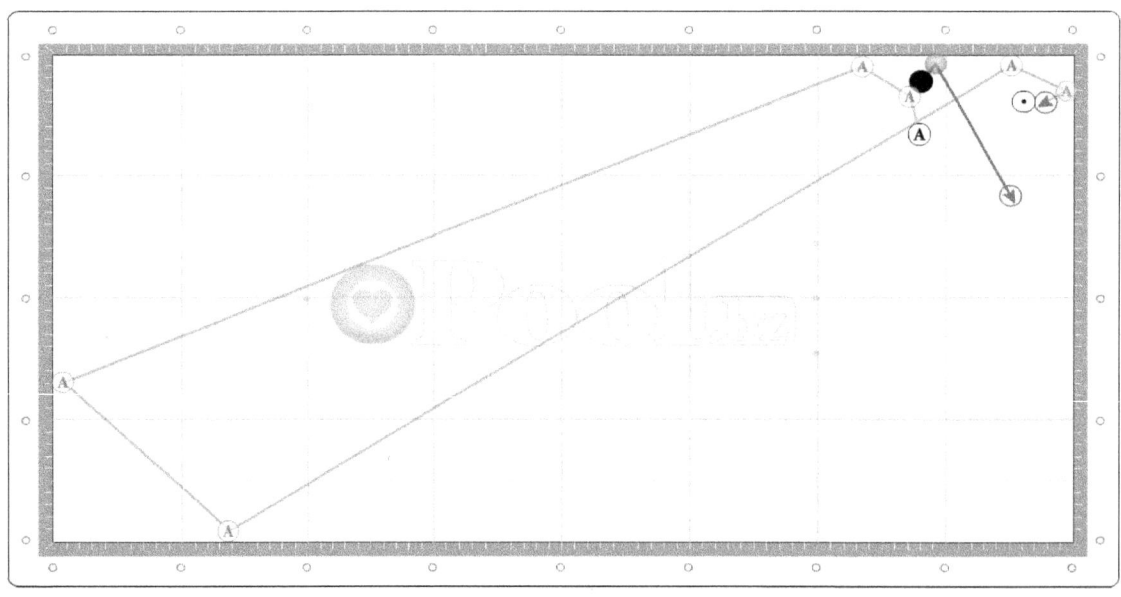

D:2c – Setup

Shot Pattern

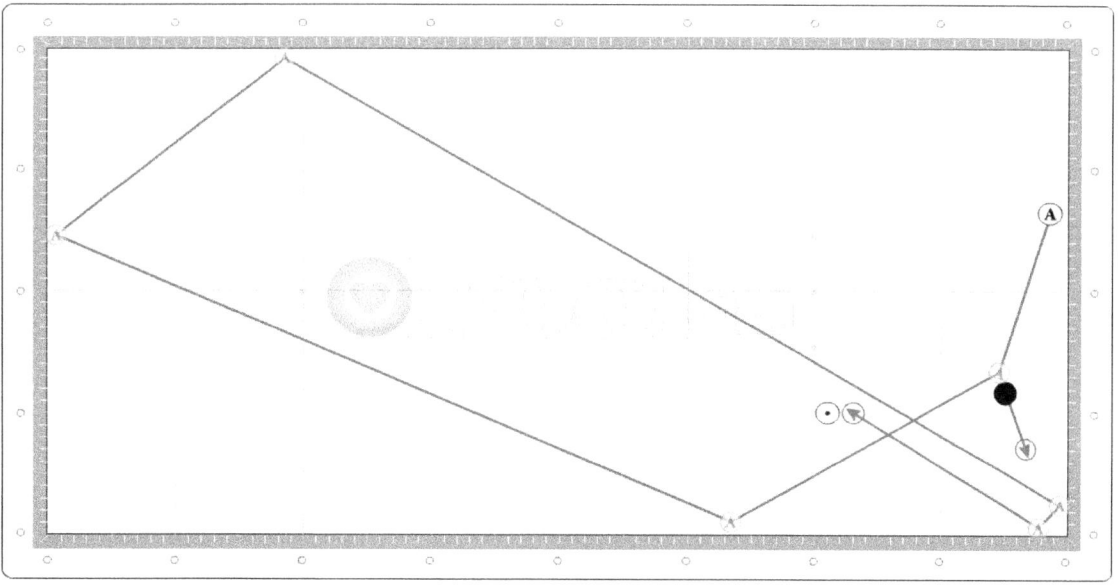

D:2d – Setup

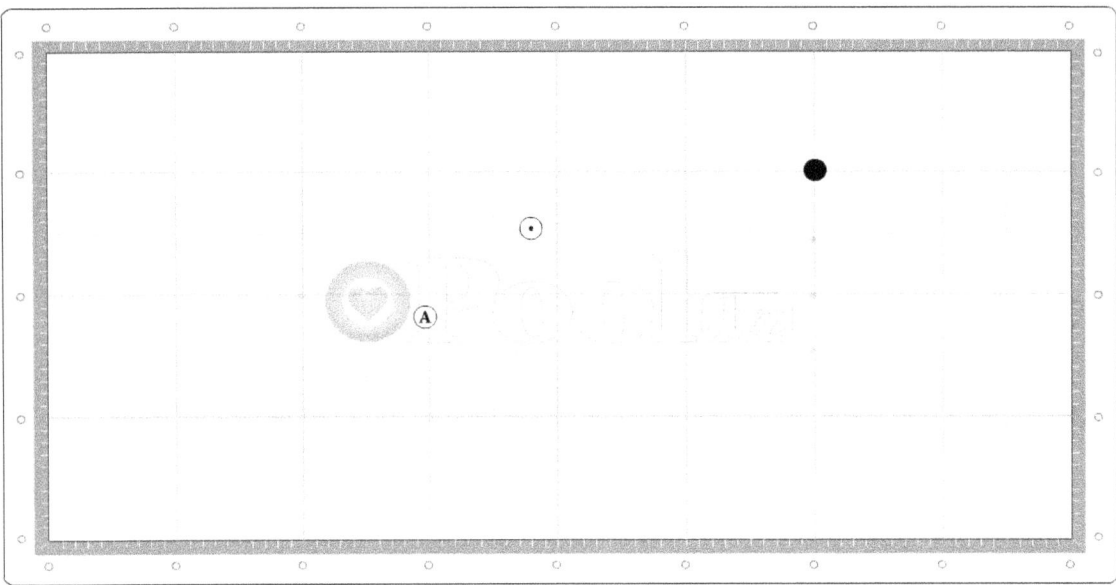

Shot Pattern

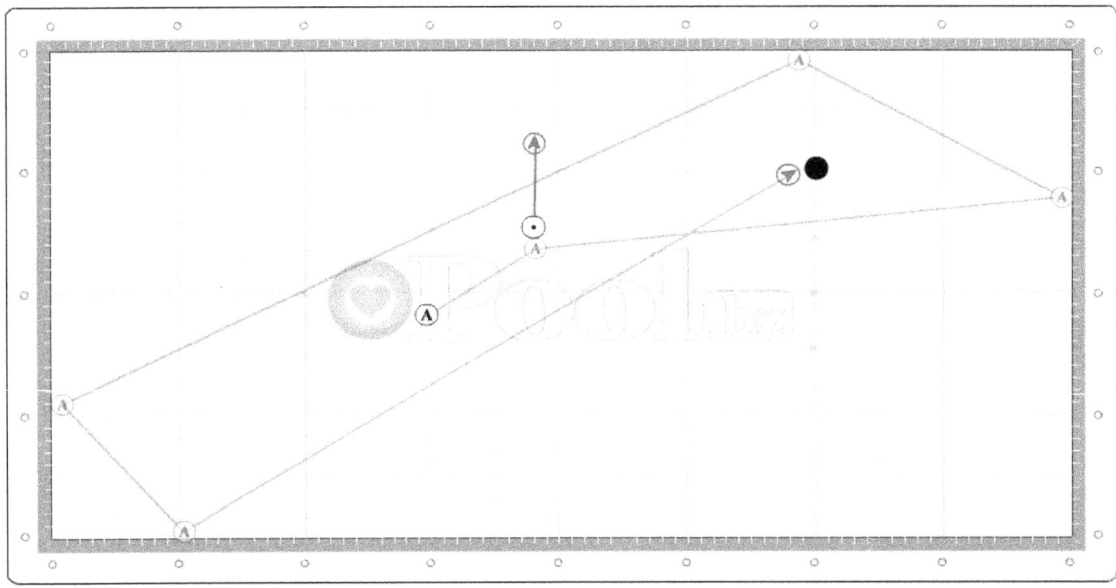

D: Group 3

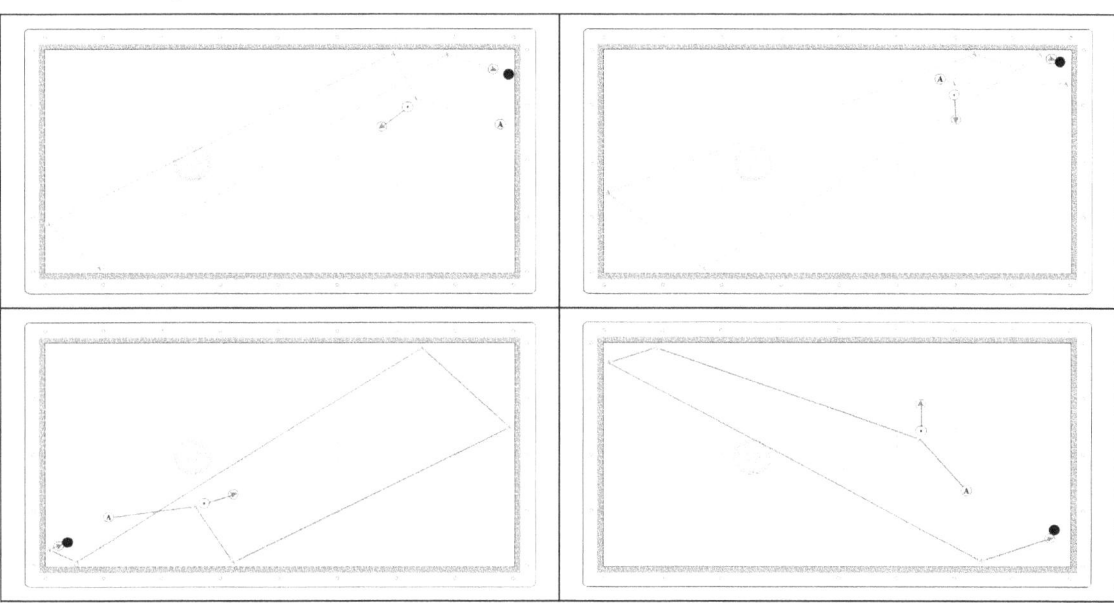

Analysis:

D:3a. _____

D:3b. _____

D:3c. _____

D:3d. _____

D:3a – Setup

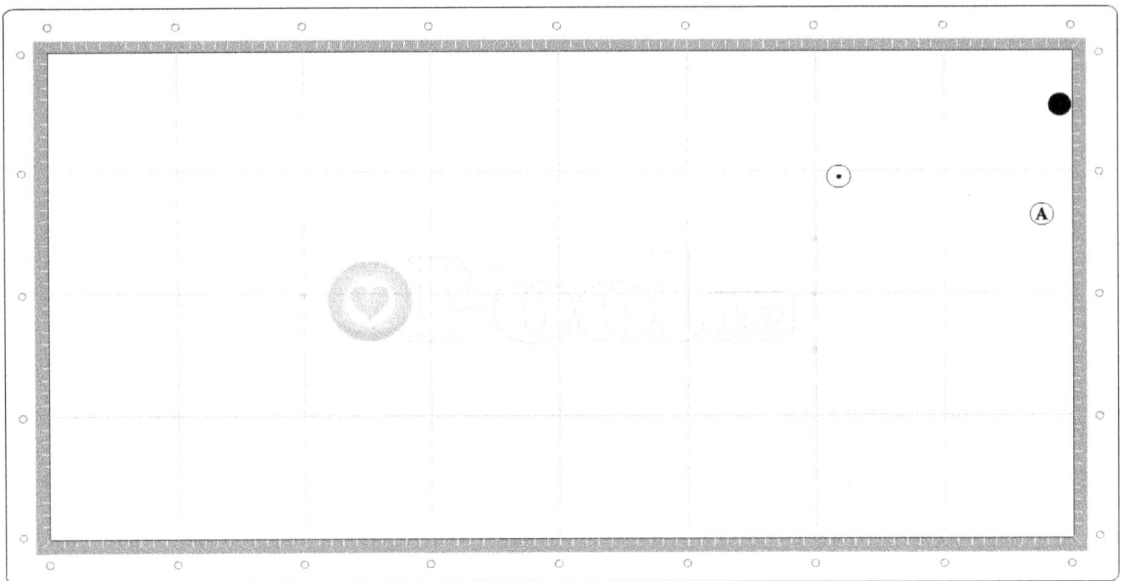

Shot Pattern

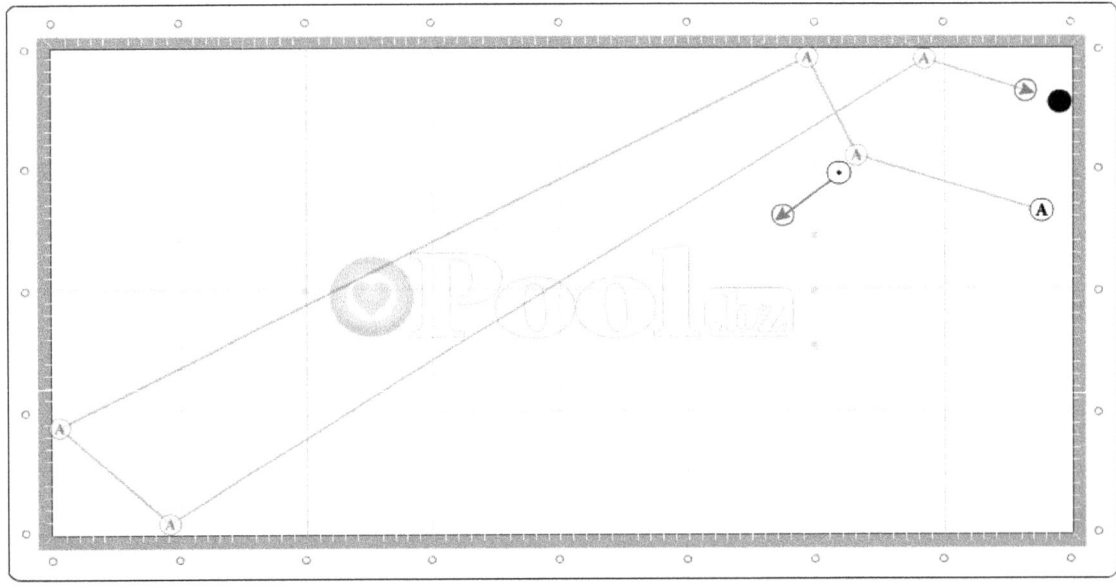

D:3b – Setup

Shot Pattern

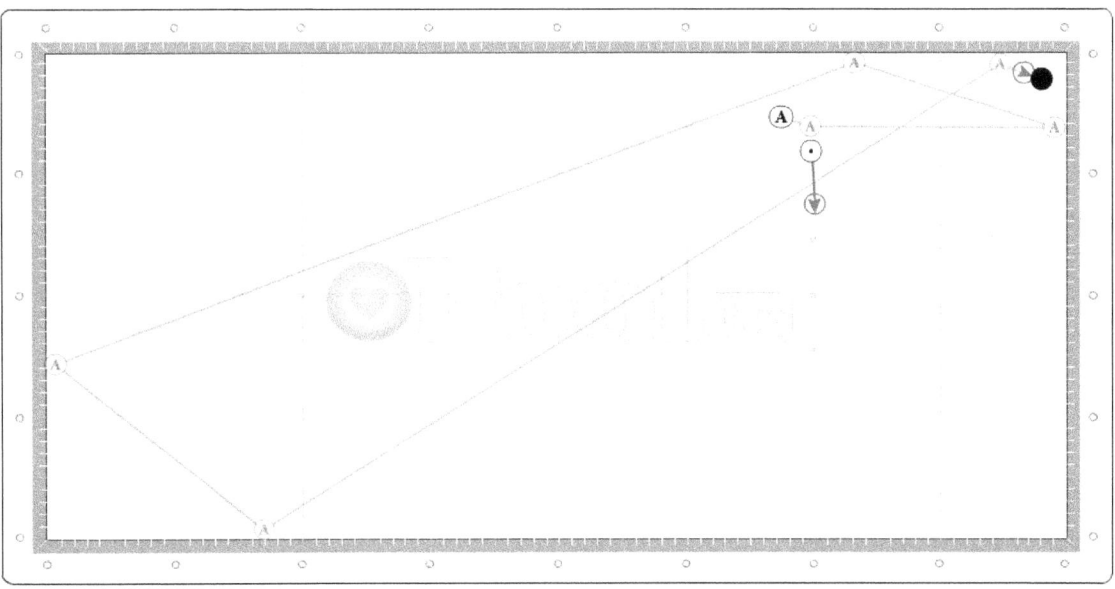

D:3c – Setup

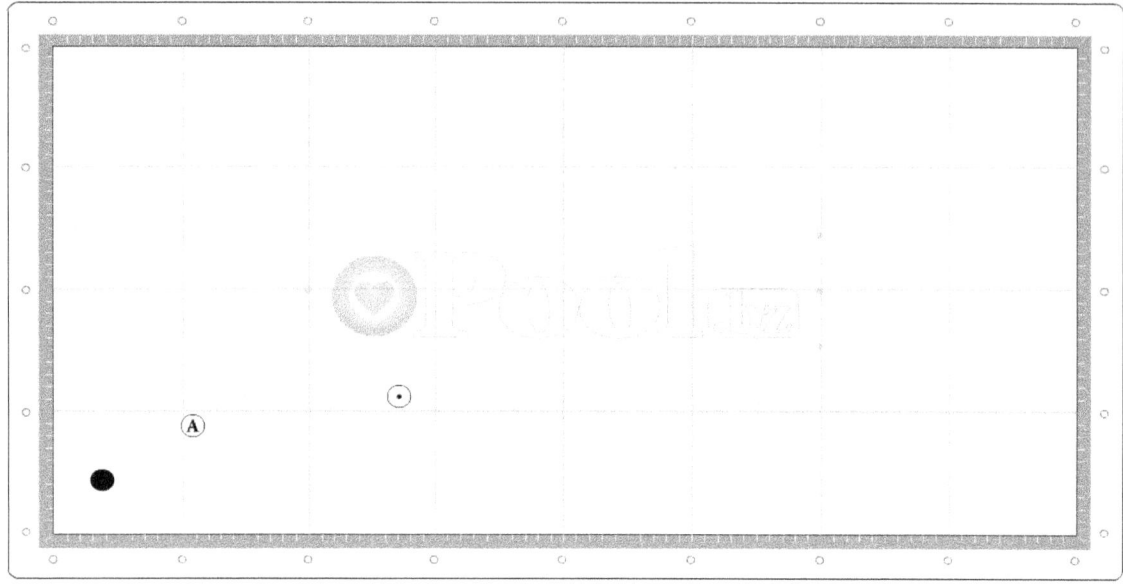

Shot Pattern

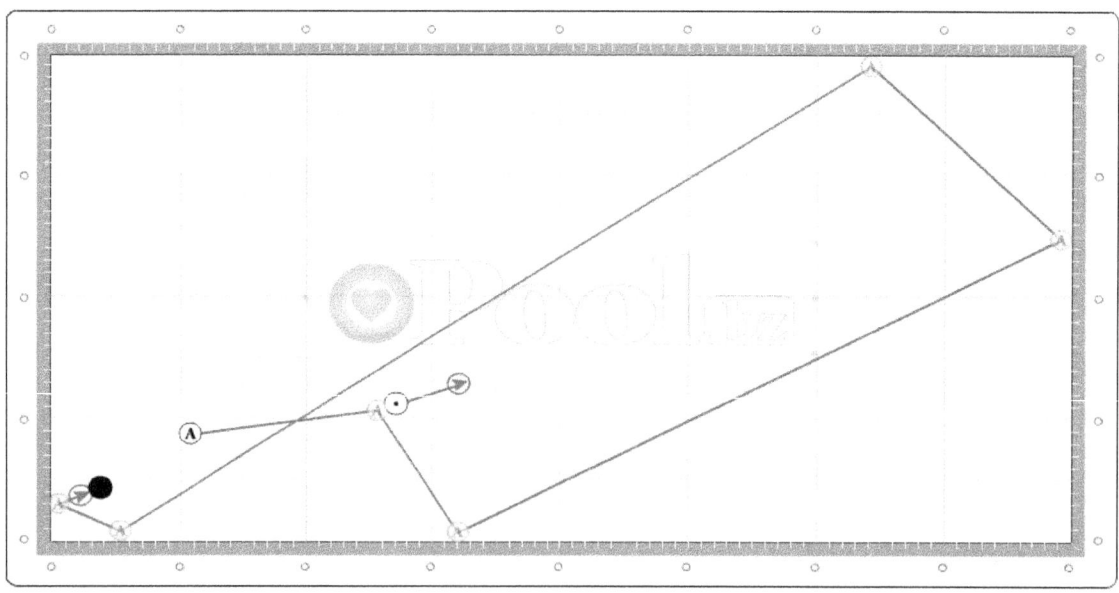

D:3d – Setup

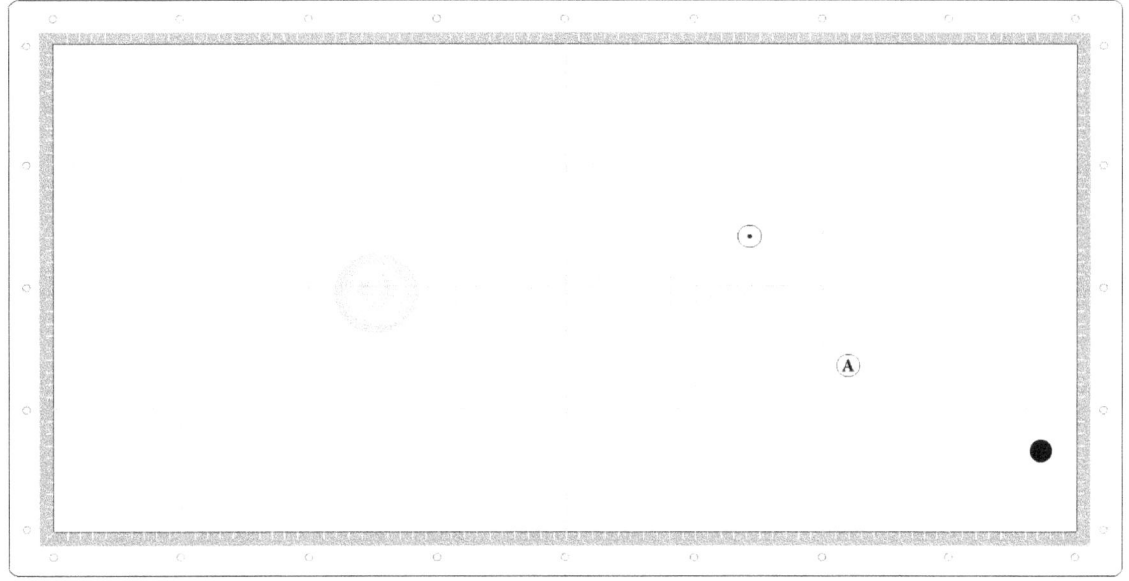

Shot Pattern

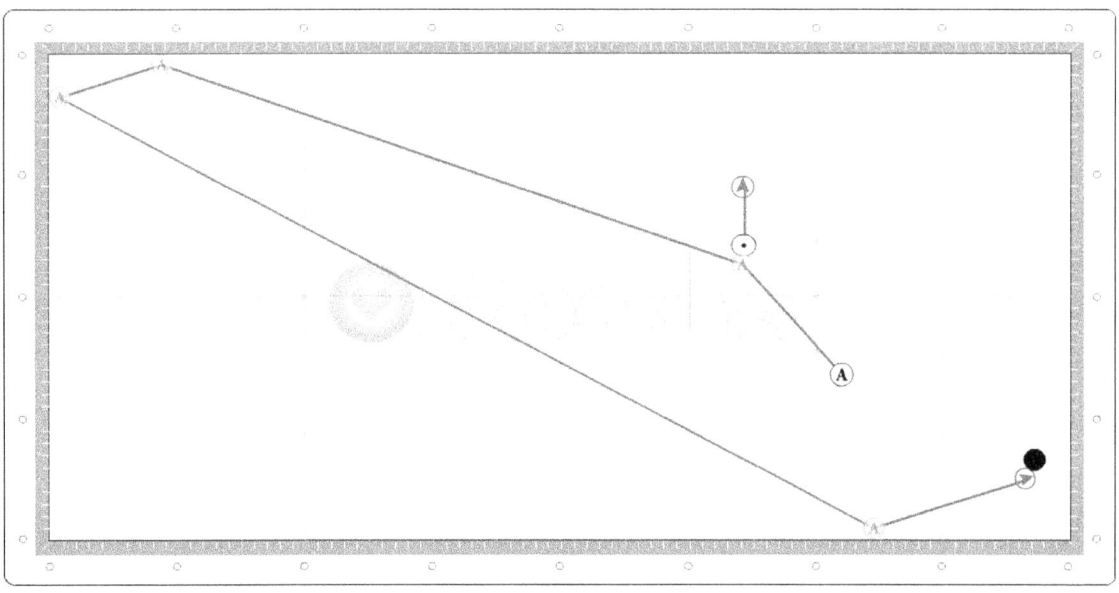

D: Group 4

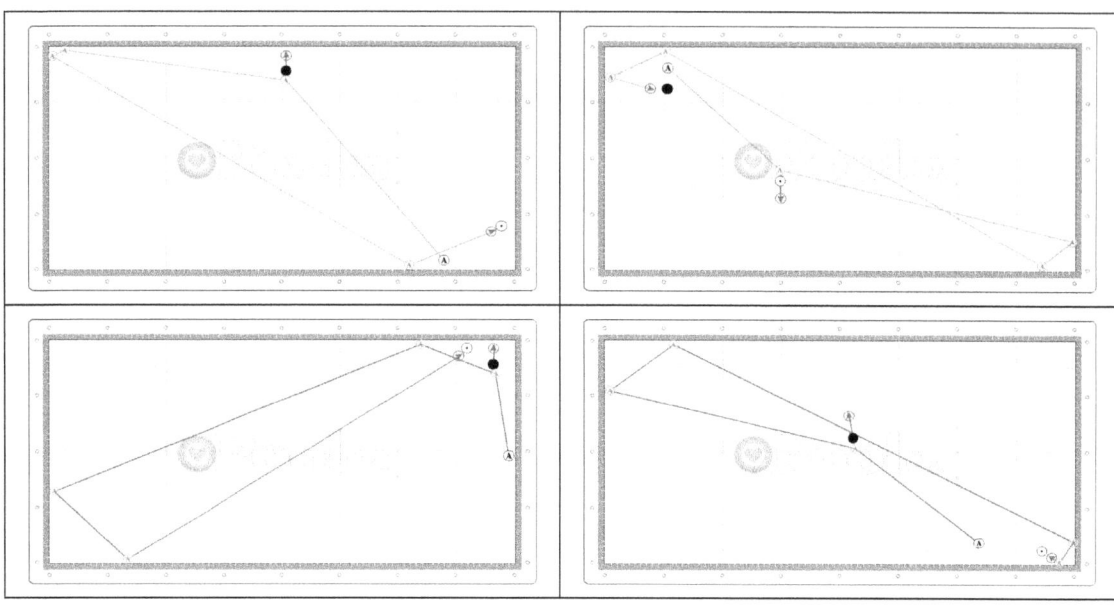

Analysis:

D:4a. _____

D:4b. _____

D:4c. _____

D:4d. _____

D:4a – Setup

Shot Pattern

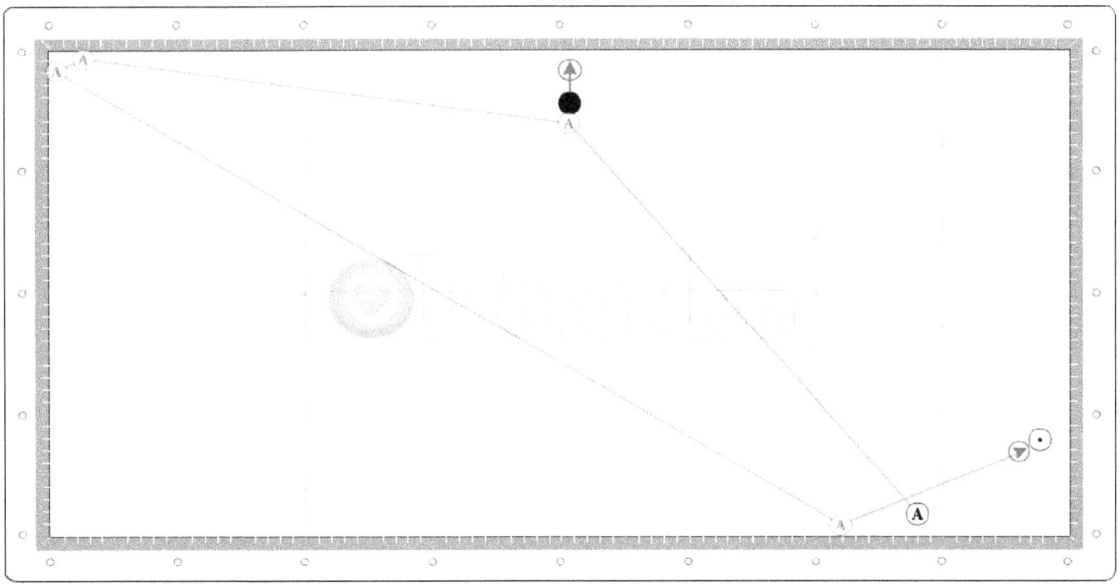

D:4b – Setup

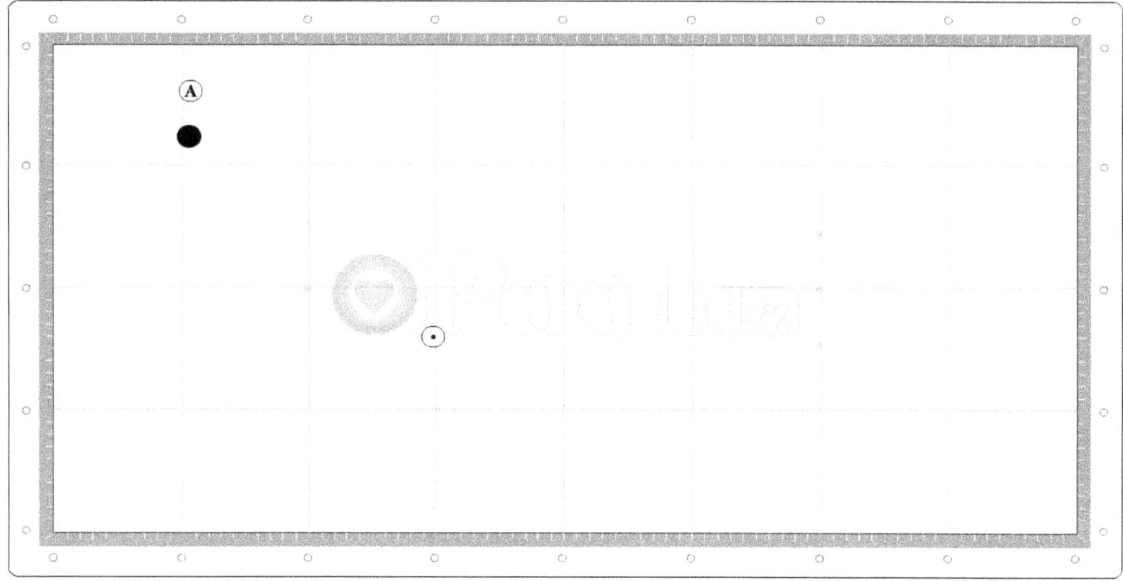

Shot Pattern

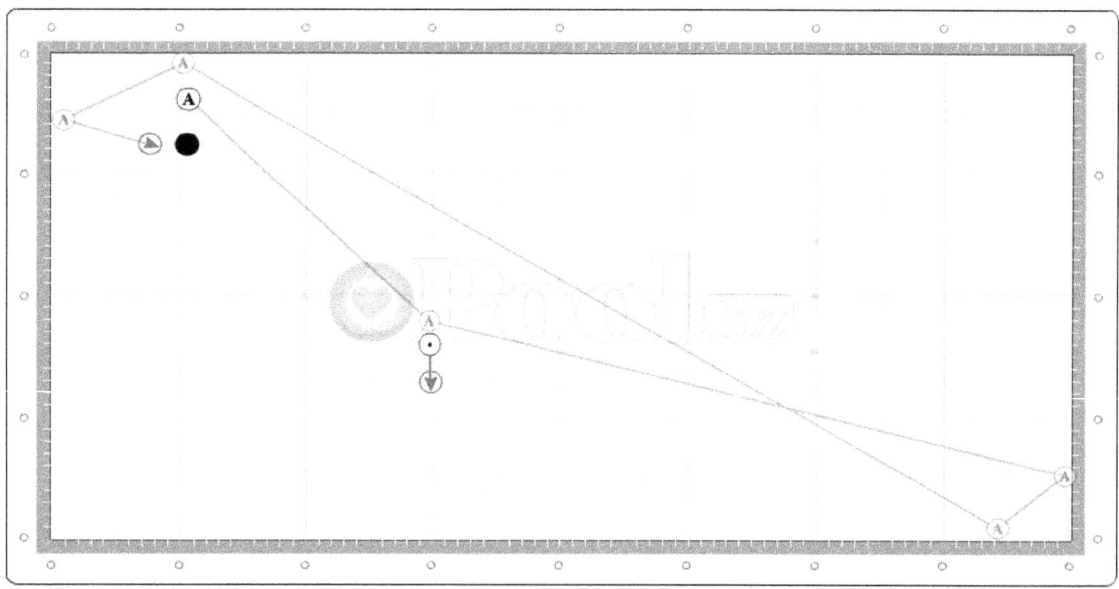

D:4c – Setup

Shot Pattern

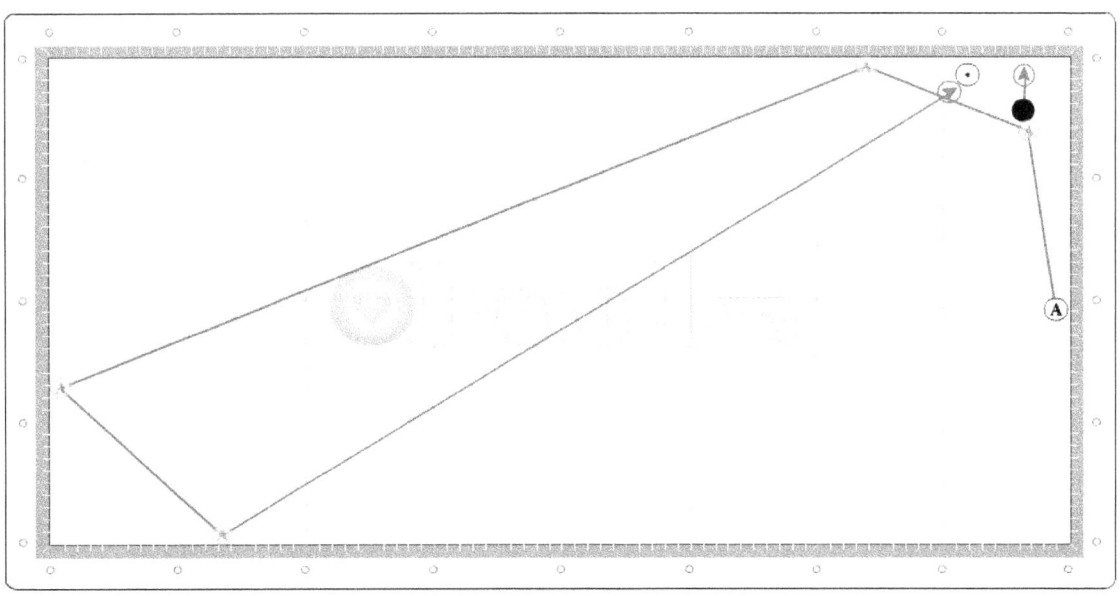

D:4d – Setup

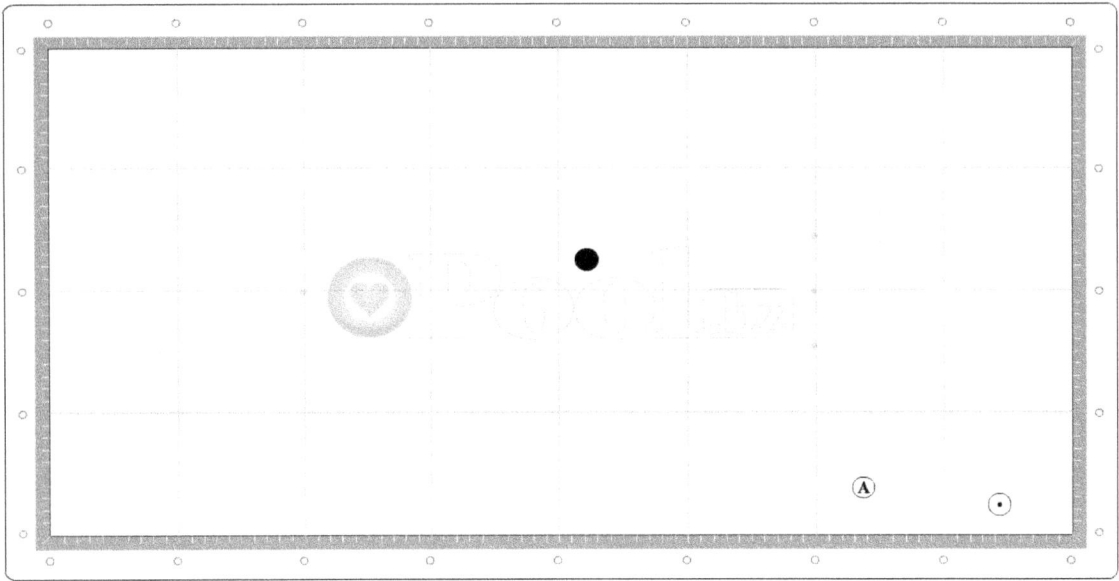

Shot Pattern

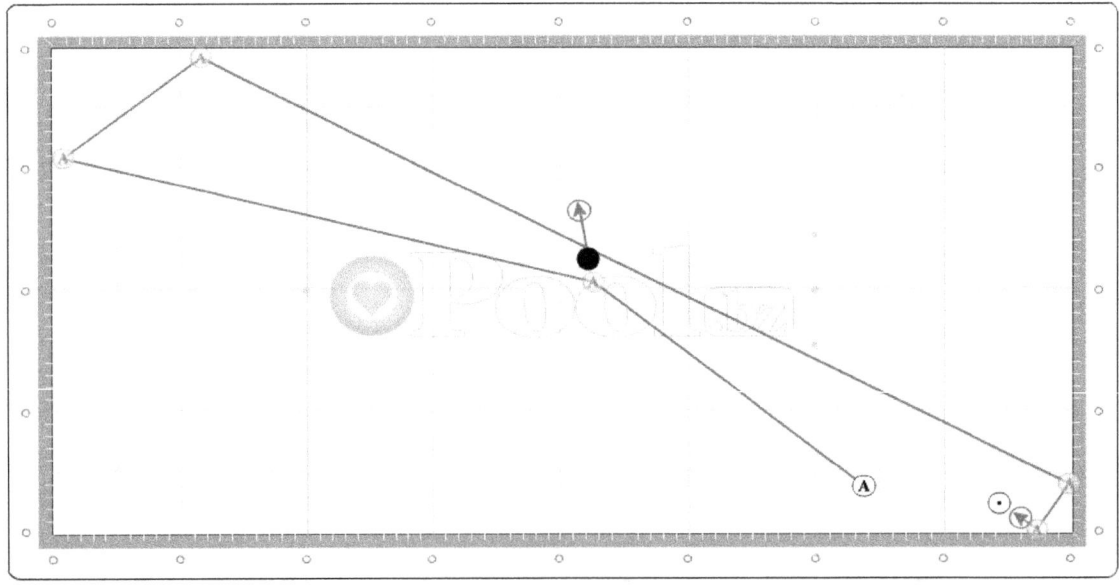

D: Group 5

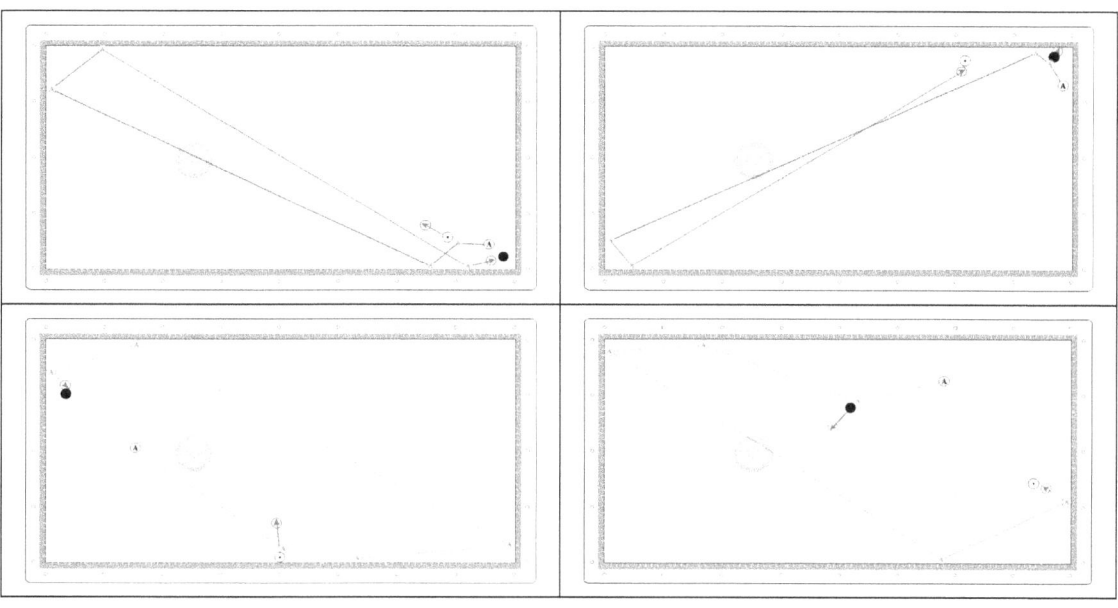

Analysis:

D:5a. _____

D:5b. _____

D:5c. _____

D:5d. _____

D:5a – Setup

Shot Pattern

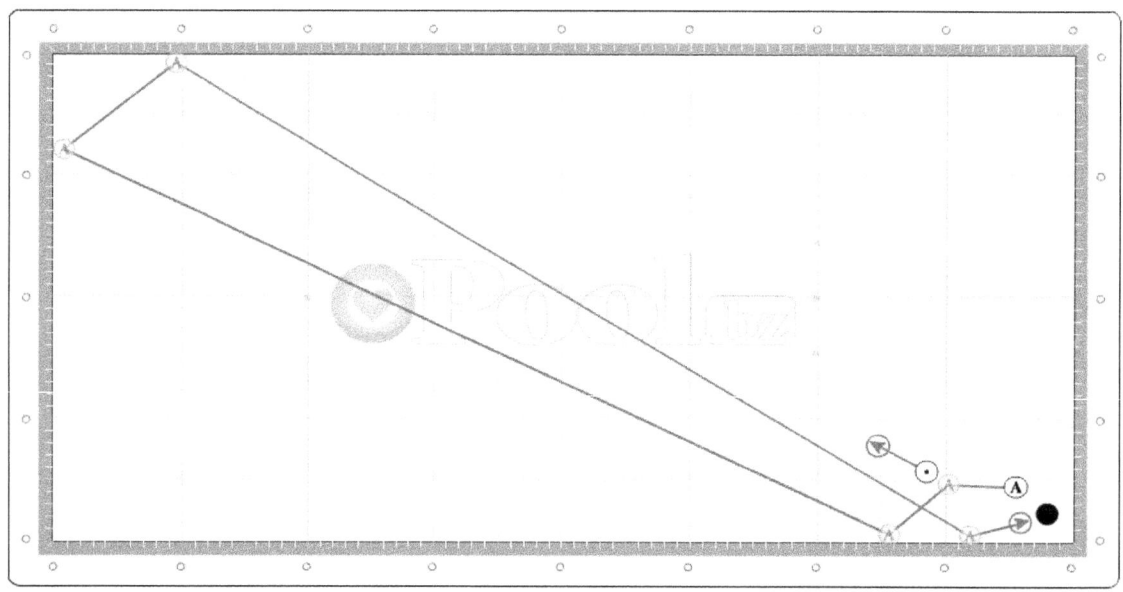

D:5b – Setup

Shot Pattern

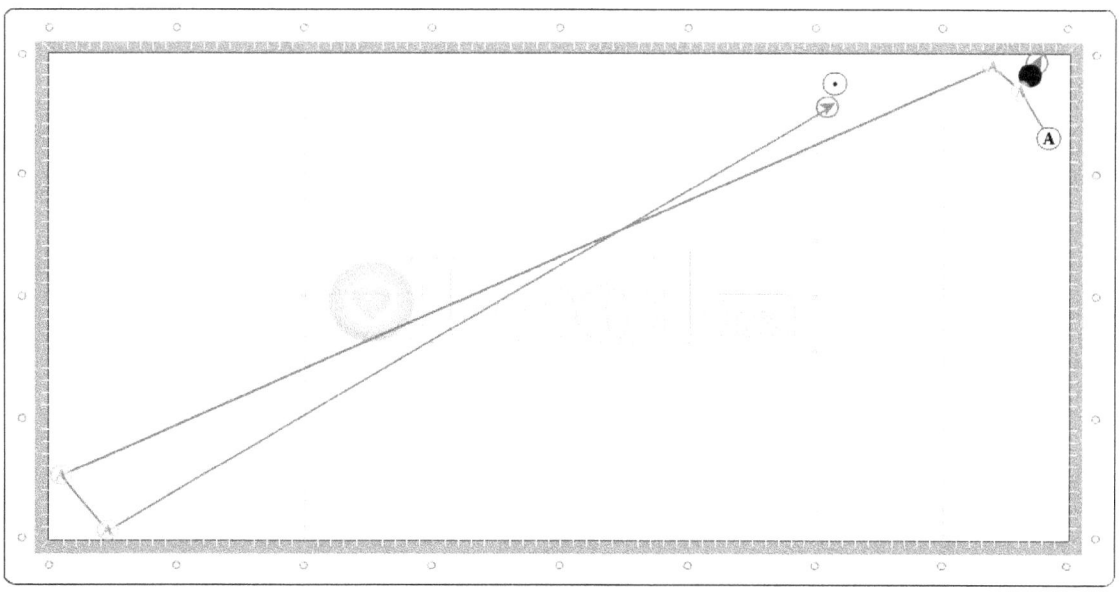

D:5c – Setup

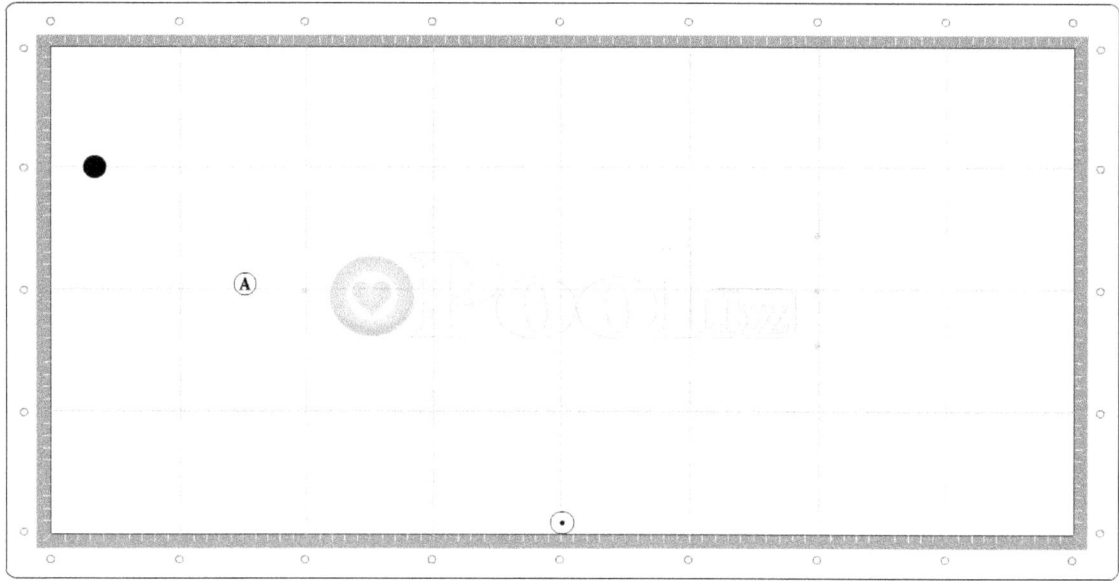

Shot Pattern

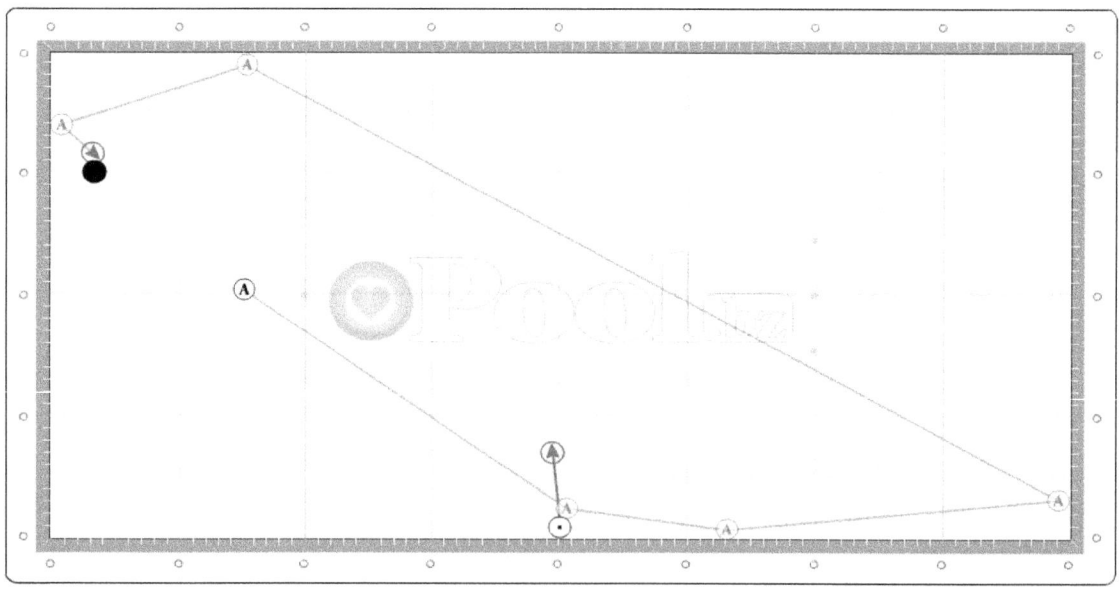

D:5d – Setup

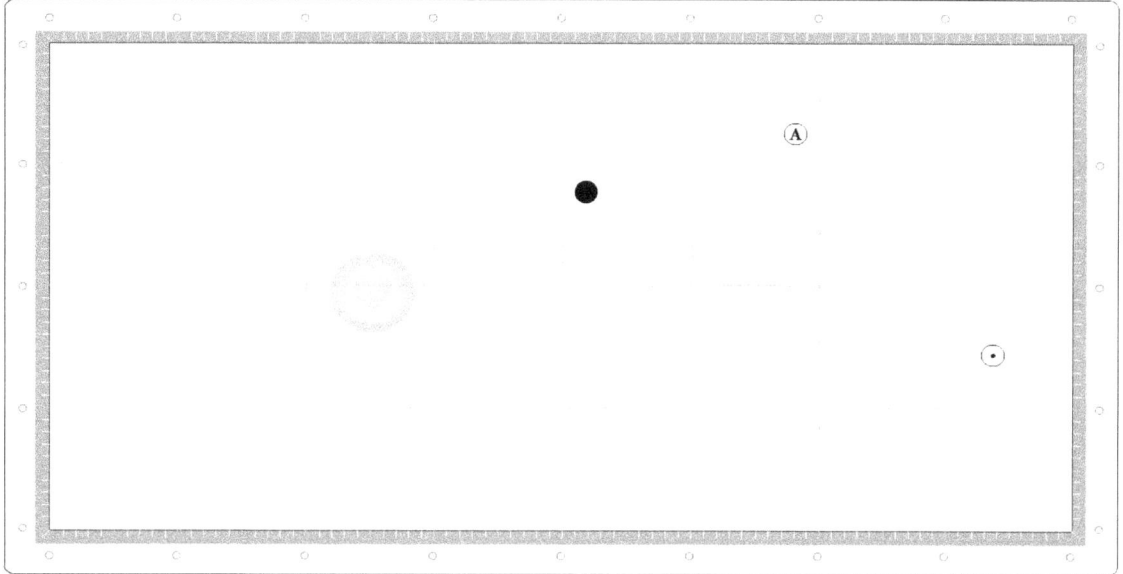

Shot Pattern

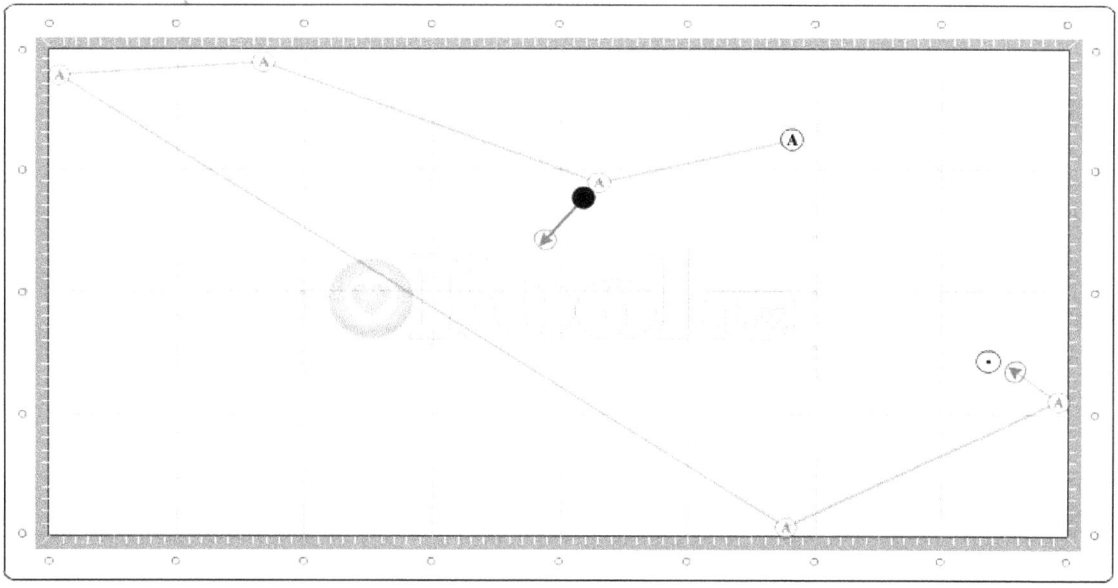

D: Group 6

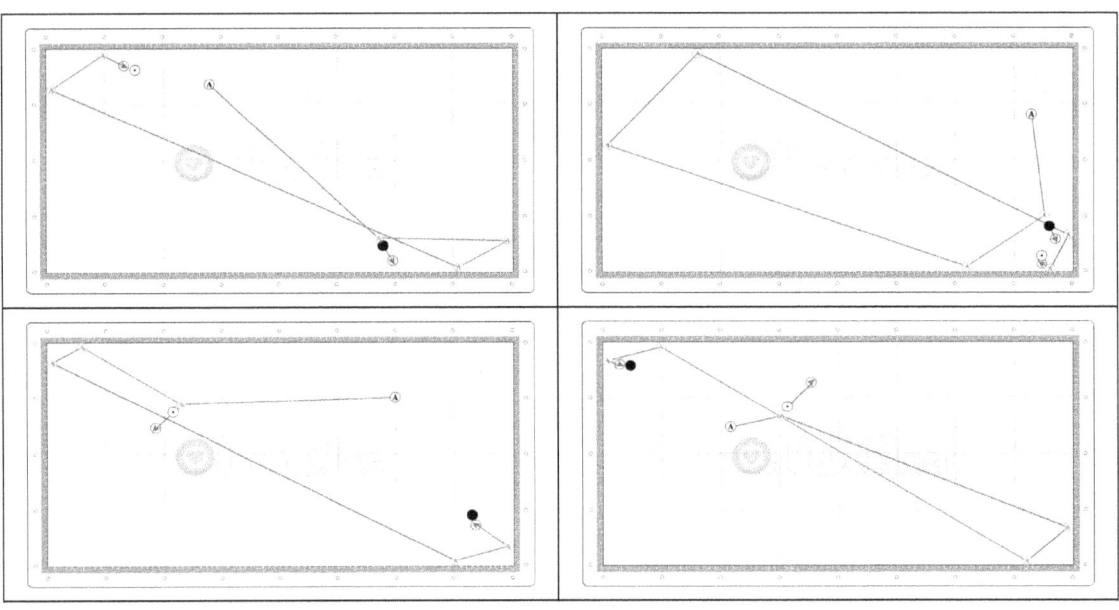

Analysis:

D:6a. _____

D:6b. _____

D:6c. _____

D:6d. _____

D:6a – Setup

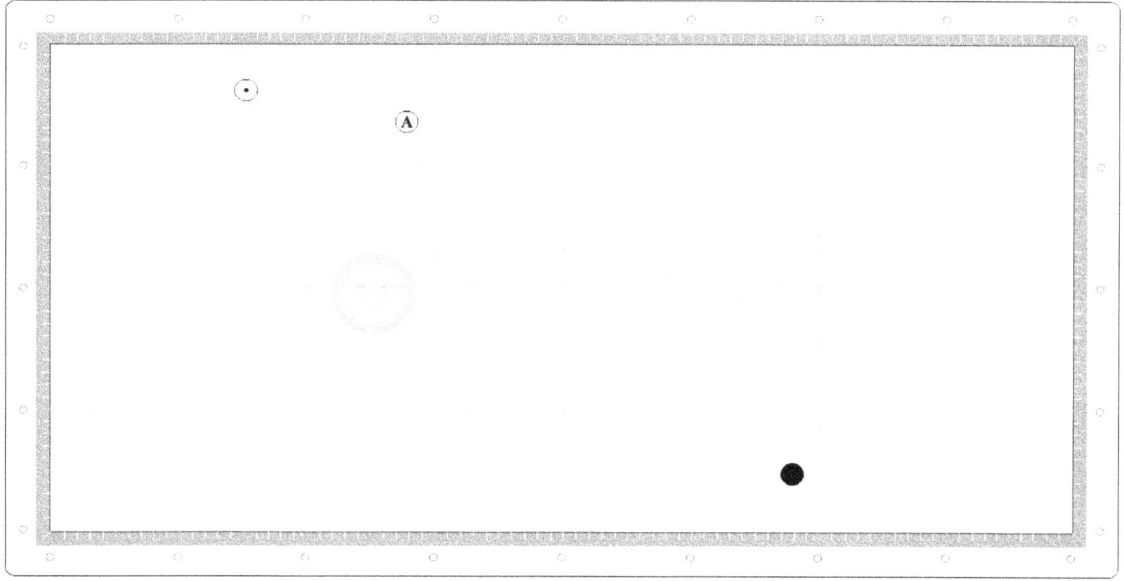

Shot Pattern

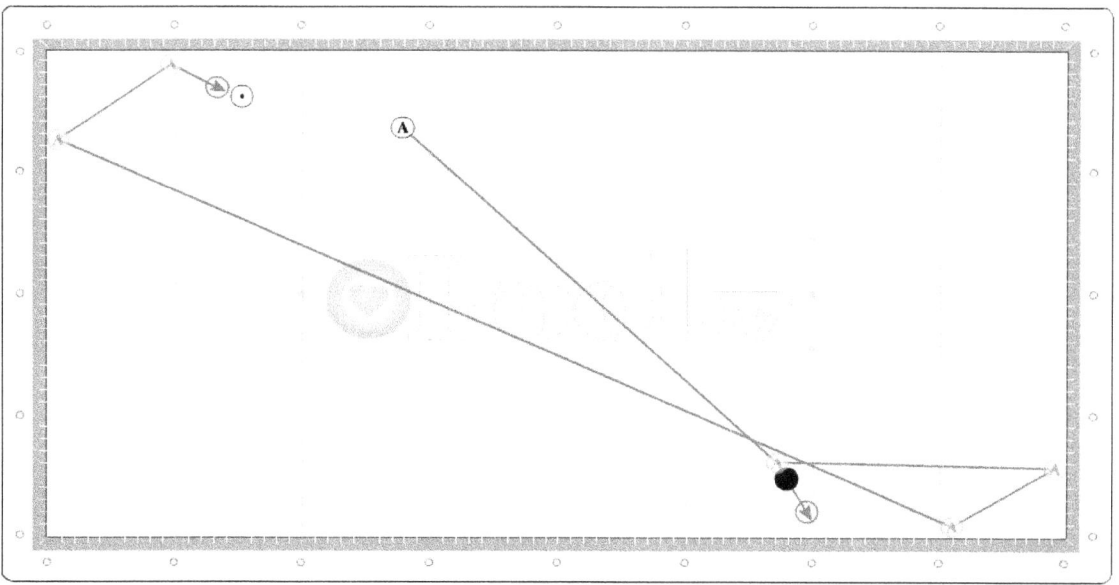

D:6b – Setup

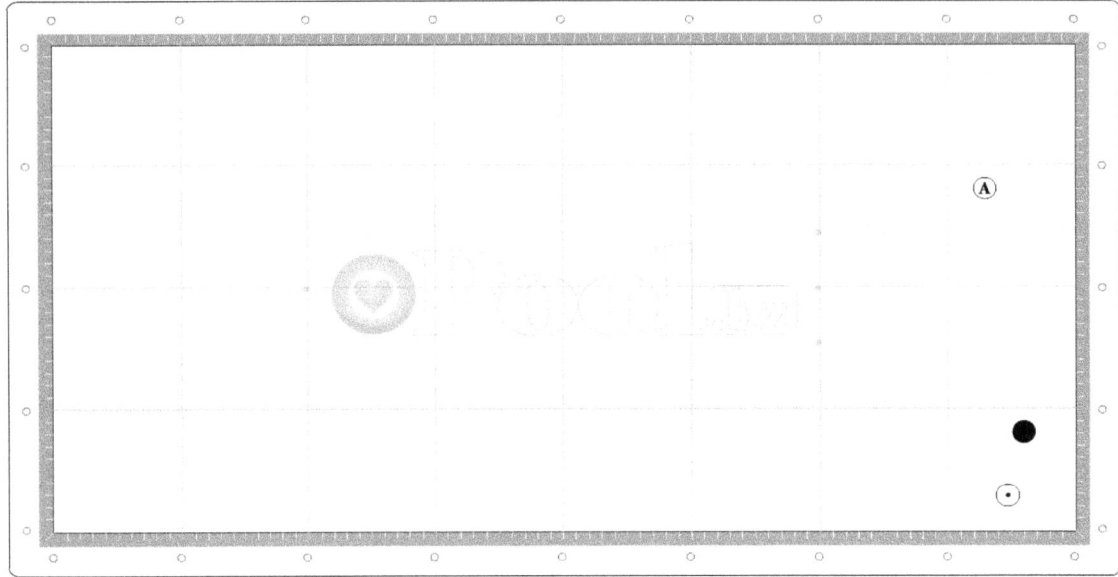

Shot Pattern

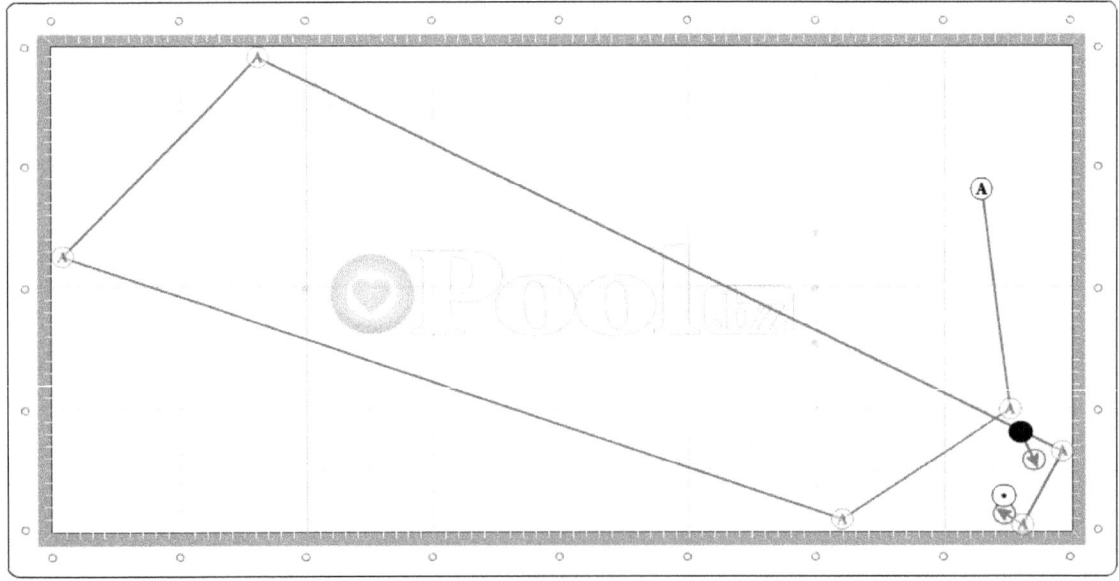

D:6c – Setup

Shot Pattern

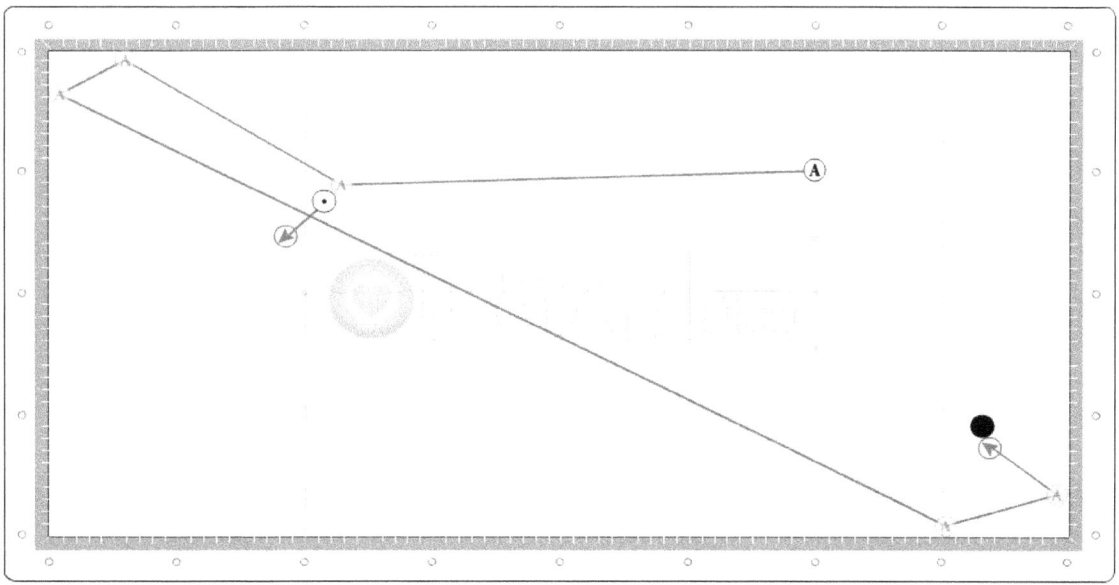

D:6d – Setup

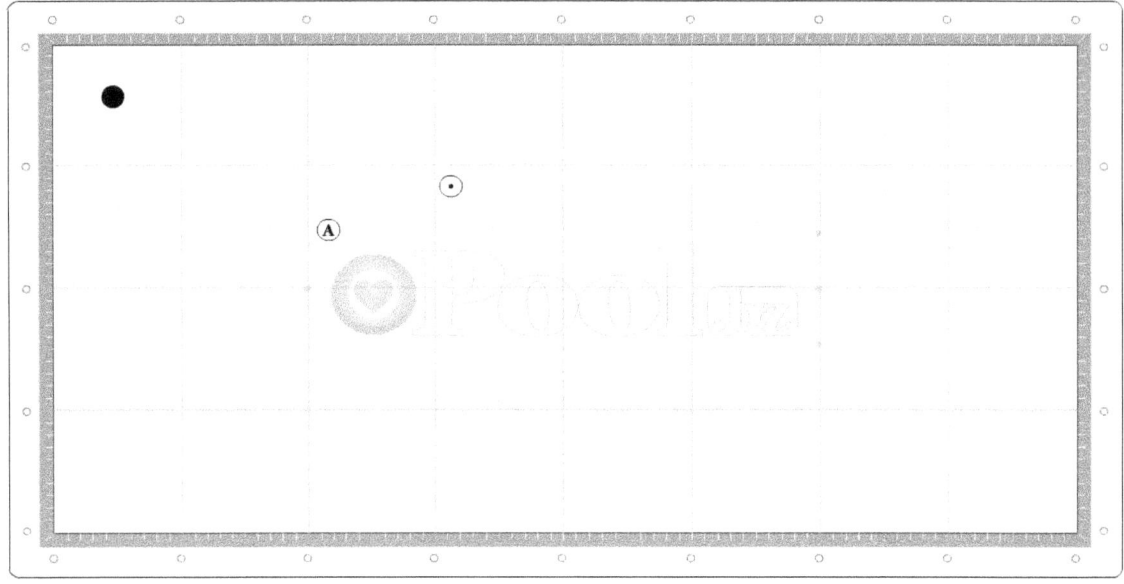

Shot Pattern

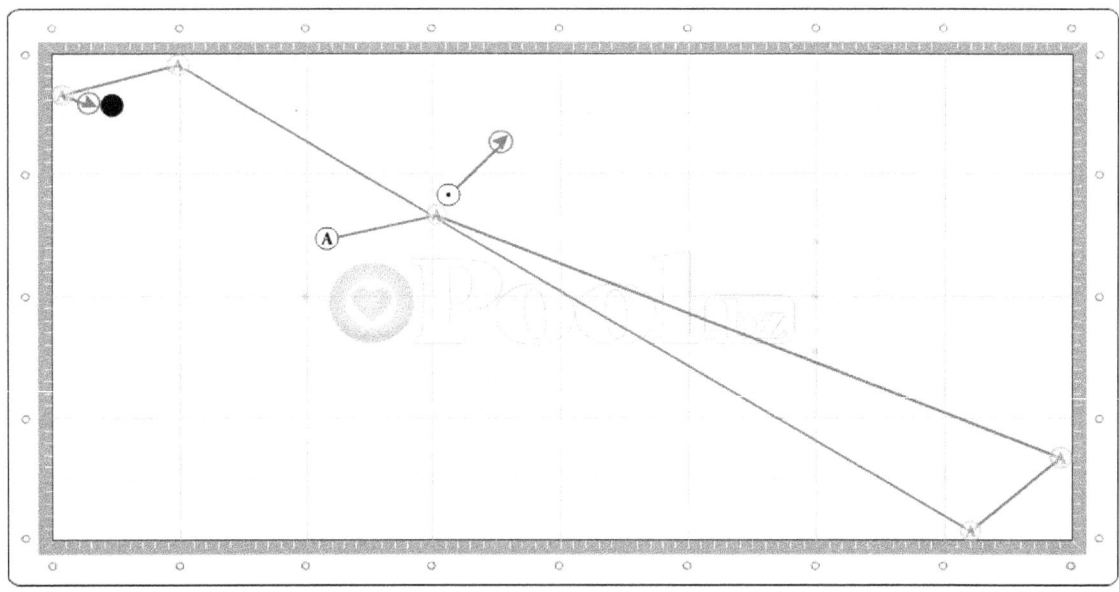

D: Group 7

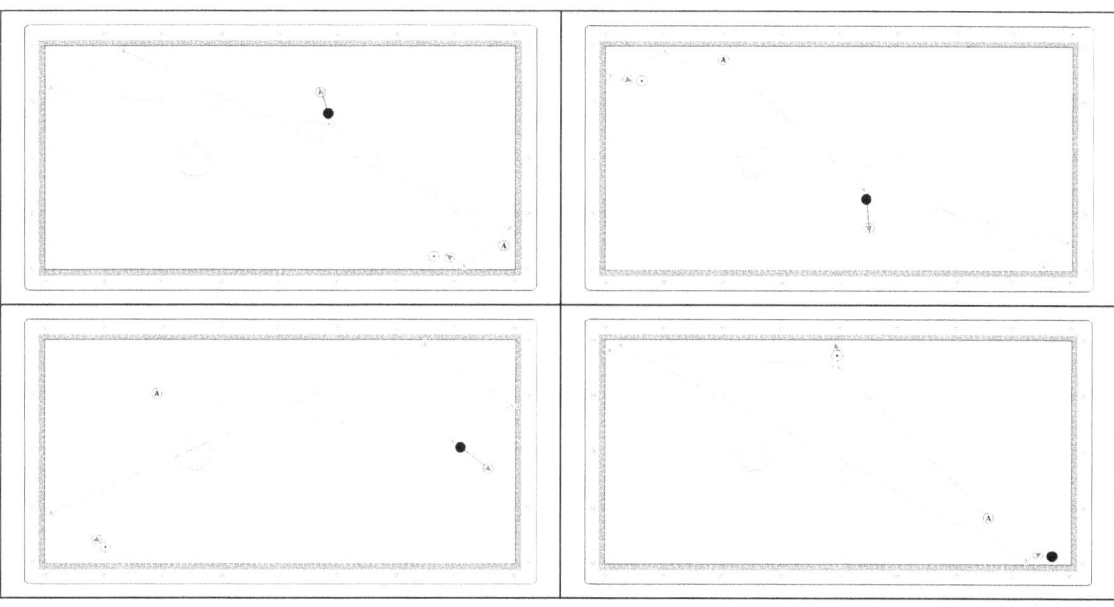

Analysis:

D:7a. _____

D:7b. _____

D:7c. _____

D:7d. _____

D:7a – Setup

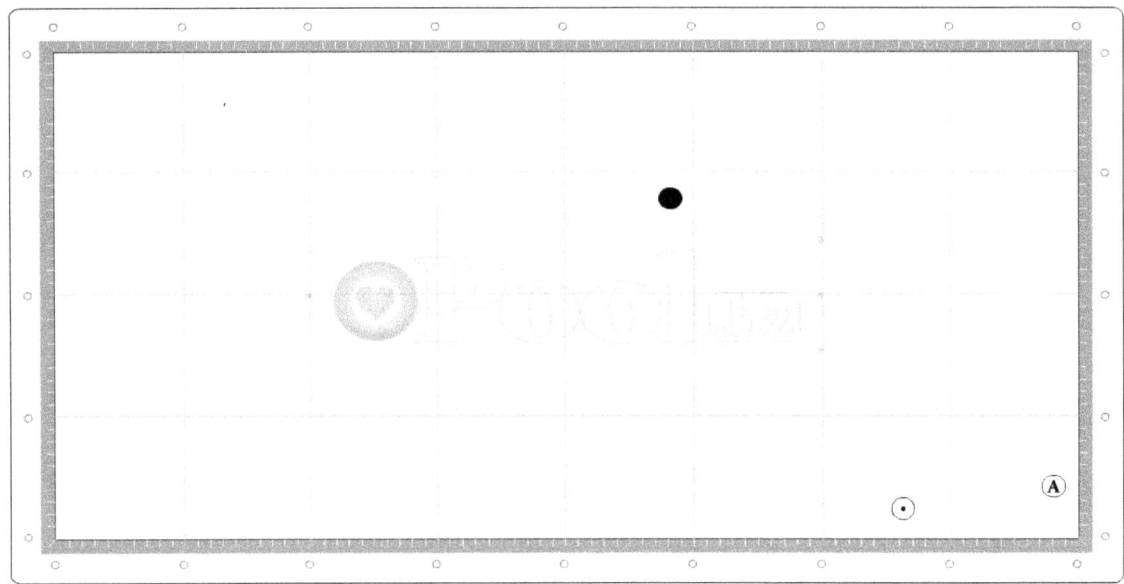

Shot Pattern

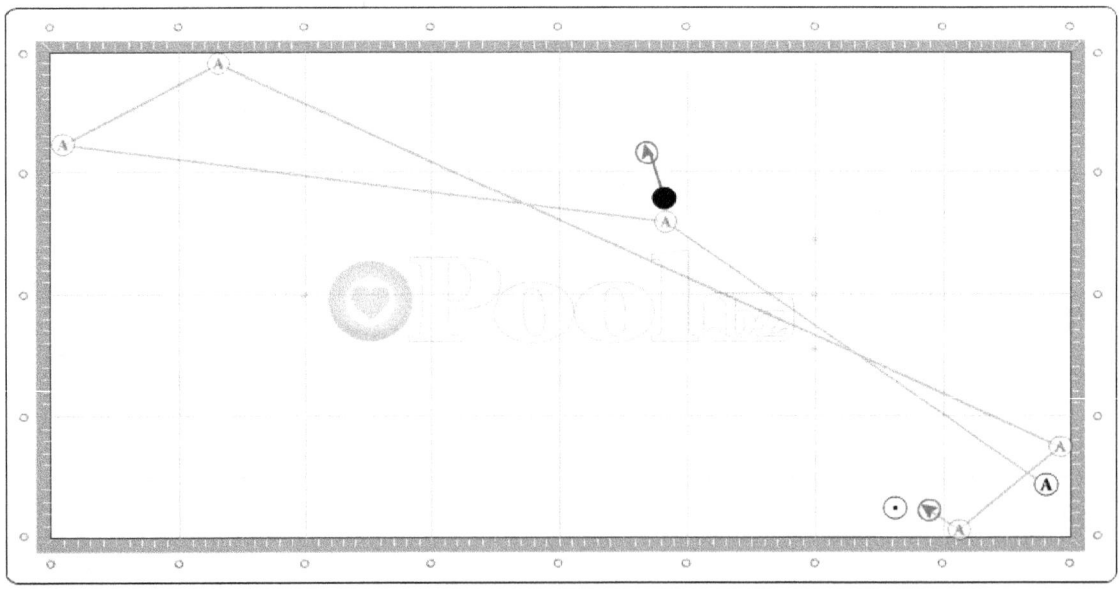

D:7b – Setup

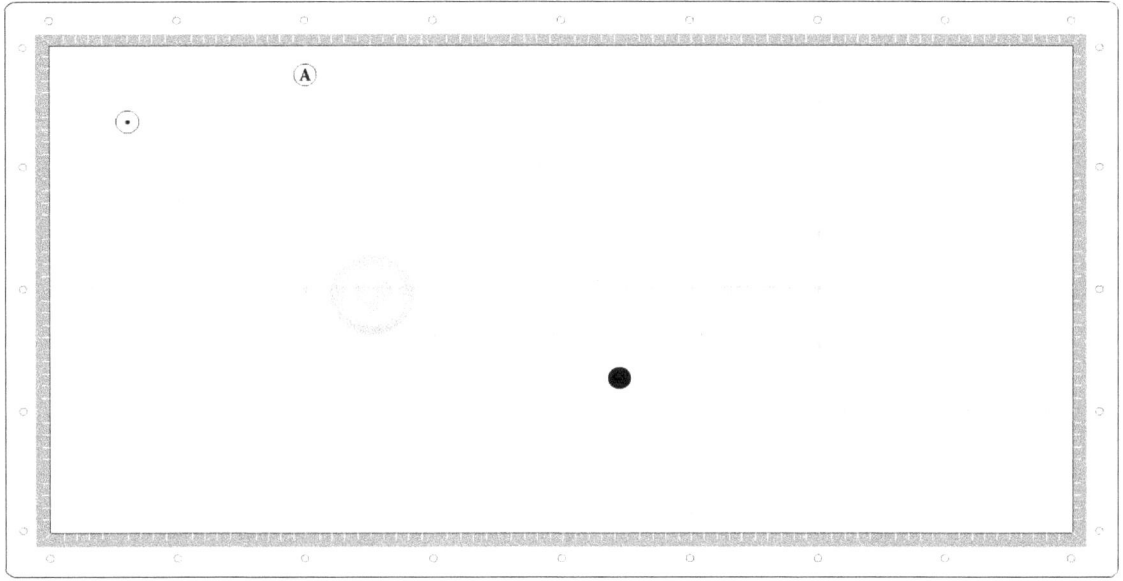

Shot Pattern

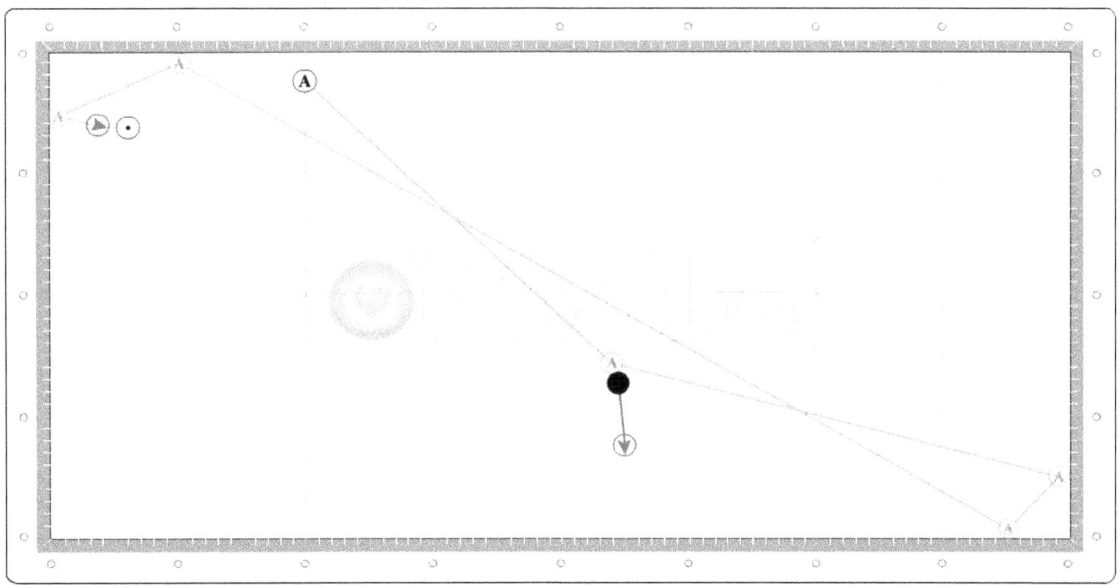

D:7c – Setup

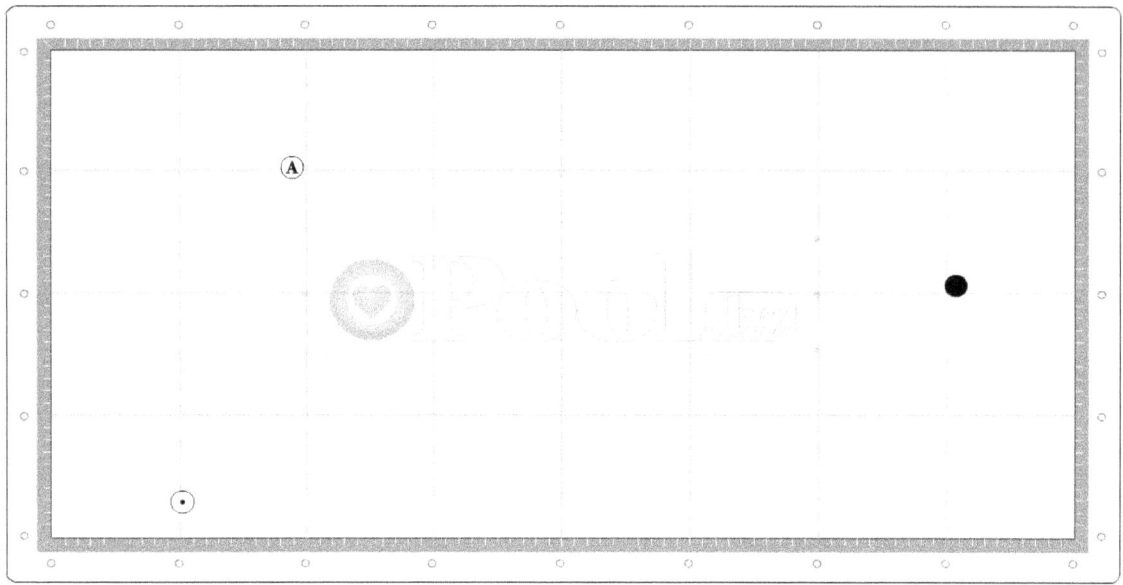

Shot Pattern

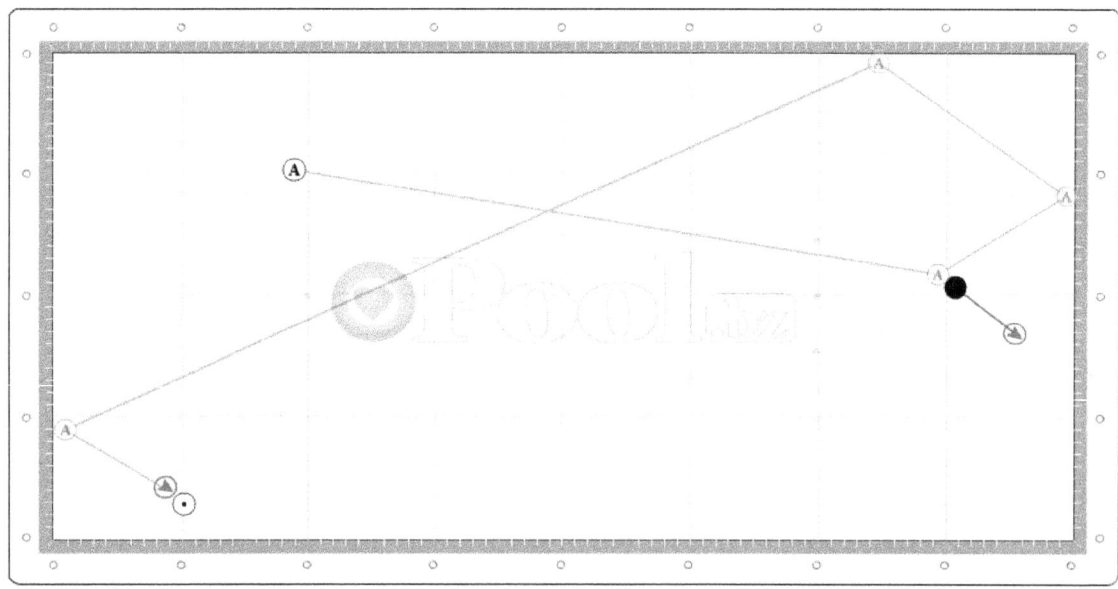

D:7d – Setup

Shot Pattern

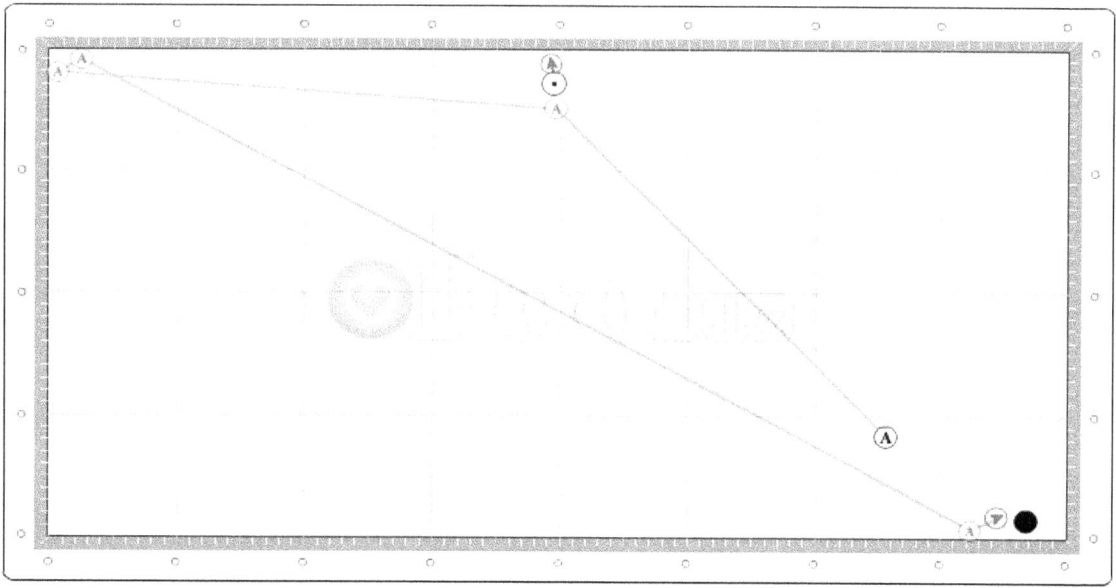

Carom Billiards: Cross-Corner Diagonal Patterns

E: Double Modified Diagonals

Like section E, the CB comes off the first OB and starts the diagonal pattern. The CB goes into the corner and then returns on a diagonal path to make contact with the second OB.

E: Group 1

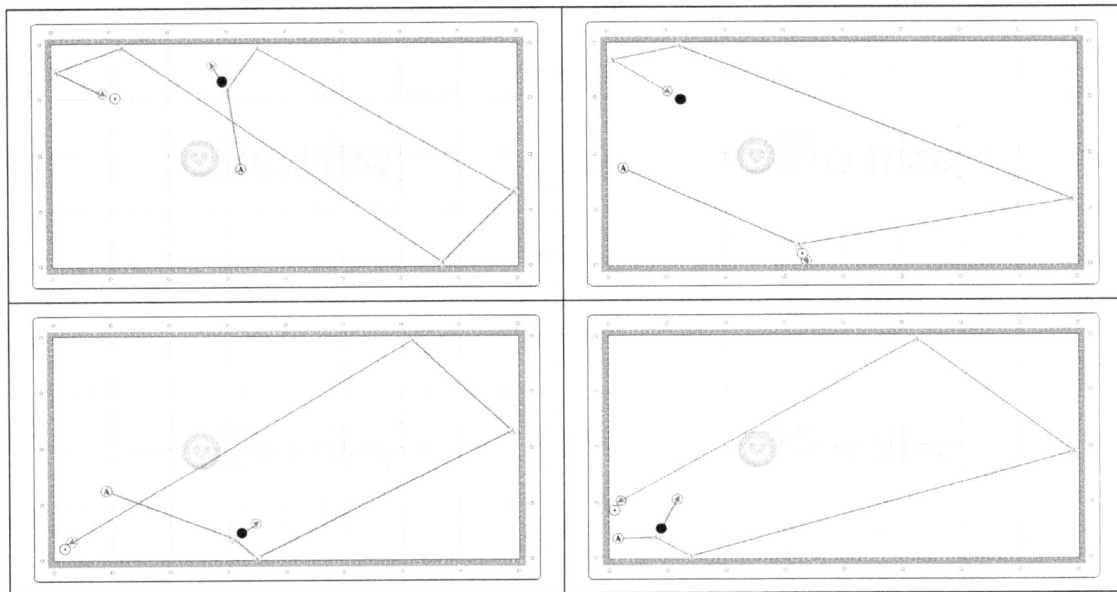

Analysis:

E:1a. _____

E:1b. _____

E:1c. _____

E:1d. _____

E:1a – Setup

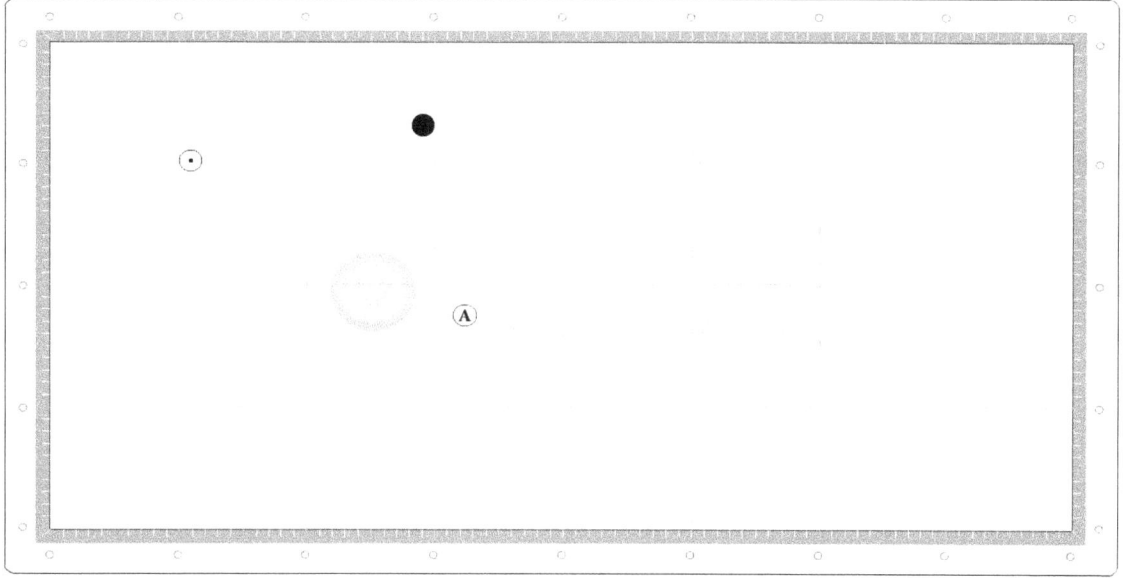

Shot Pattern

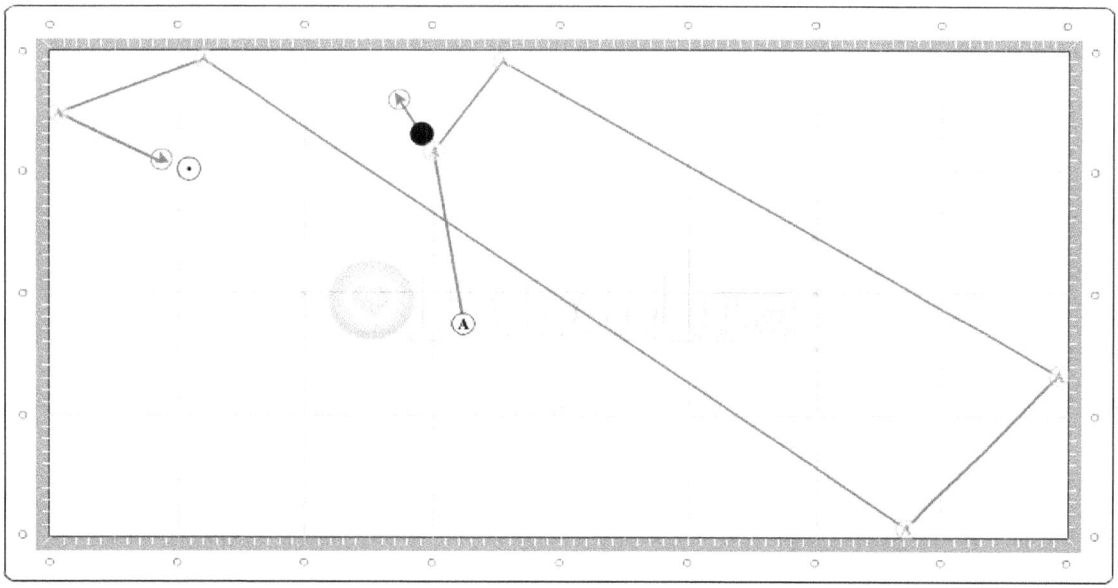

E:1b – Setup

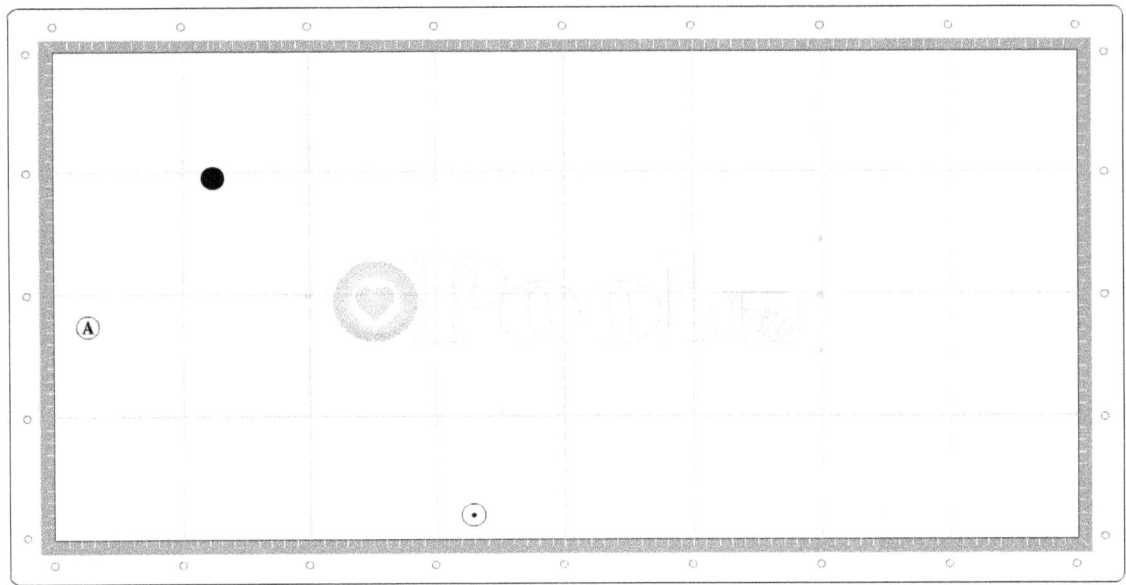

Shot Pattern

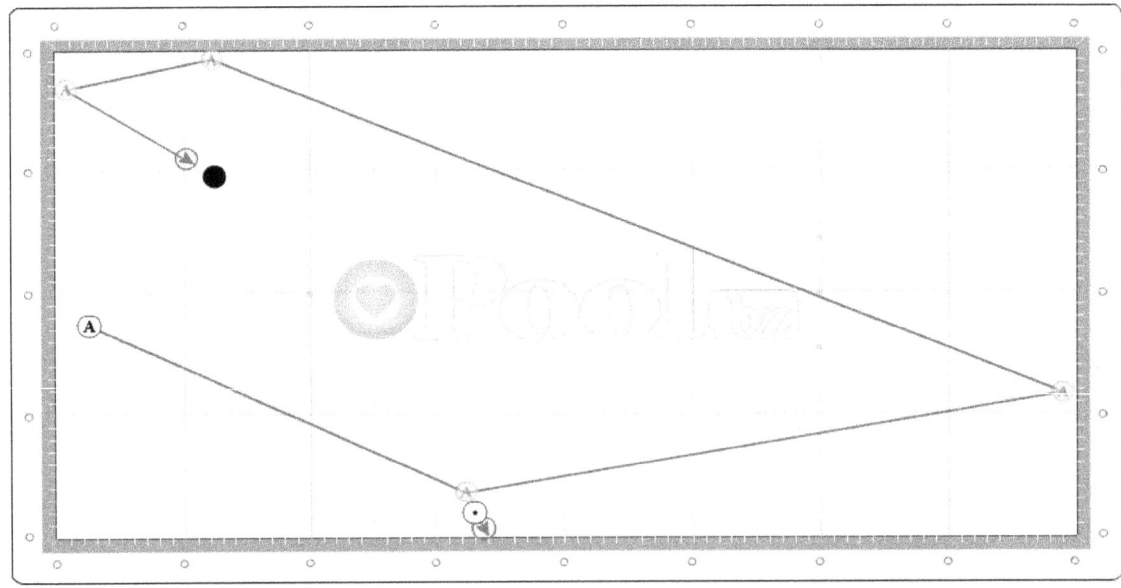

E:1c – Setup

Shot Pattern

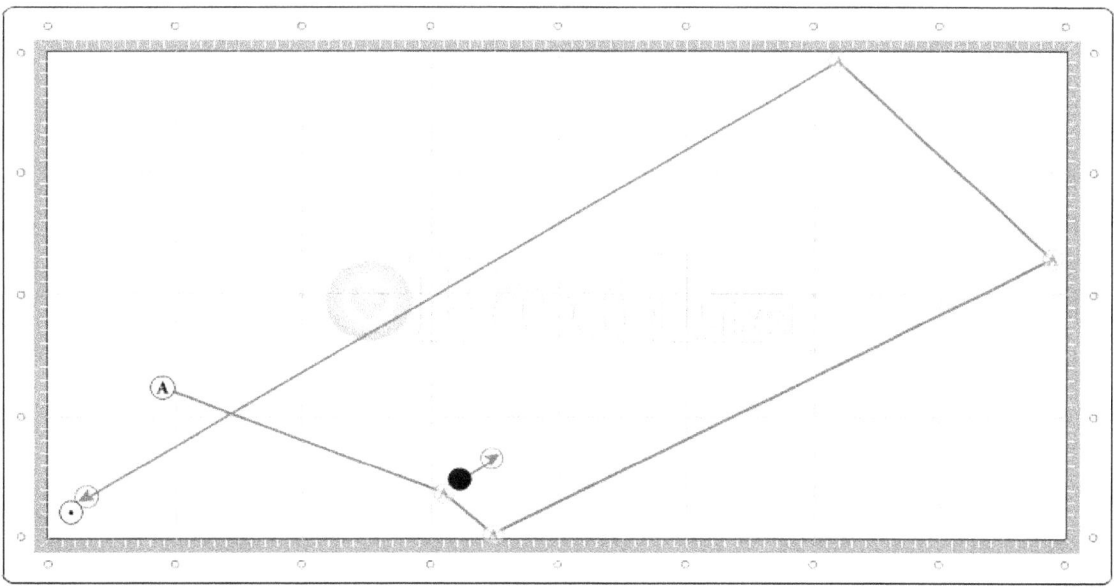

E:1d – Setup

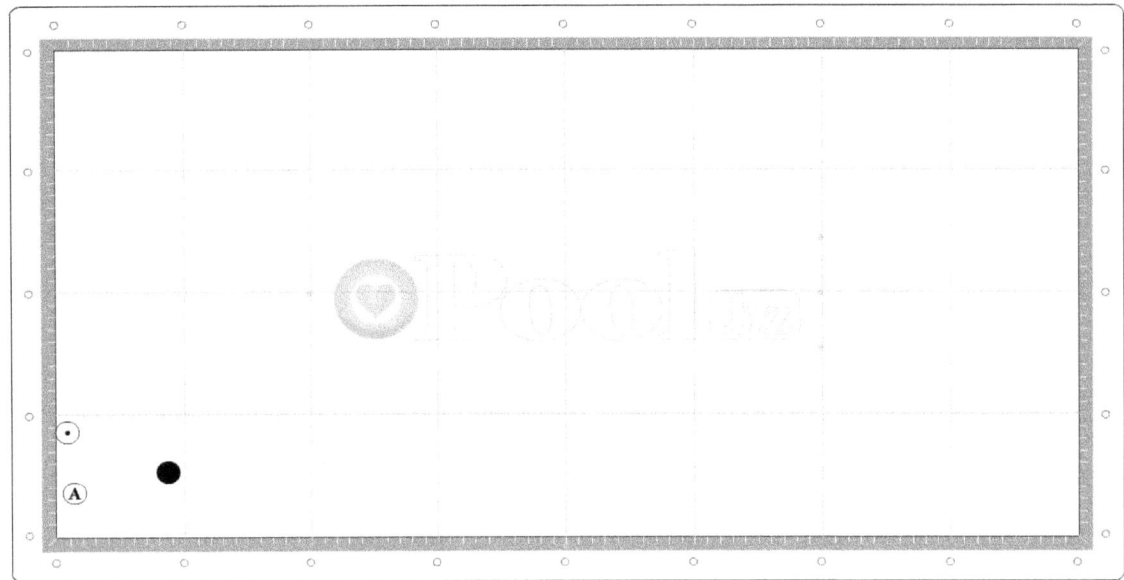

Shot Pattern

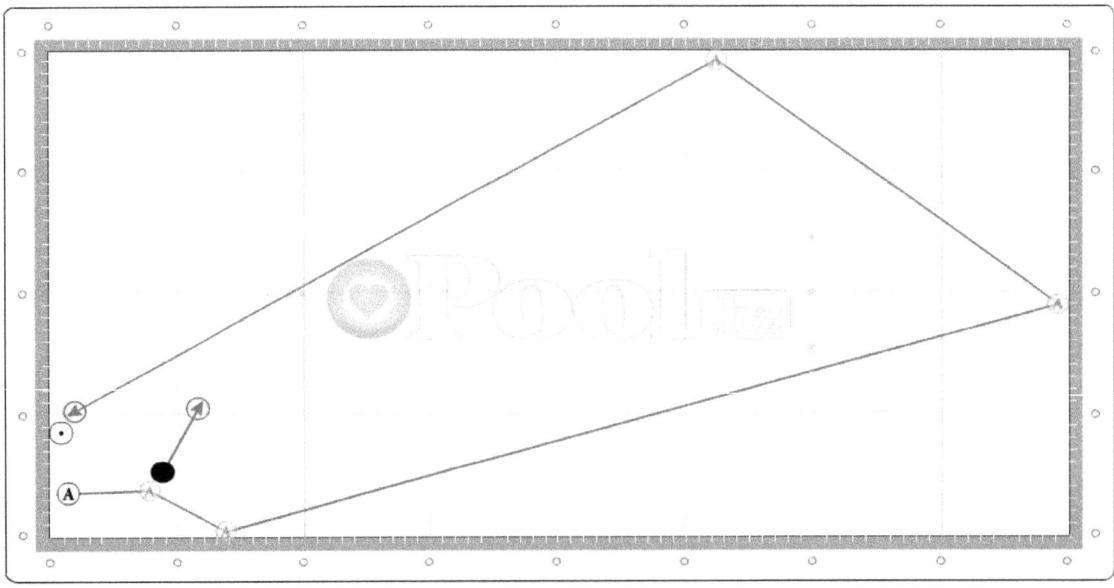

E: Group 2

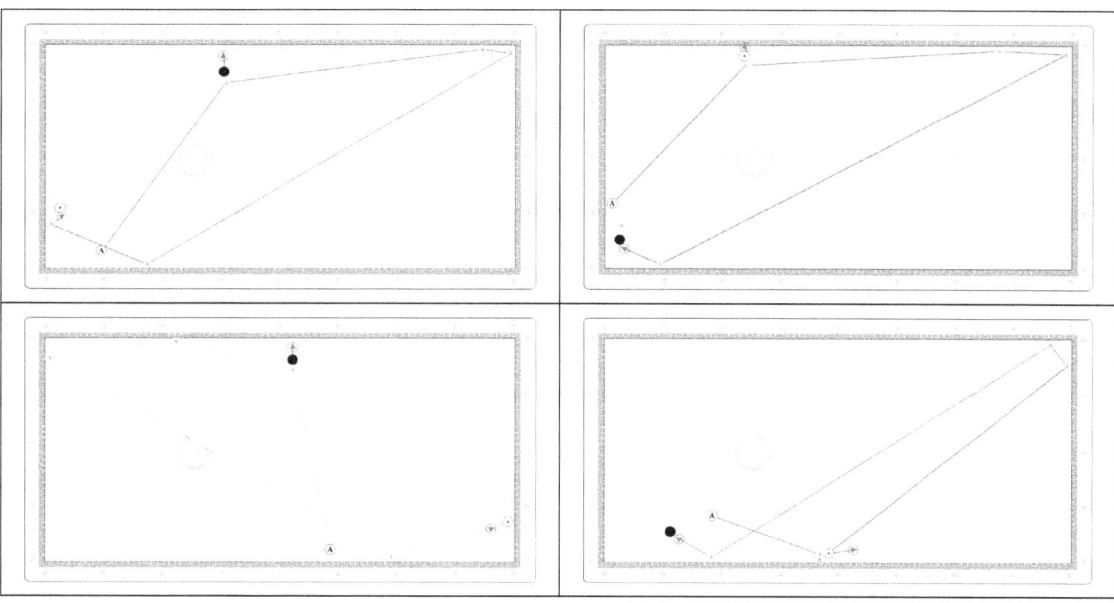

Analysis:

E:2a. _____

E:2b. _____

E:2c. _____

E:2d. _____

E:2a – Setup

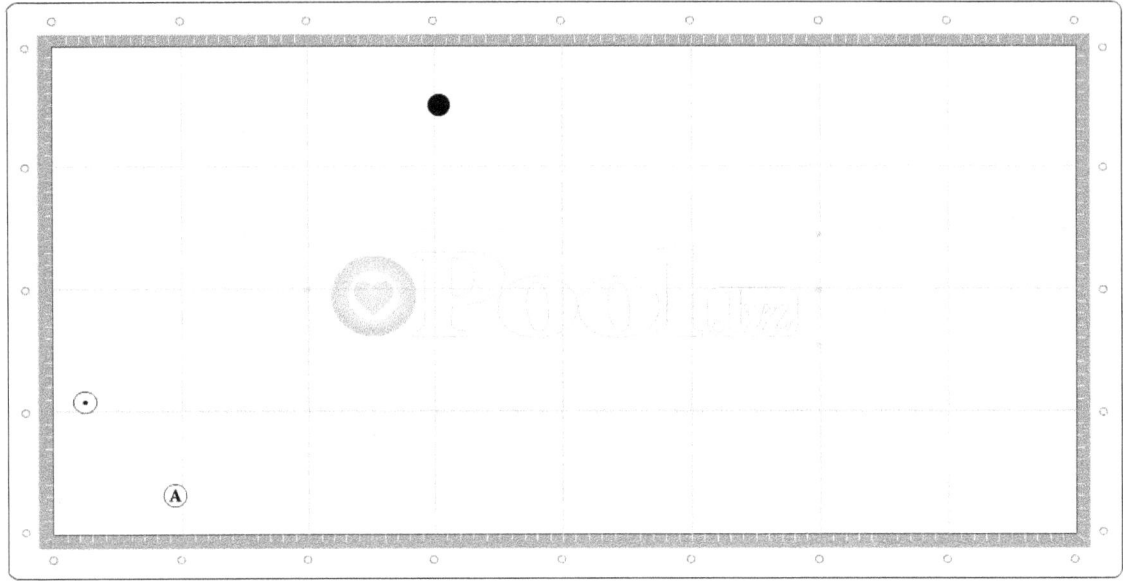

Shot Pattern

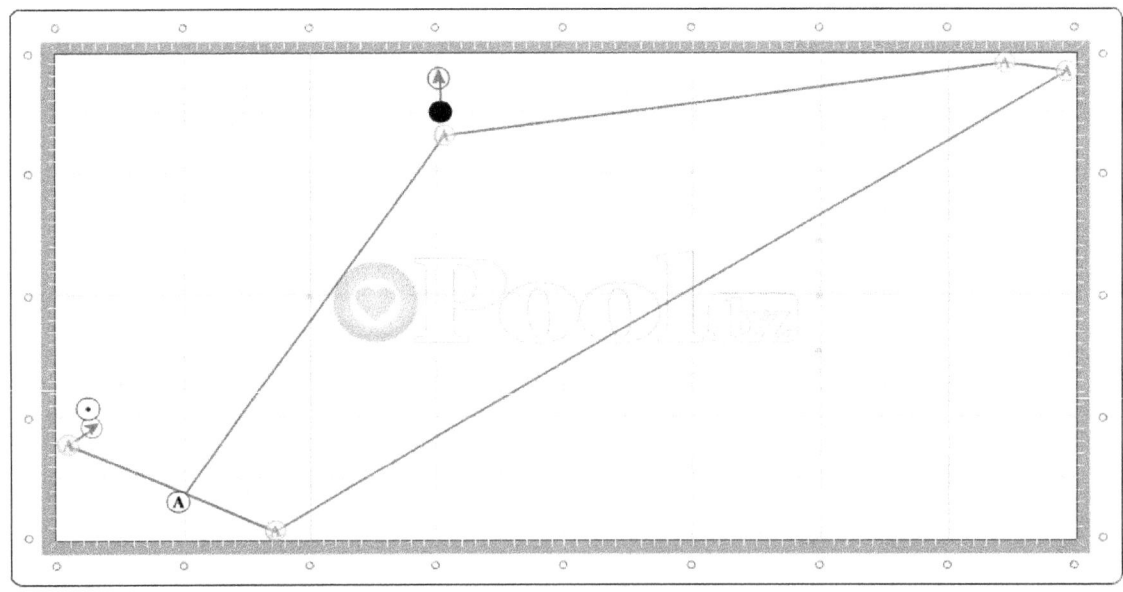

E:2b – Setup

Shot Pattern

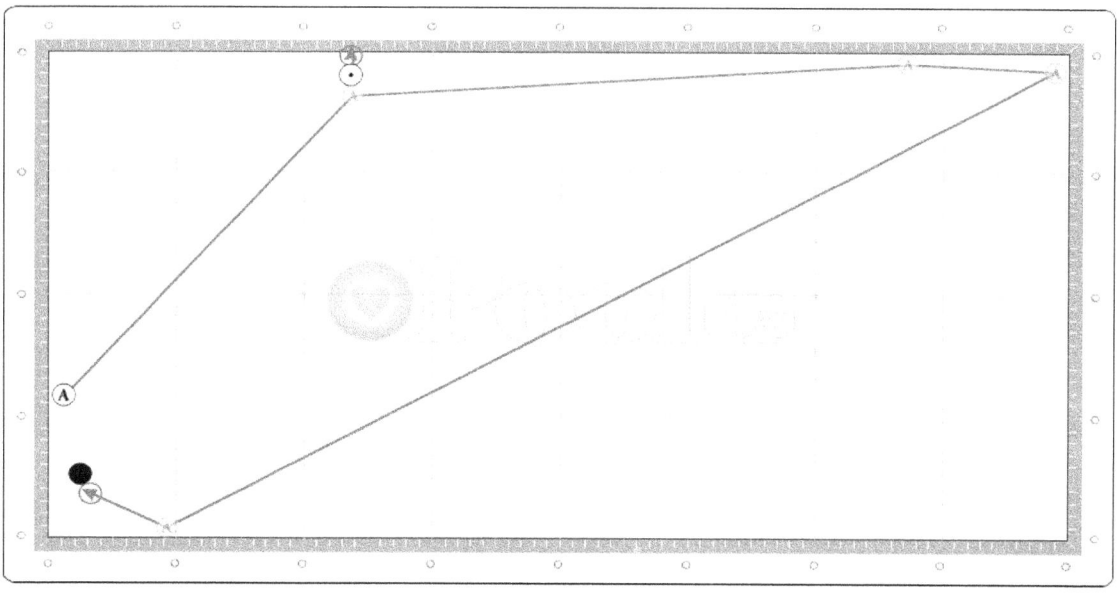

E:2c – Setup

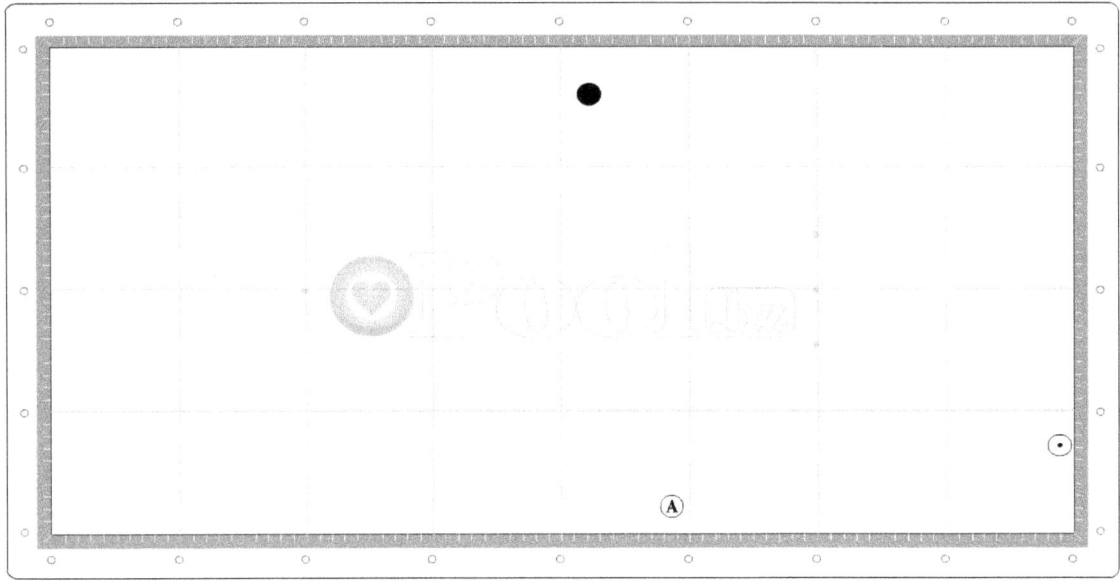

Shot Pattern

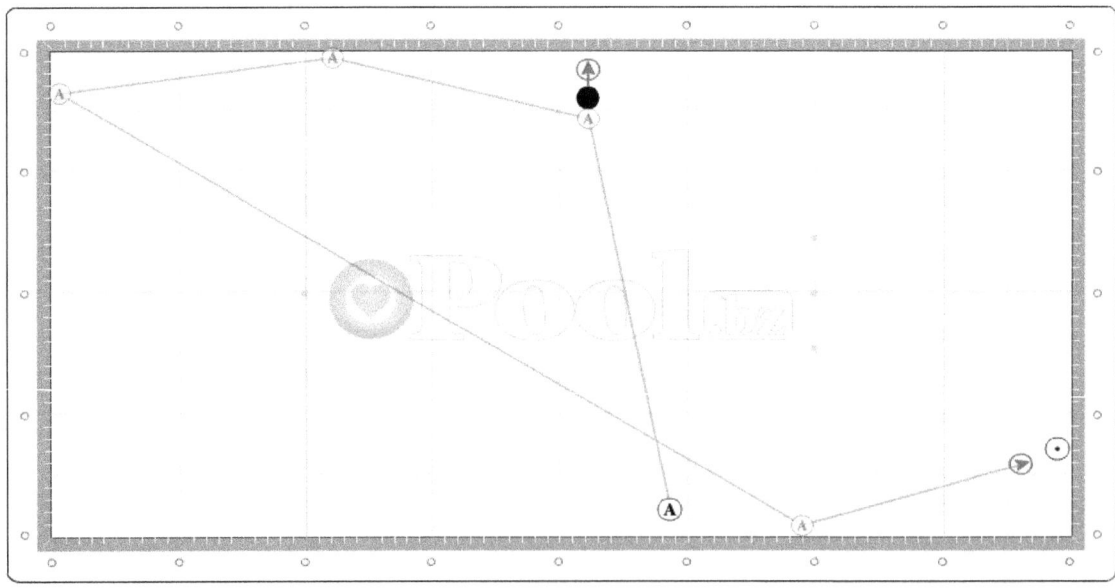

E:2d – Setup

Shot Pattern

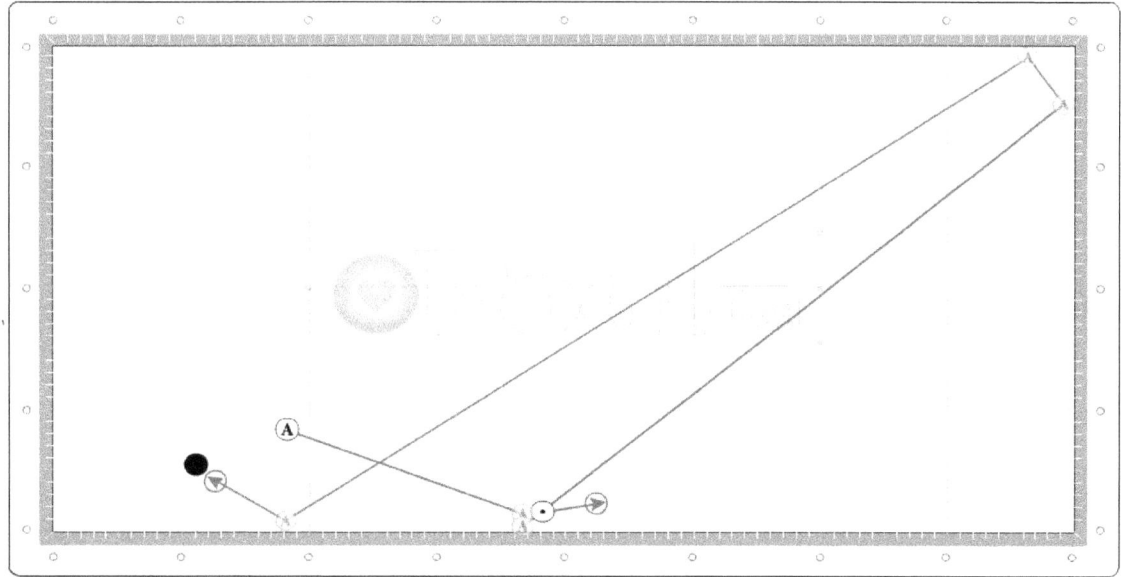

E: Group 3

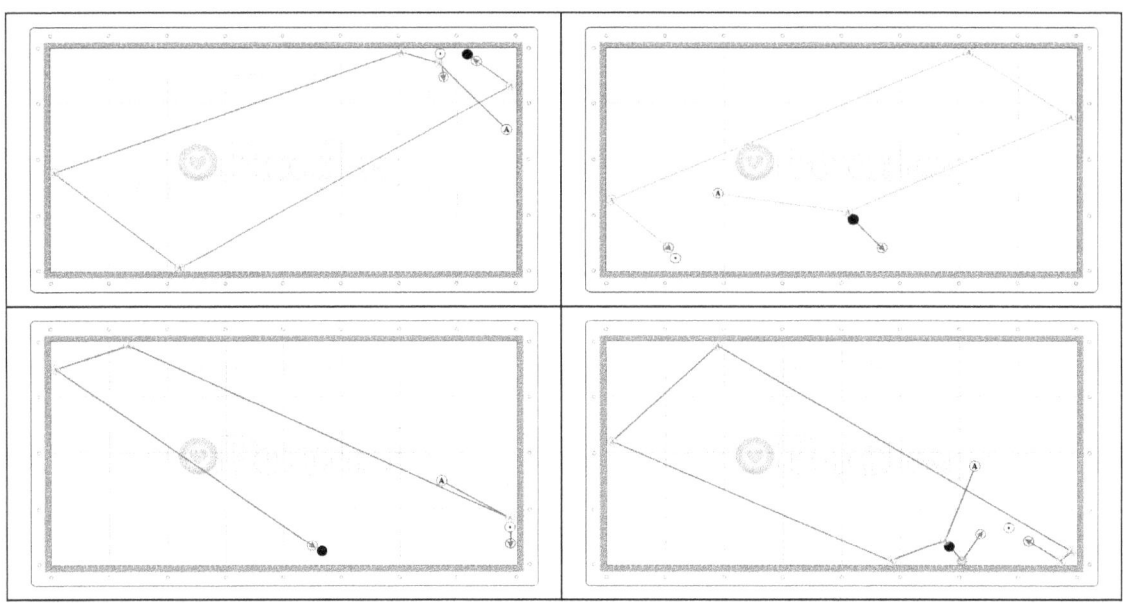

Analysis:

E:3a. _____

E:3b. _____

E:3c. _____

E:3d. _____

E:3a – Setup

Shot Pattern

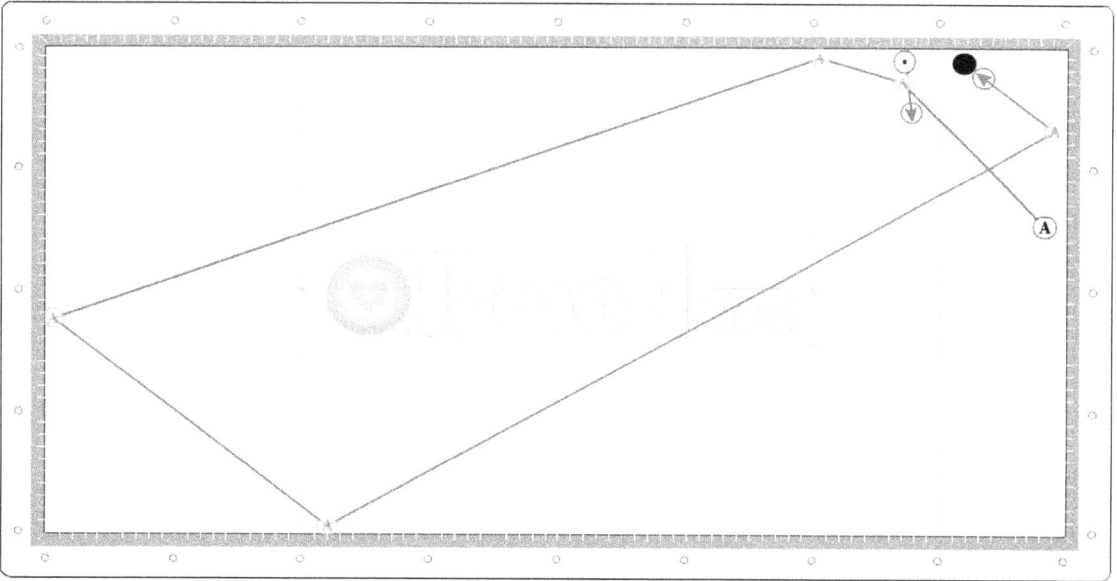

E:3b – Setup

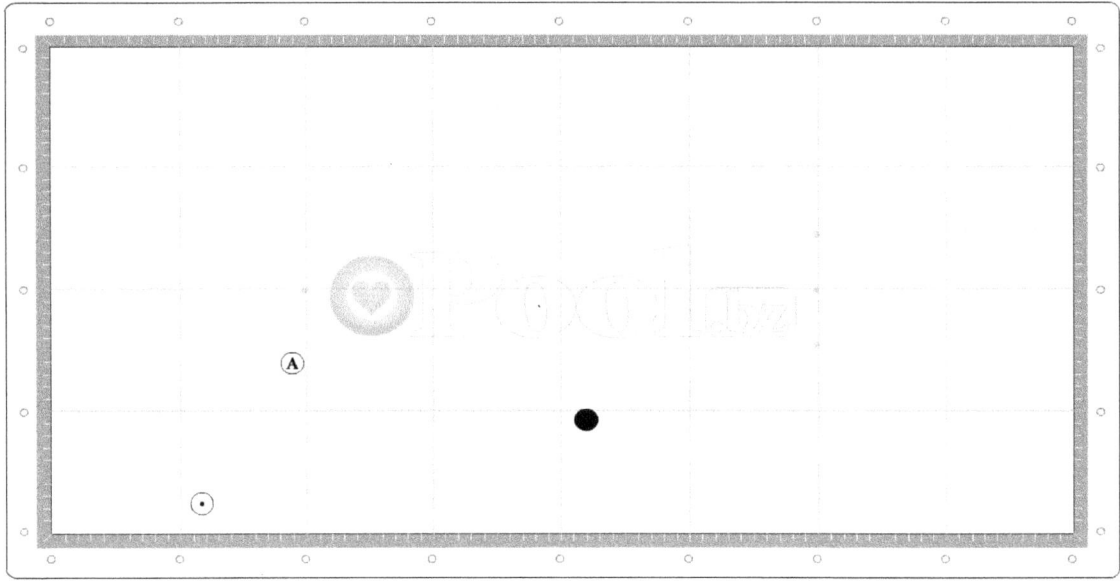

Shot Pattern

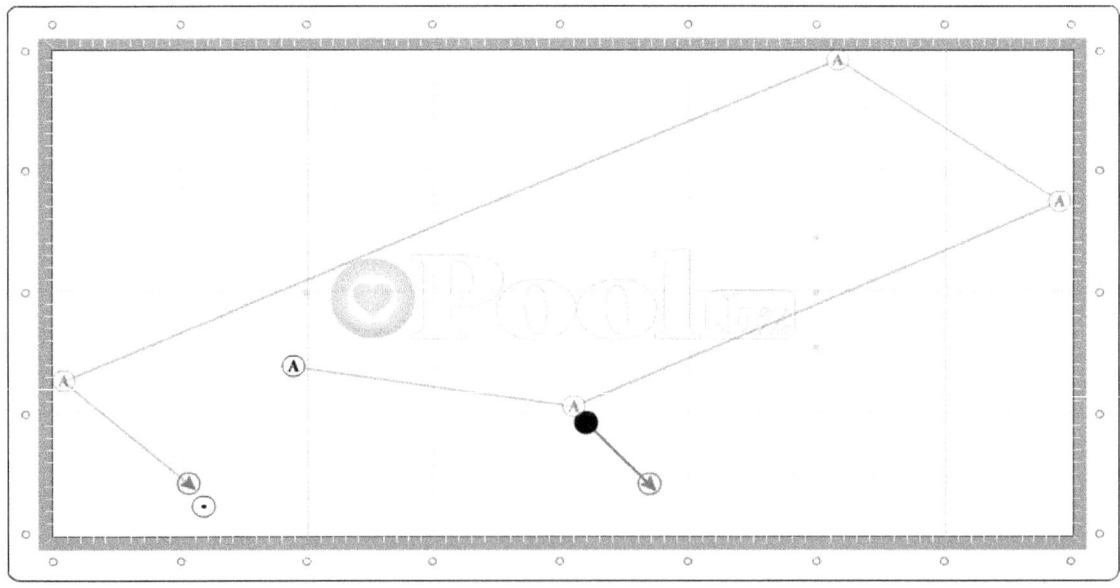

E:3c – Setup

Shot Pattern

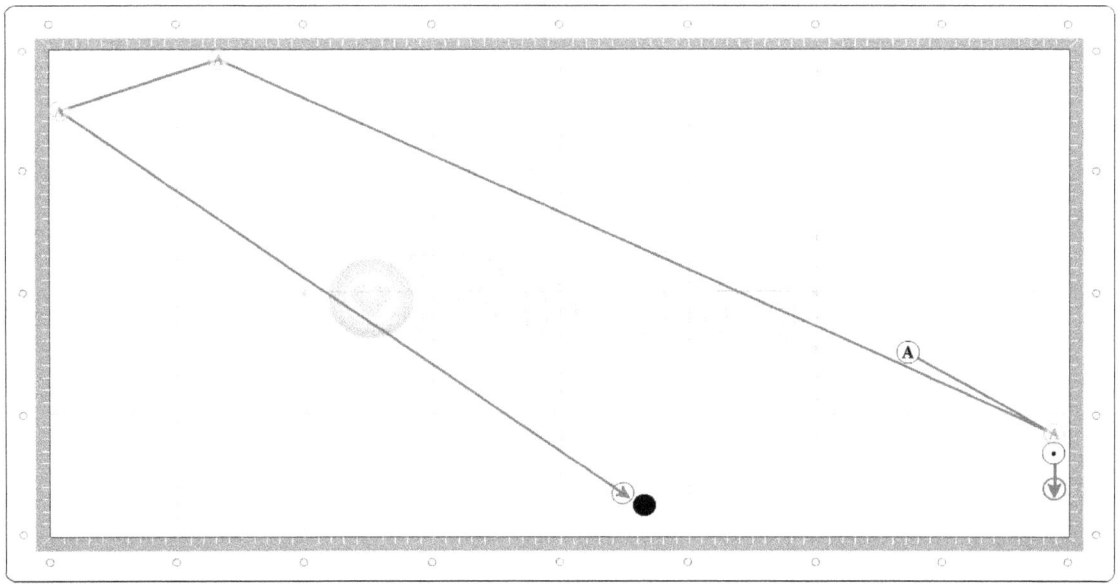

E:3d – Setup

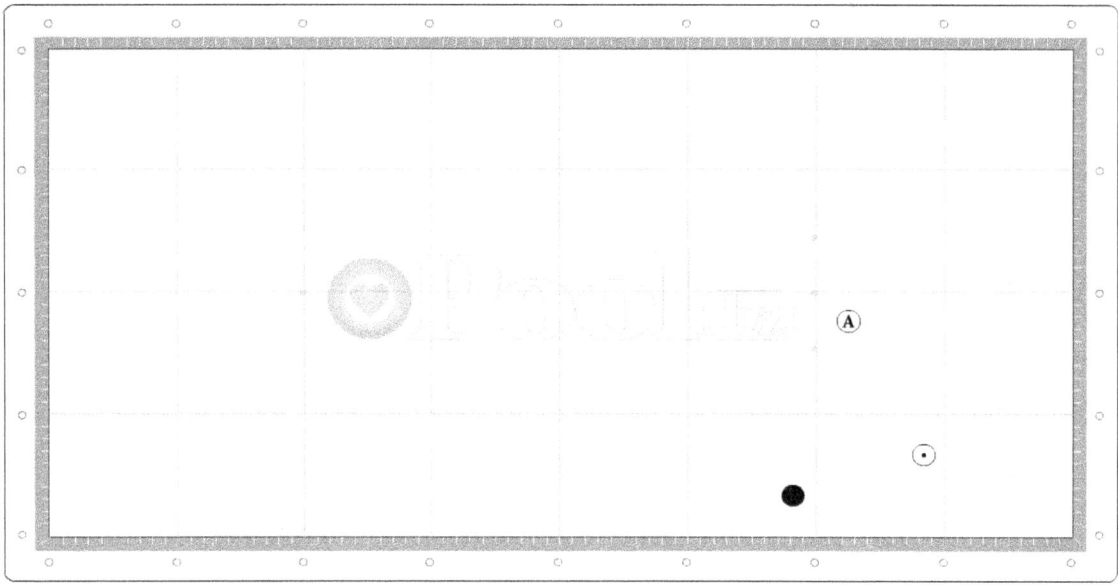

Shot Pattern

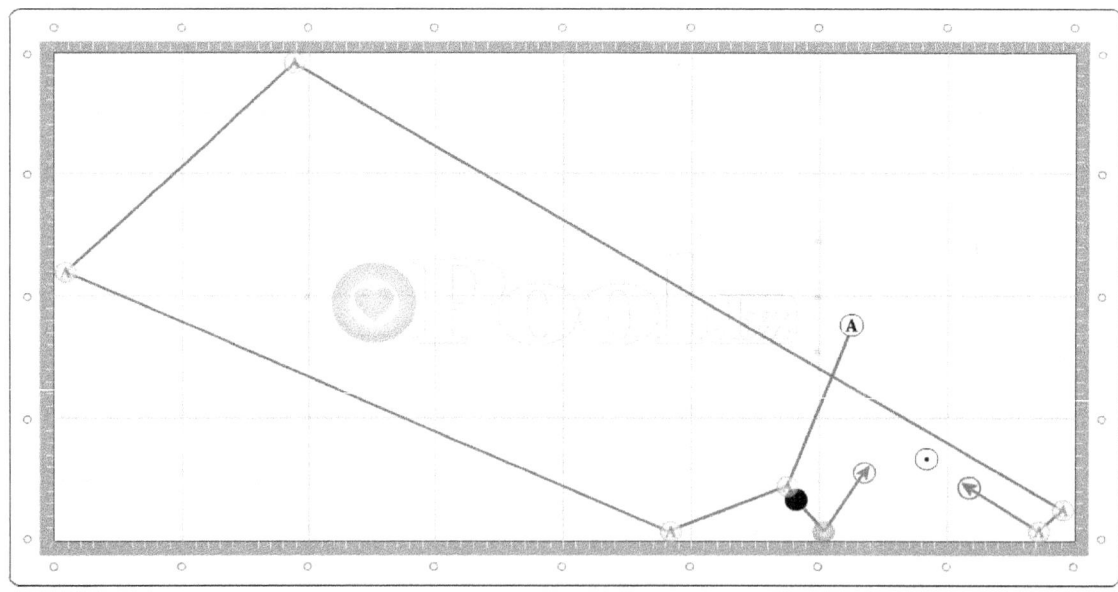

E: Group 4

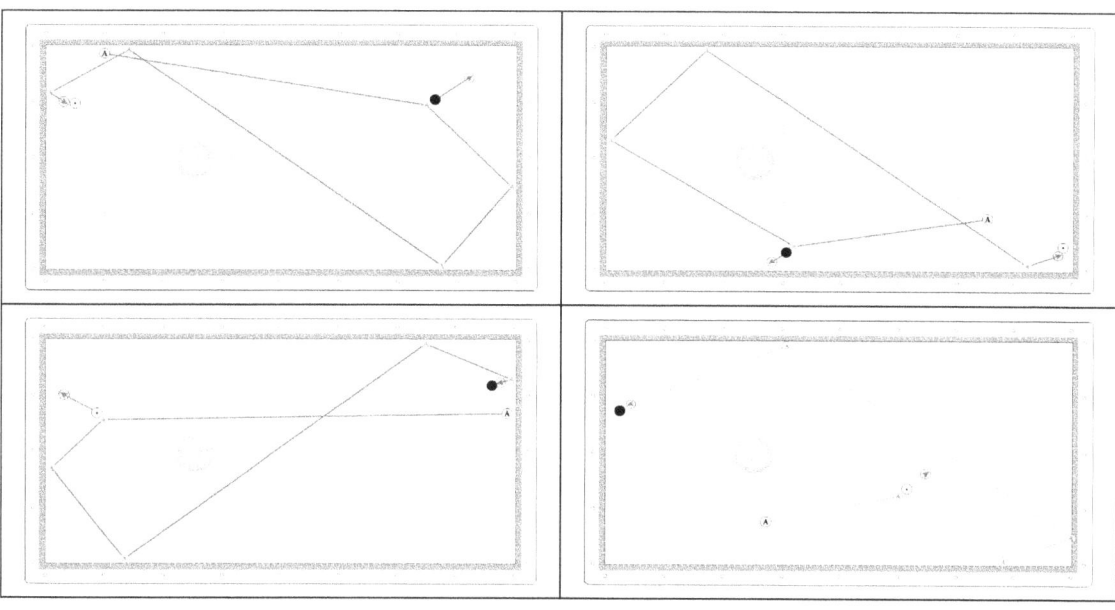

Analysis:

E:4a. _____

E:4b. _____

E:4c. _____

E:4d. _____

E:4a – Setup

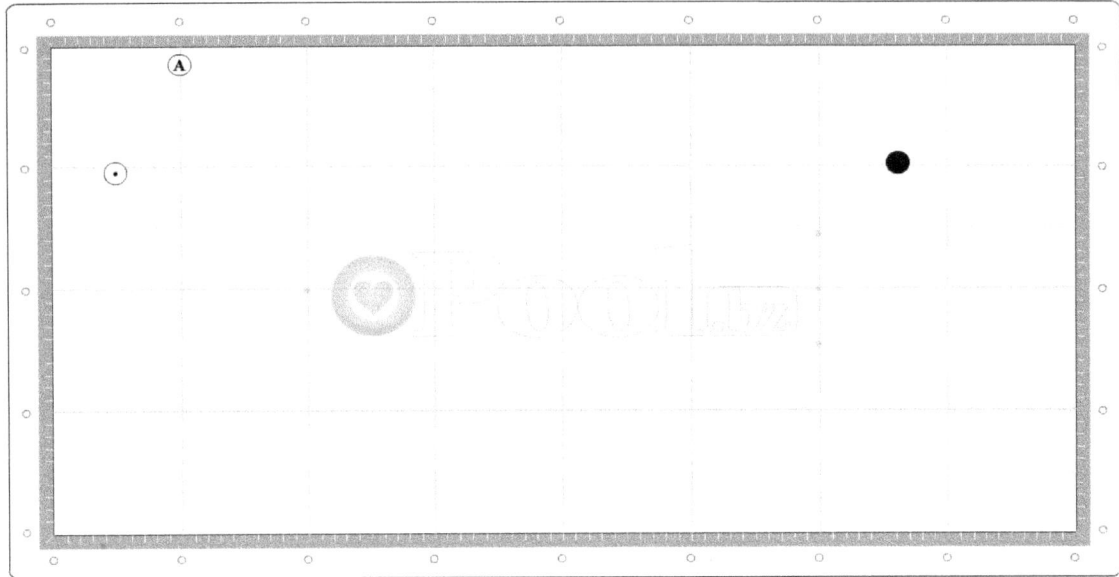

Shot Pattern

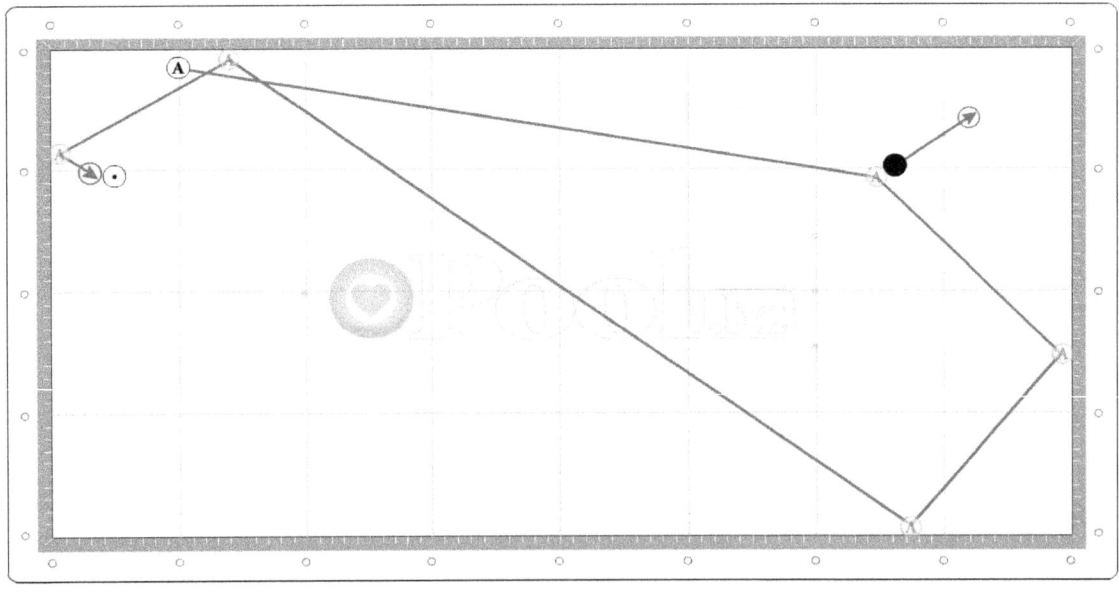

E:4b – Setup

Shot Pattern

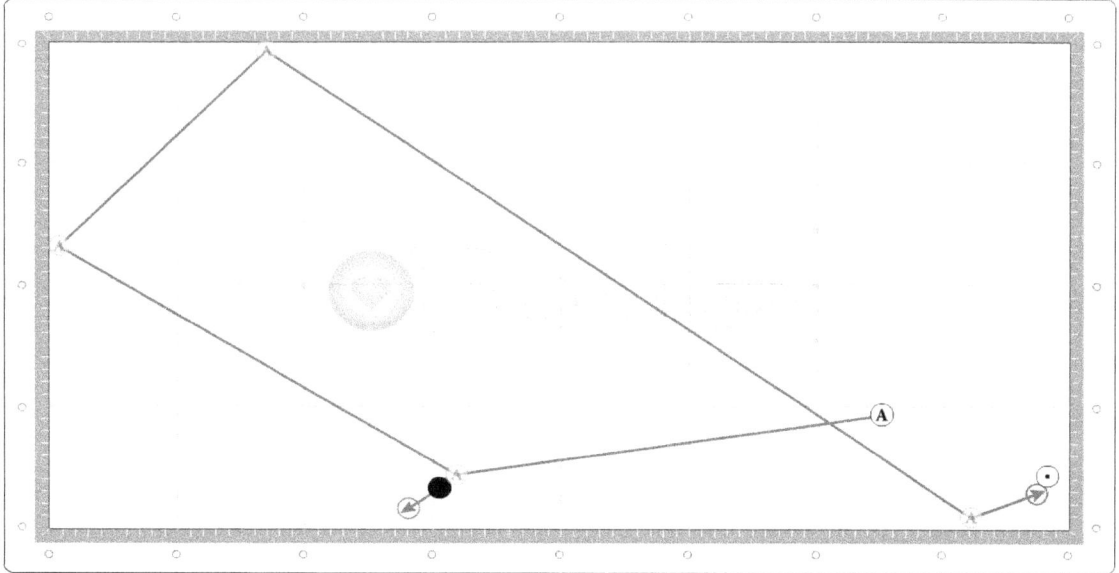

E:4c – Setup

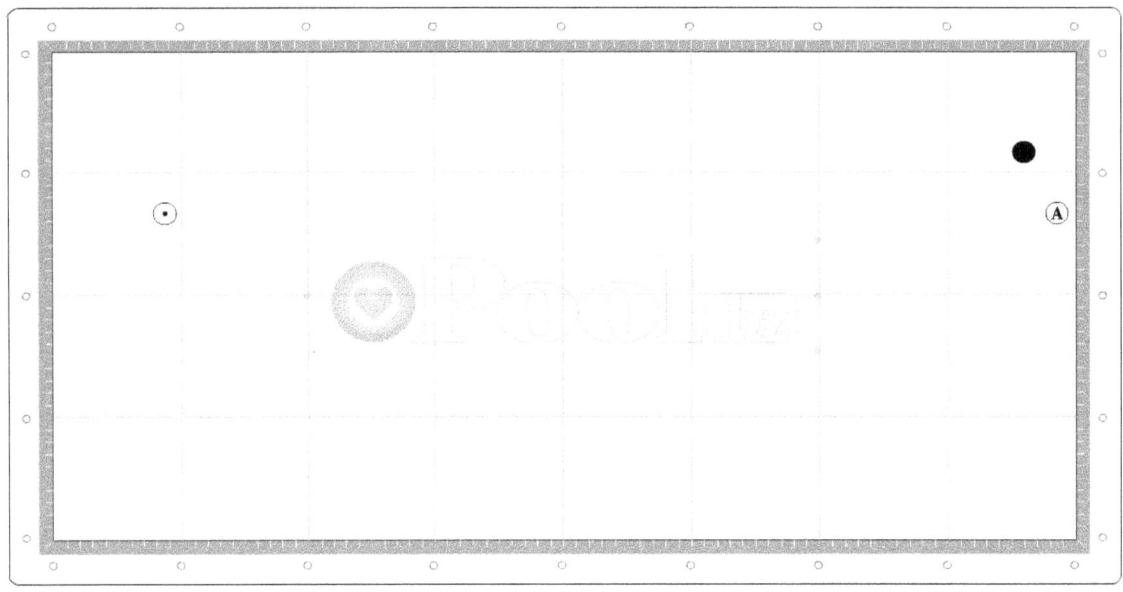

Shot Pattern

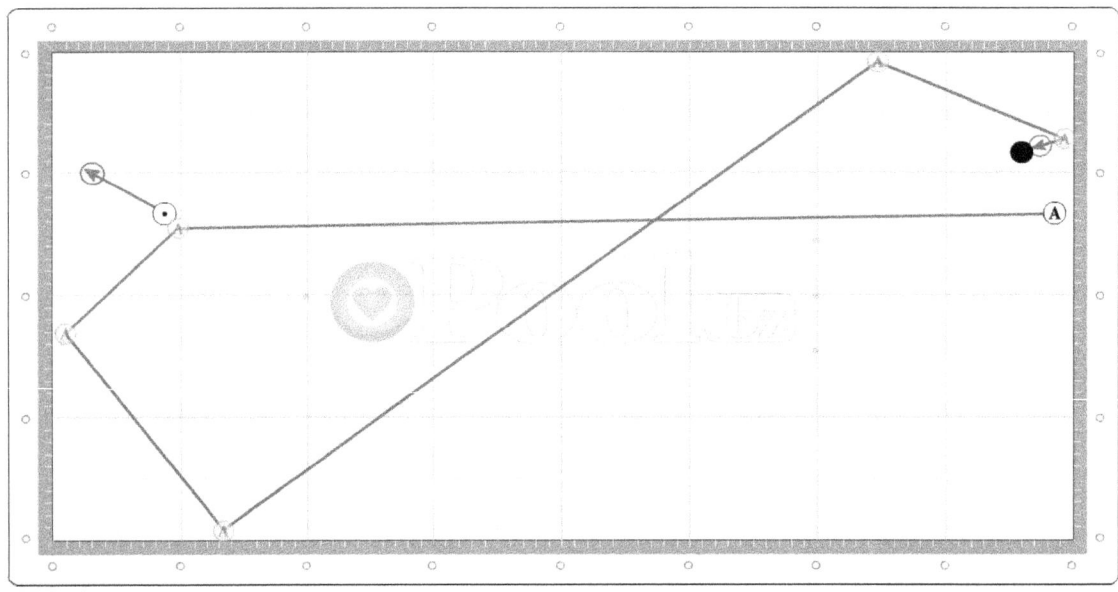

E:4d – Setup

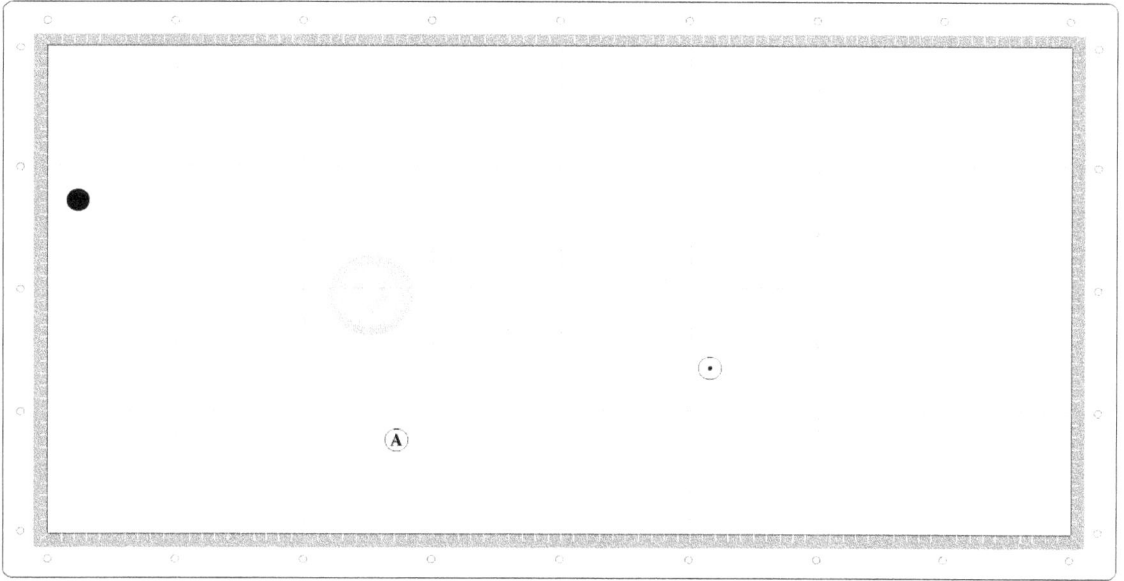

Shot Pattern

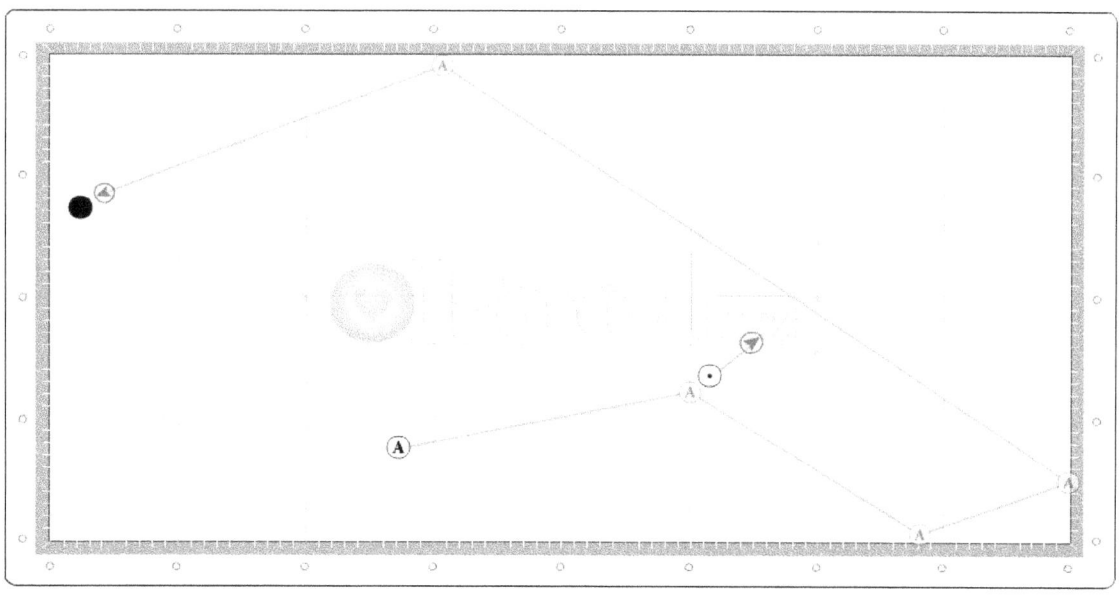

E: Group 5

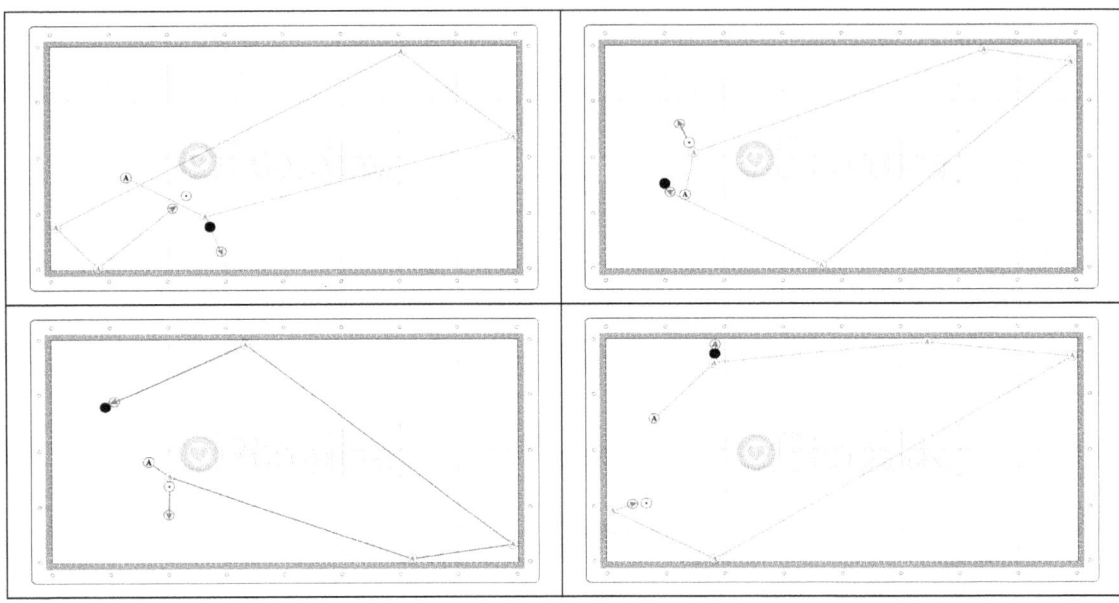

Analysis:

E:5a. _____

E:5b. _____

E:5c. _____

E:5d. _____

E:5a – Setup

Shot Pattern

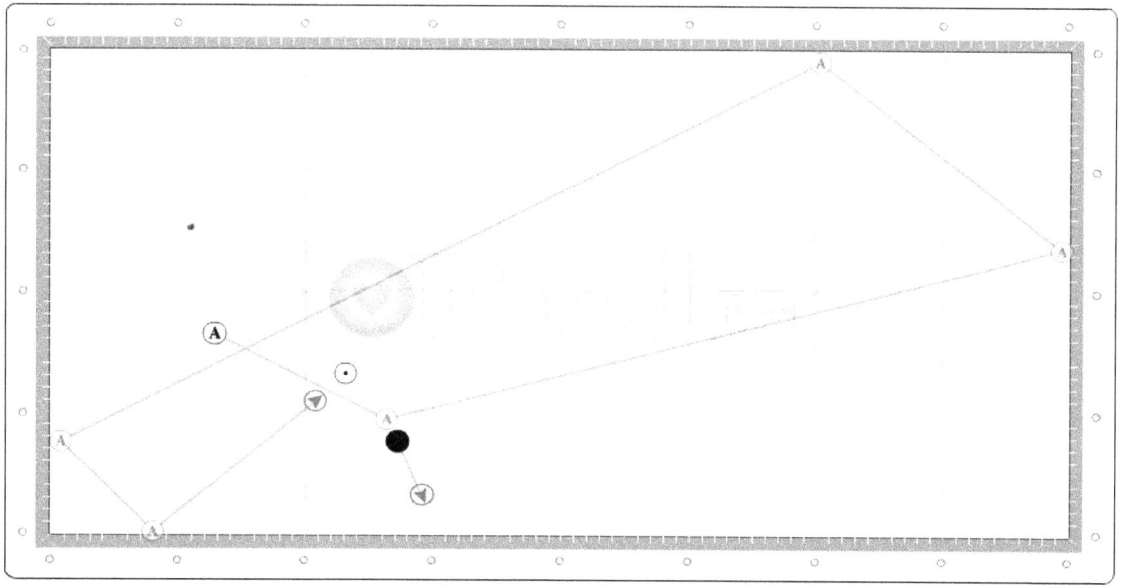

E:5b – Setup

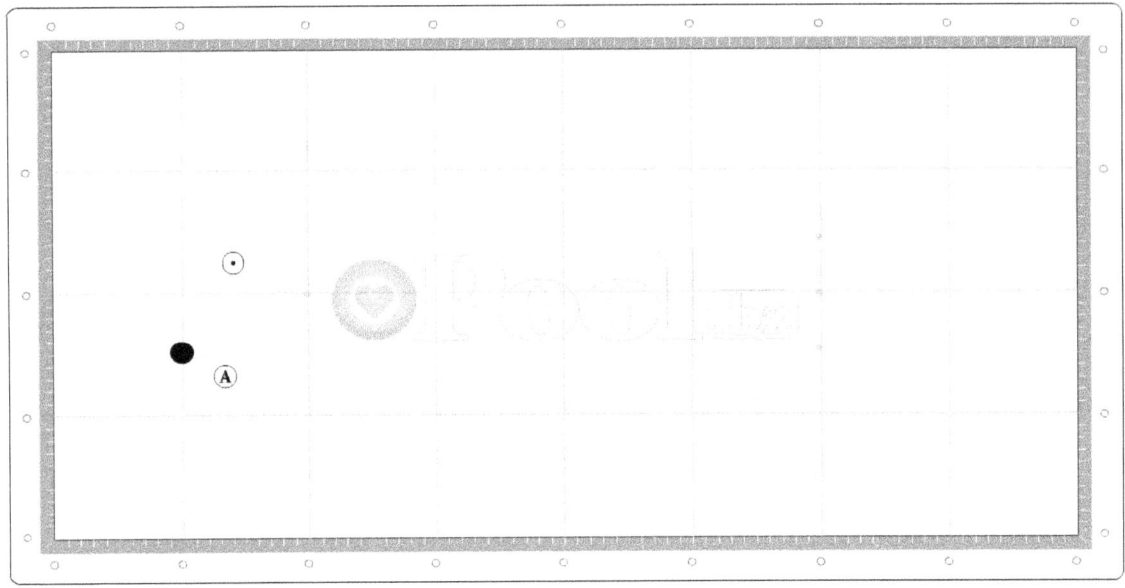

Shot Pattern

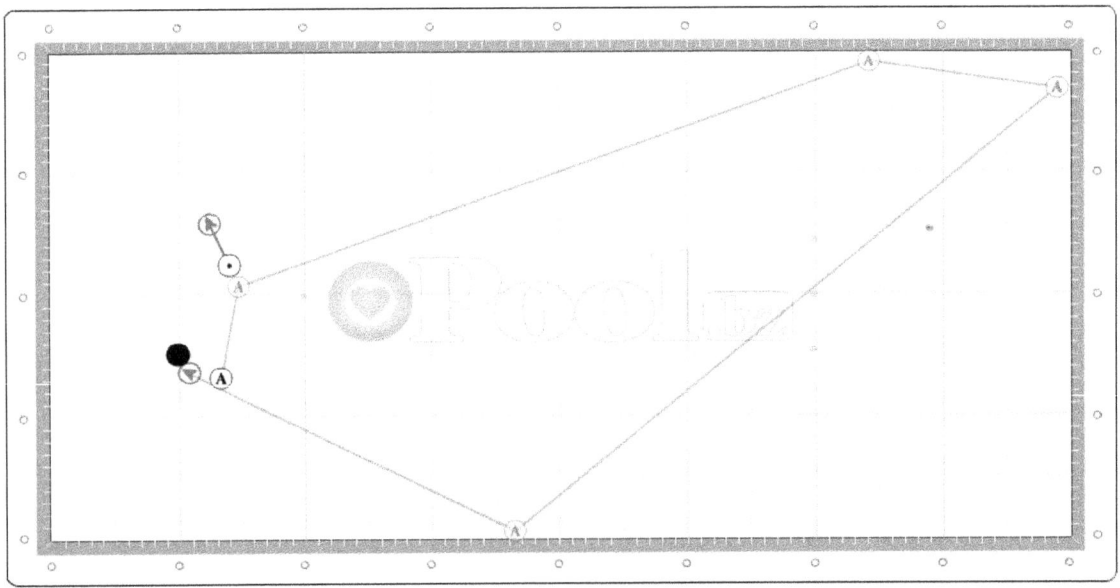

E:5c – Setup

Shot Pattern

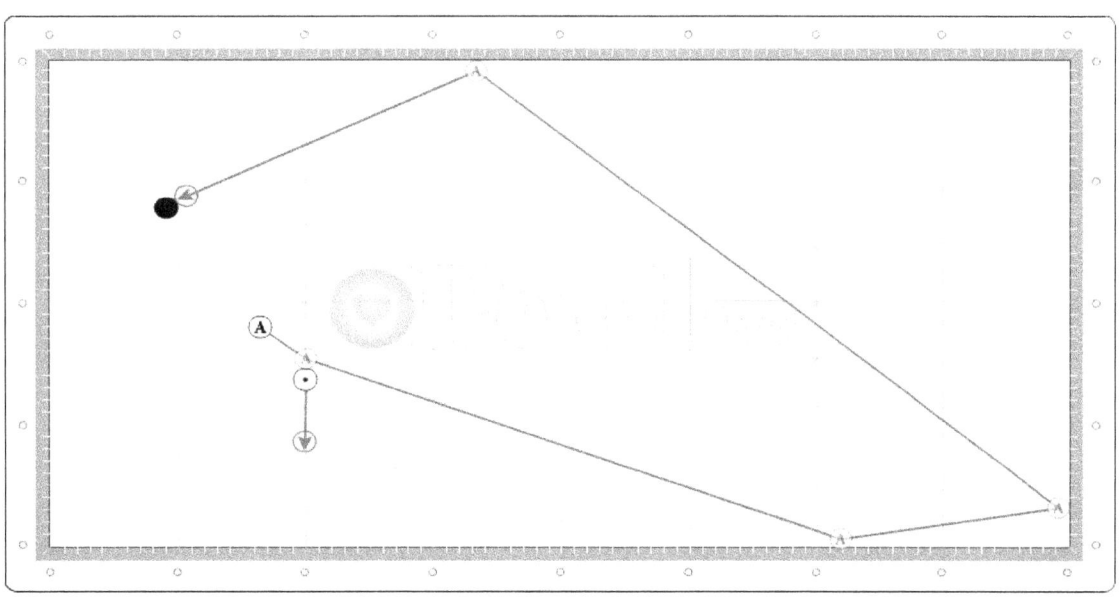

E:5d – Setup

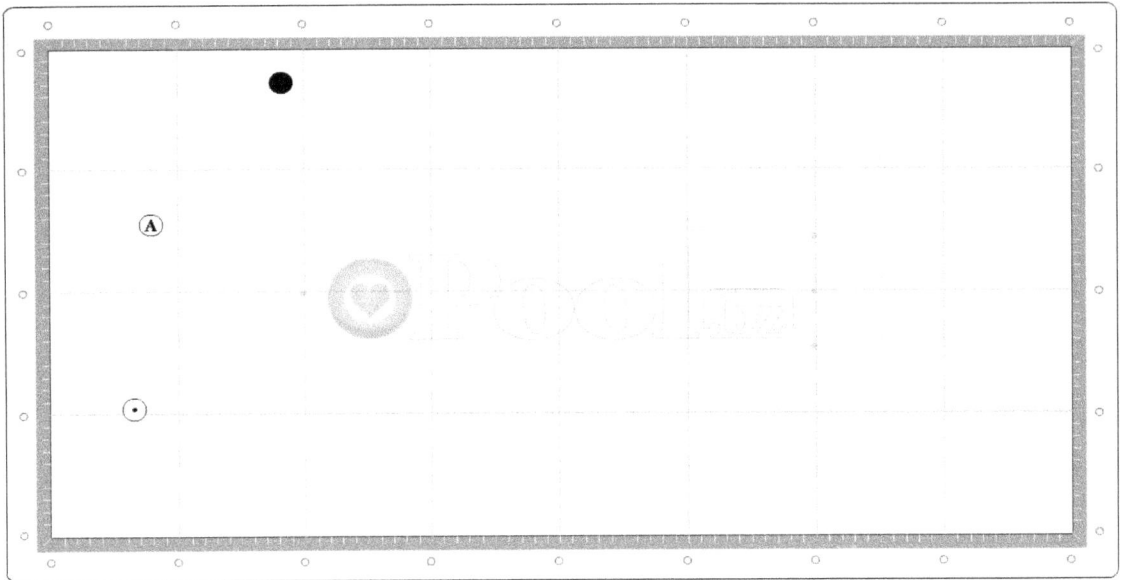

Shot Pattern

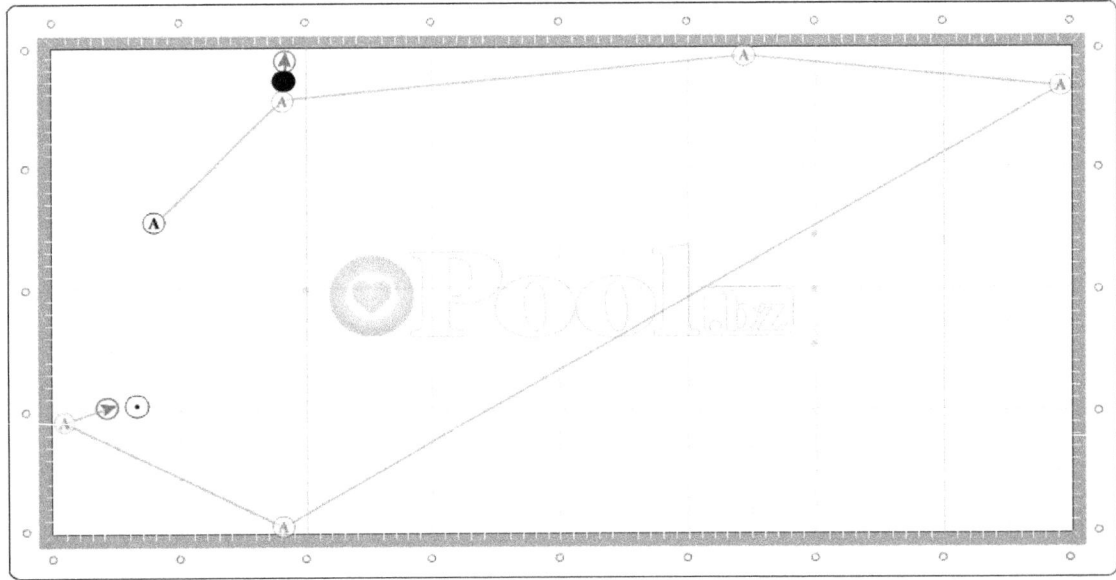

E: Group 6

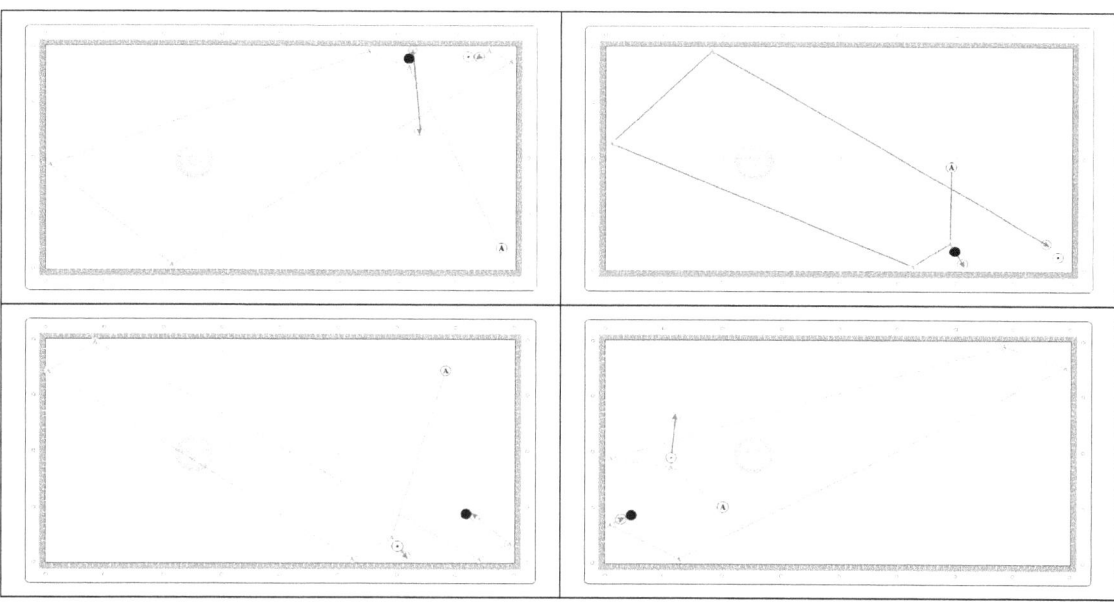

Analysis:

E:6a. _____

E:6b. _____

E:6c. _____

E:6d. _____

E:6a – Setup

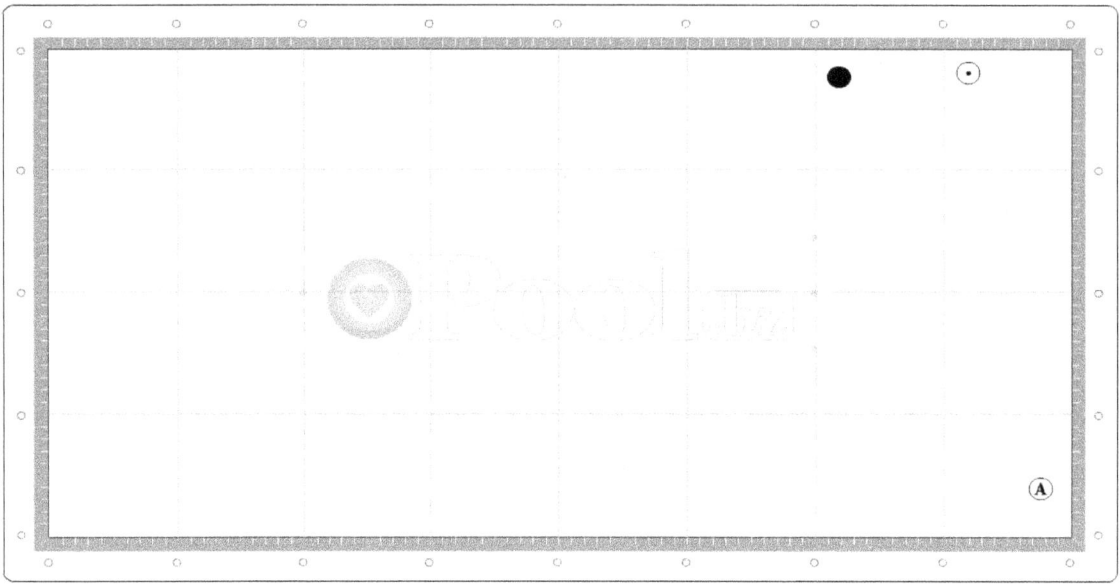

Shot Pattern

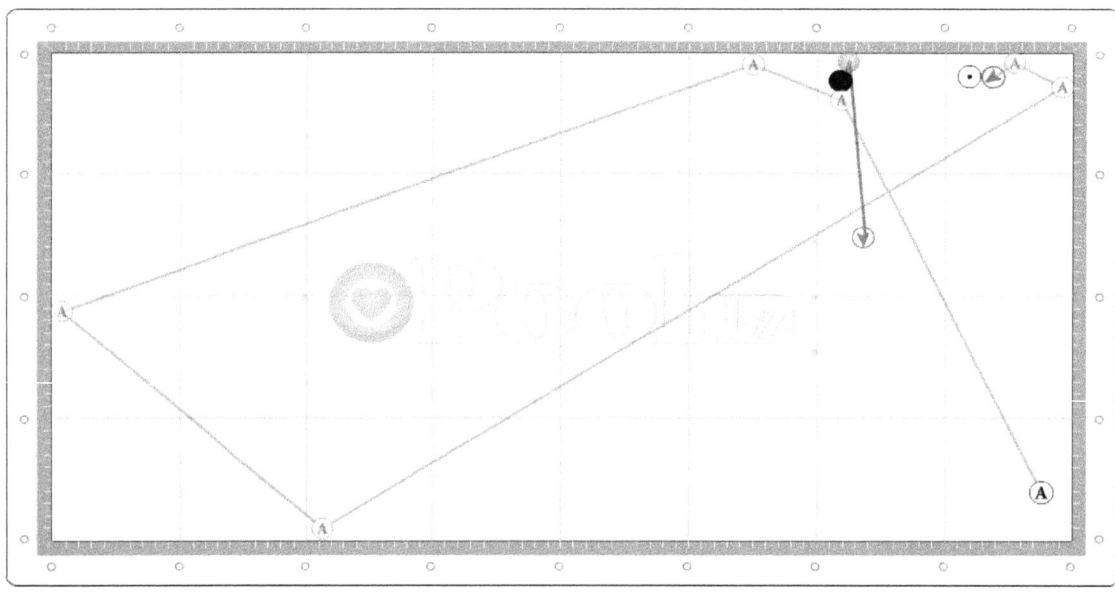

E:6b – Setup

Shot Pattern

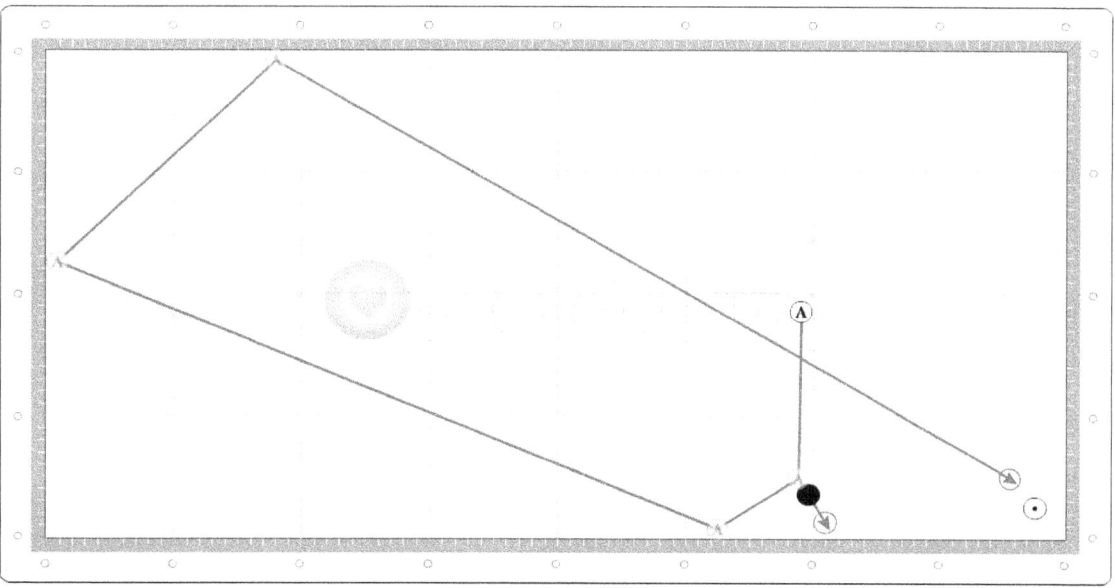

E:6c – Setup

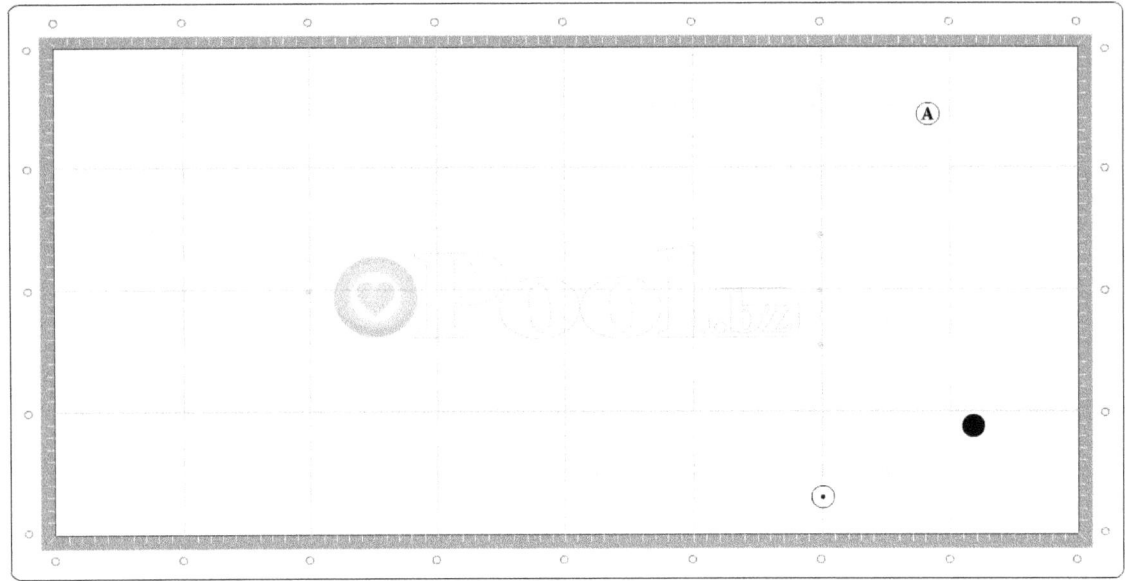

Shot Pattern

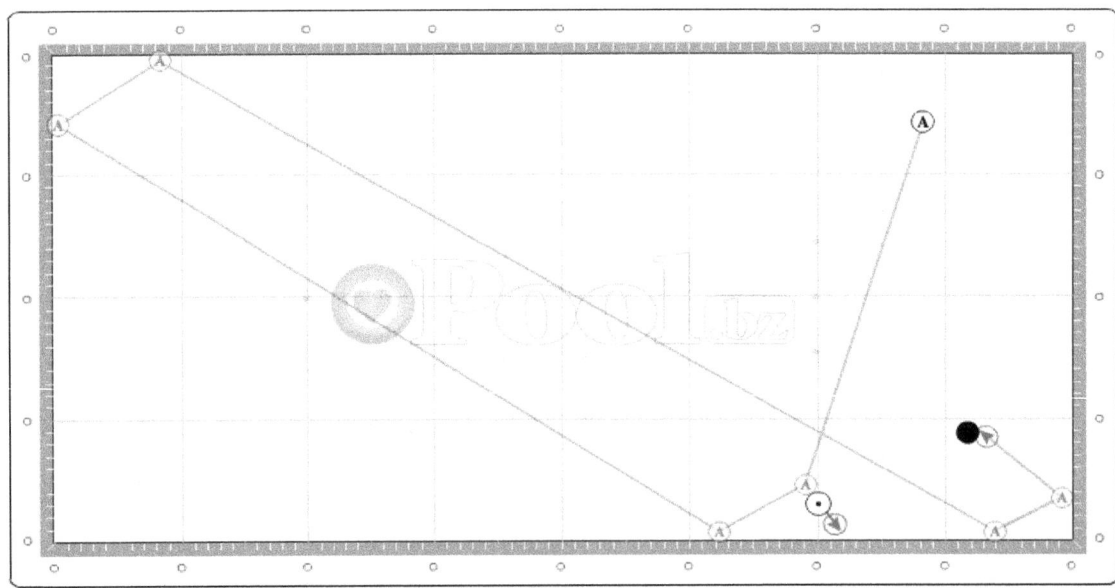

E:6d – Setup

Shot Pattern

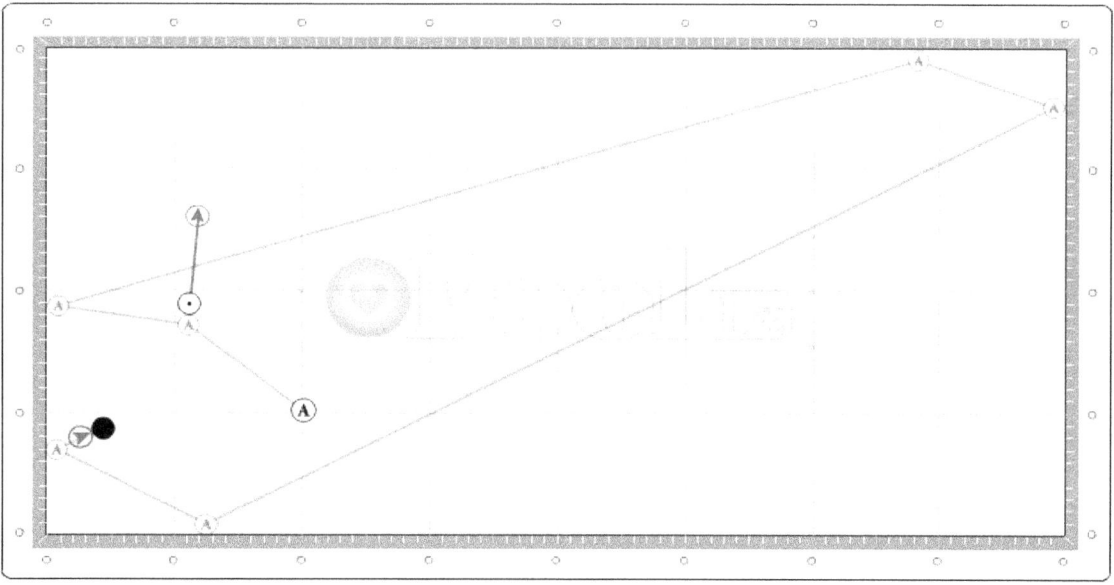

F: Triple Diagonals

The CB comes off the first OB and then enters the diagonal pattern. These are interesting shots because the CB is moving up and down the table three times.

F: Group 1

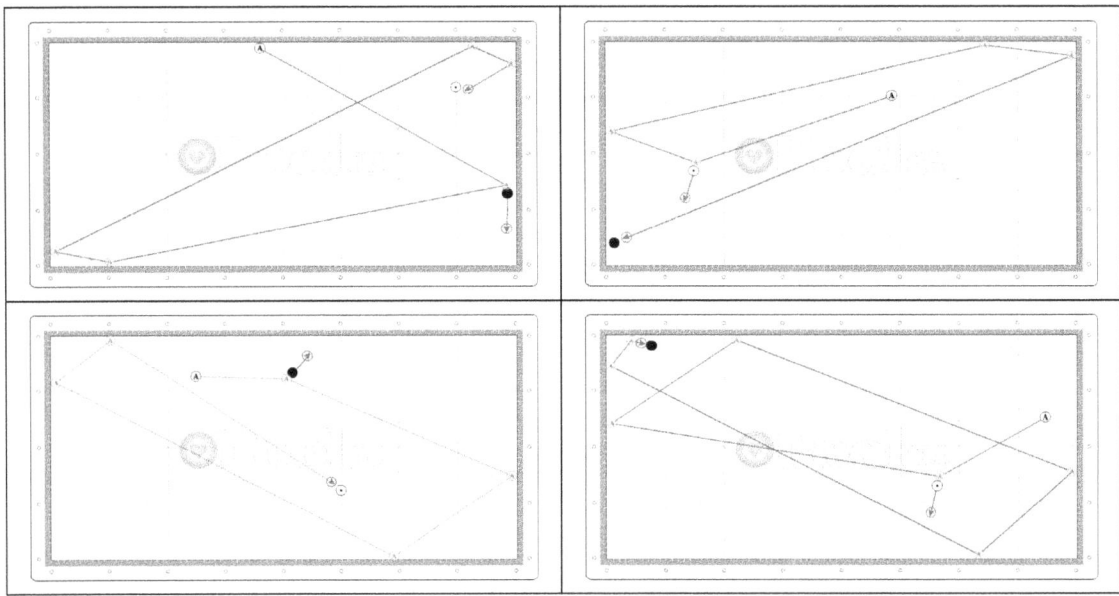

Analysis:

F:1a. _____

F:1b. _____

F:1c. _____

F:1d. _____

F:1a – Setup

Shot Pattern

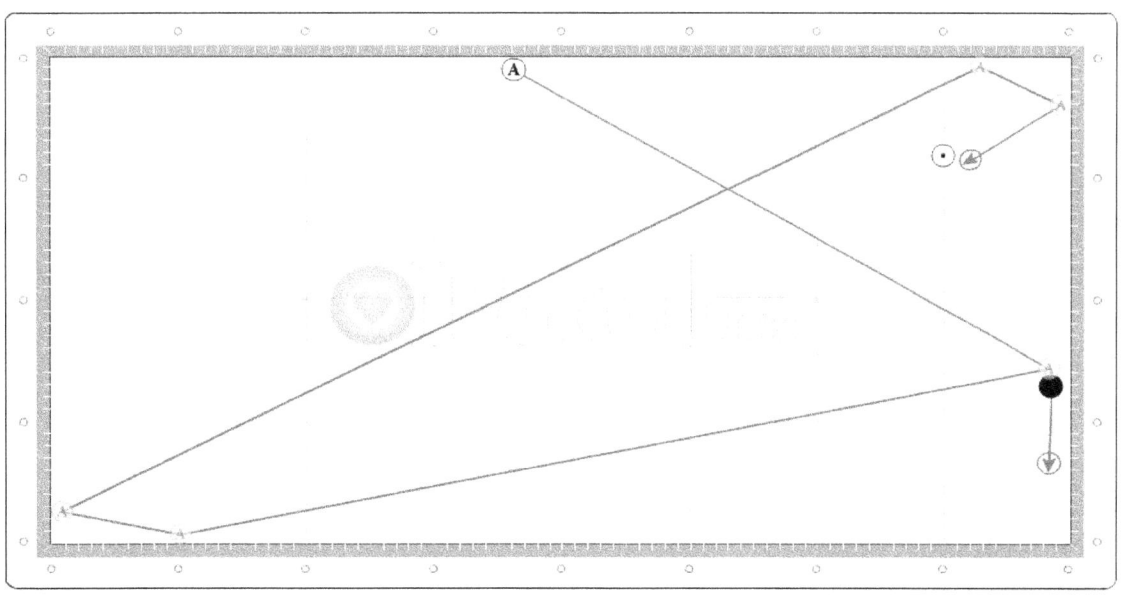

F:1b – Setup

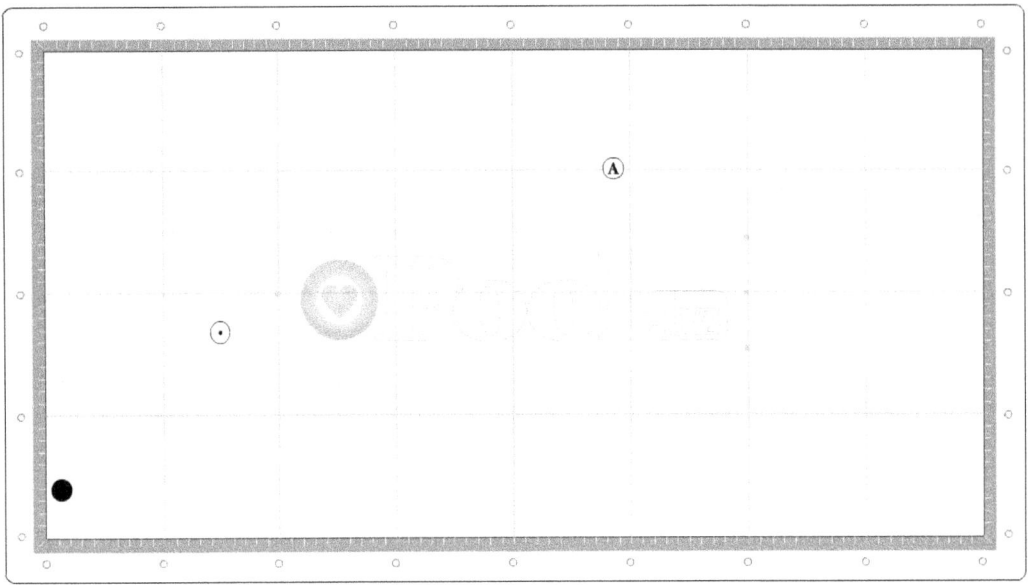

Shot Pattern

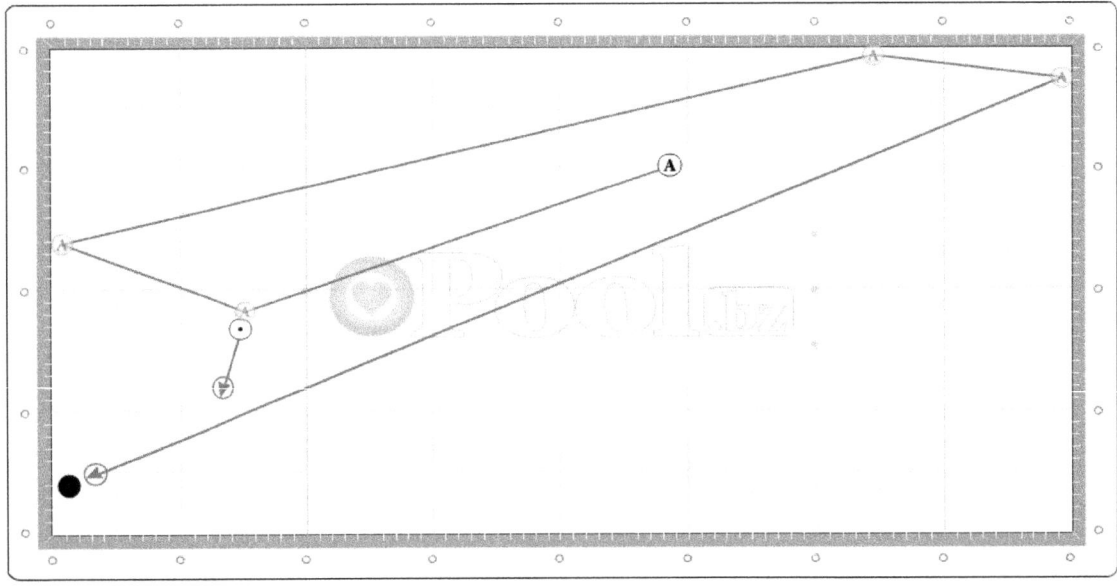

F:1c – Setup

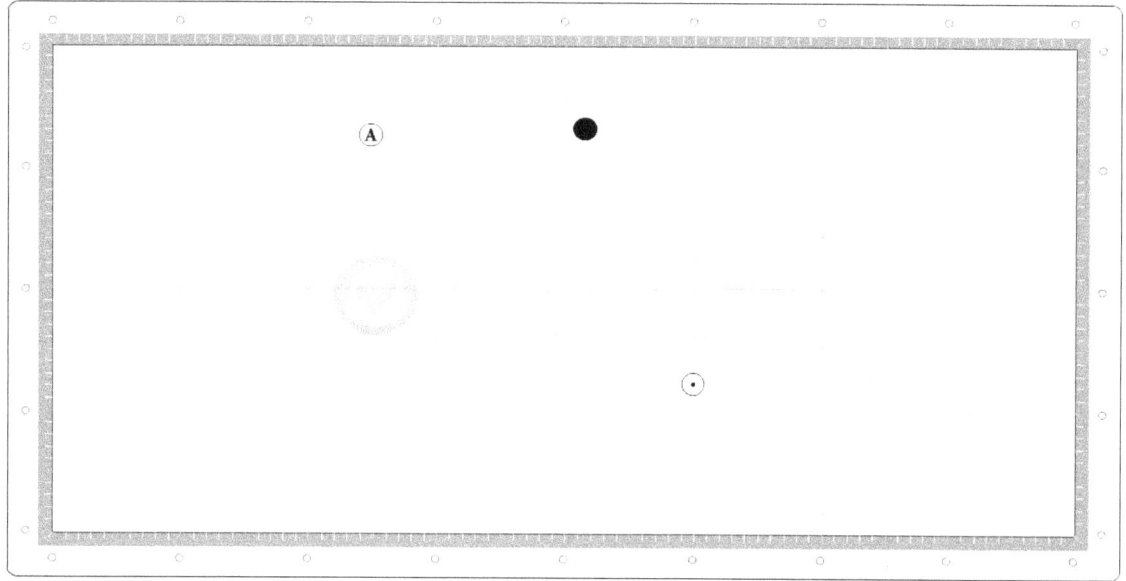

Shot Pattern

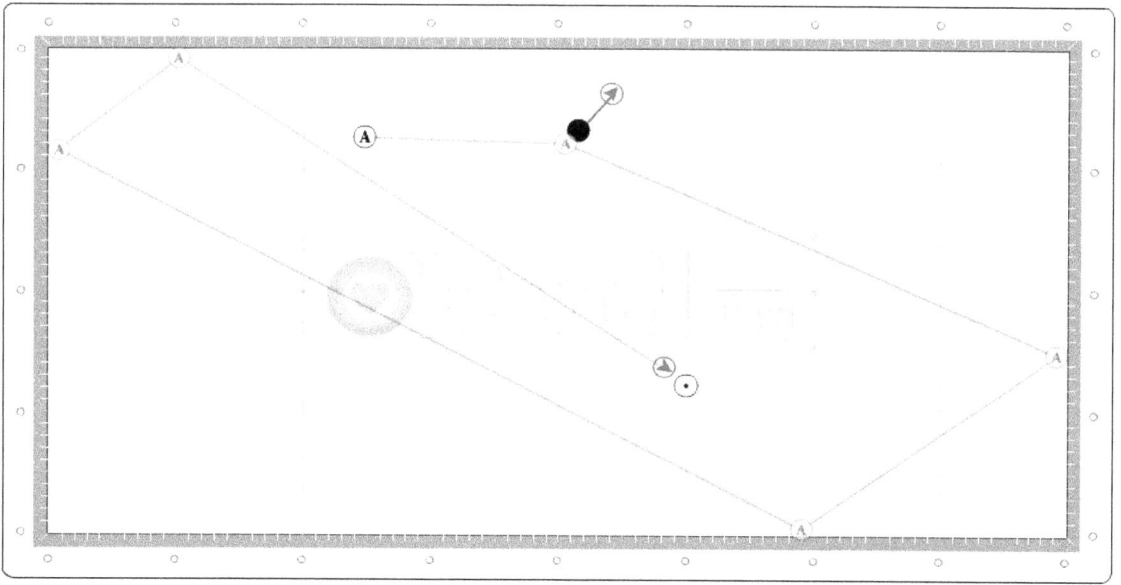

F:1d – Setup

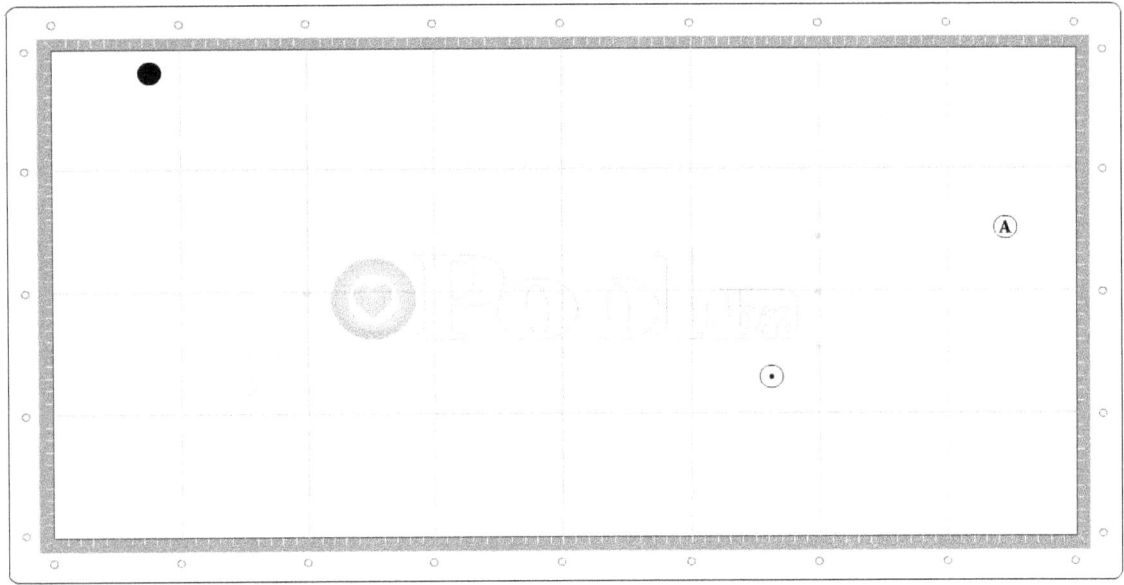

Shot Pattern

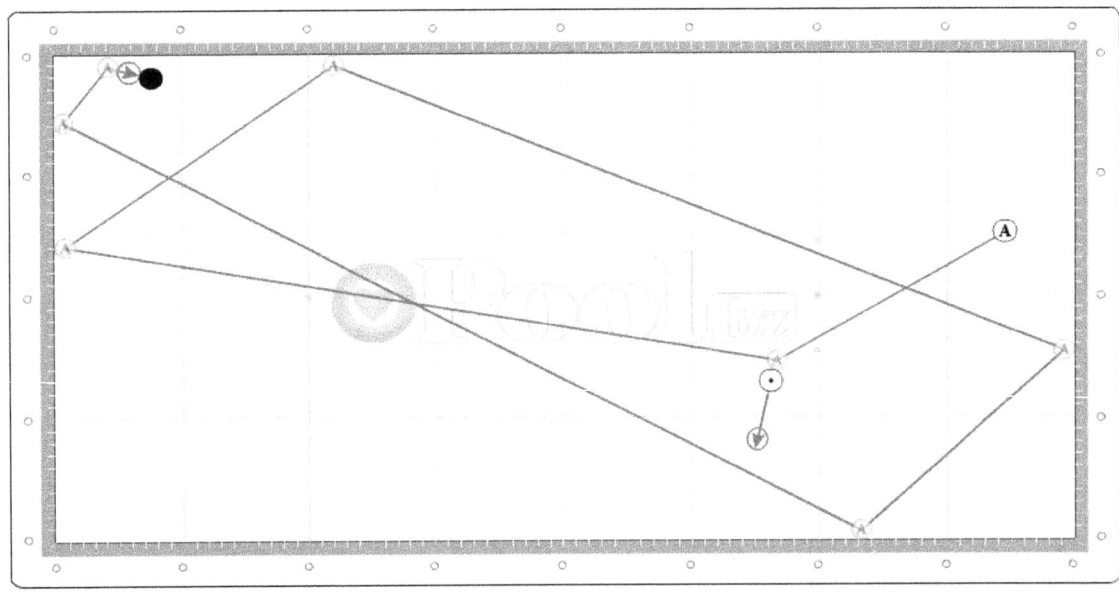

F: Group 2

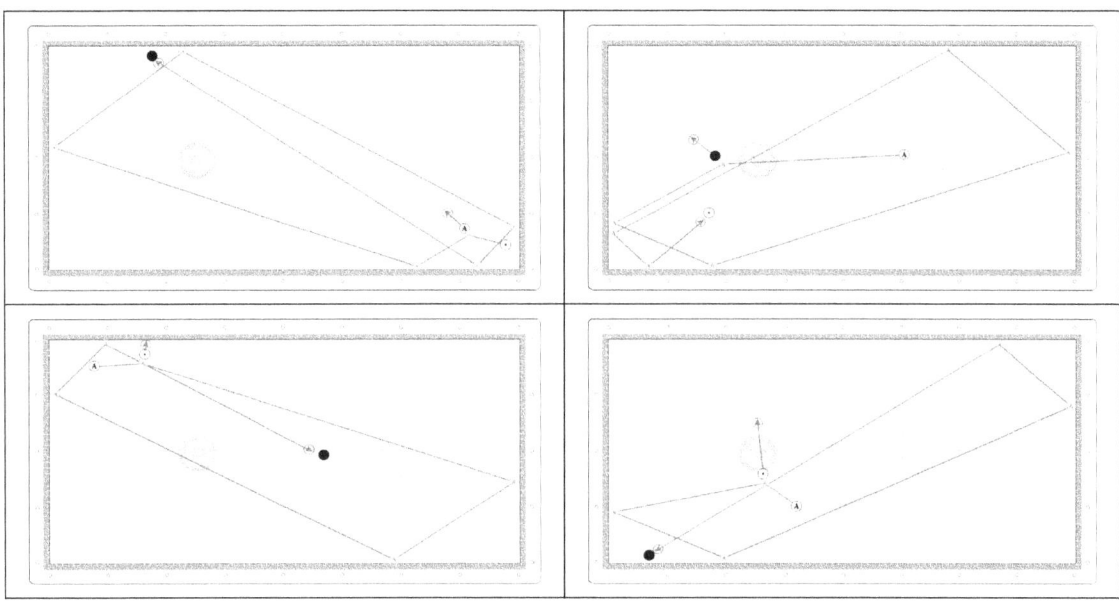

Analysis:

F:2a. _____

F:2b. _____

F:2c. _____

F:2d. _____

F:2a – Setup

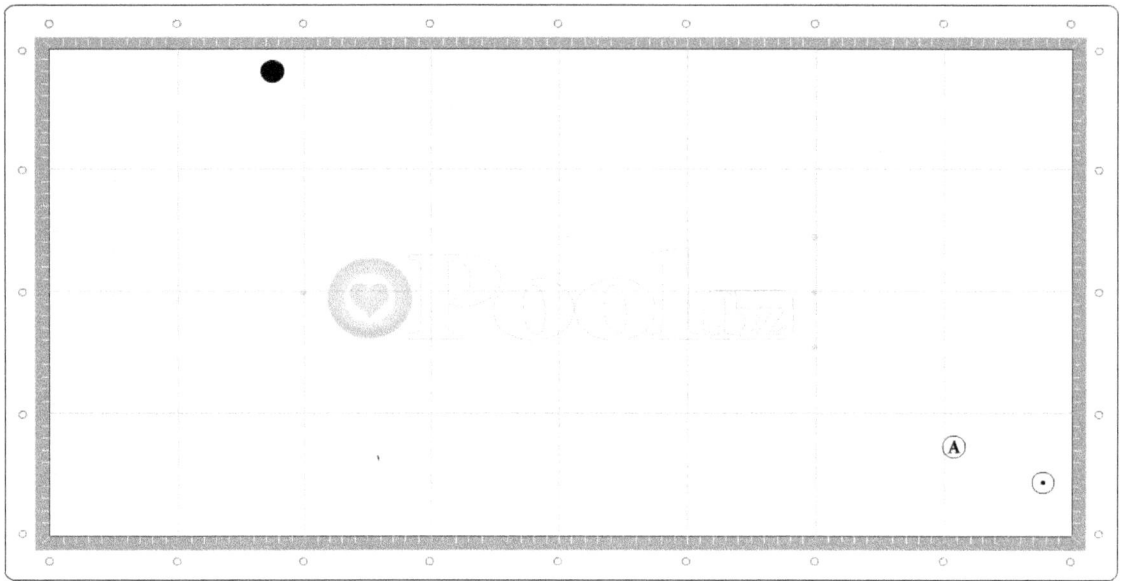

Shot Pattern

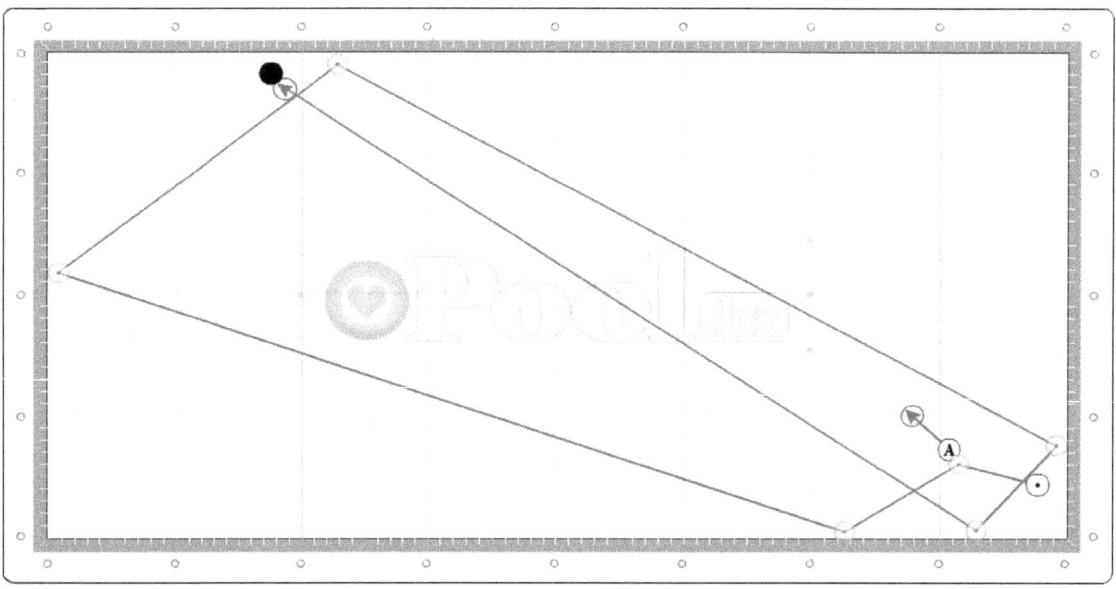

F:2b – Setup

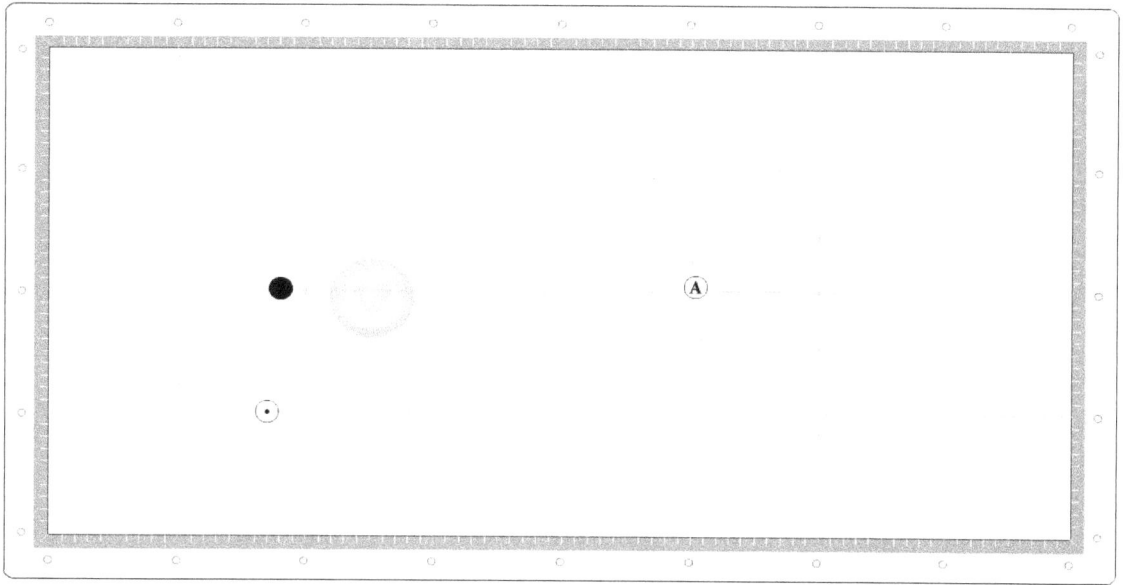

Shot Pattern

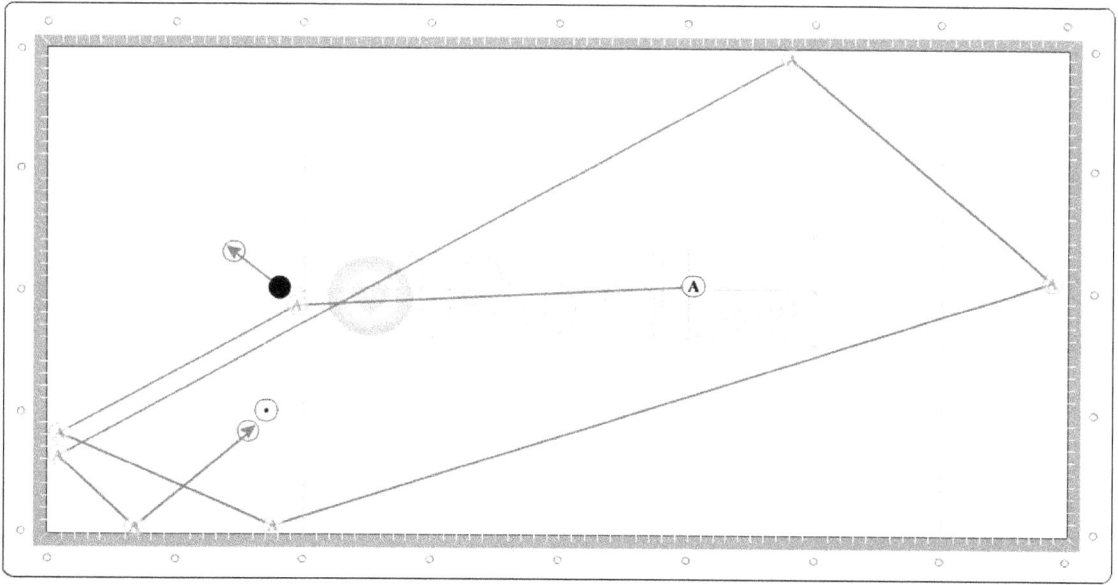

F:2c – Setup

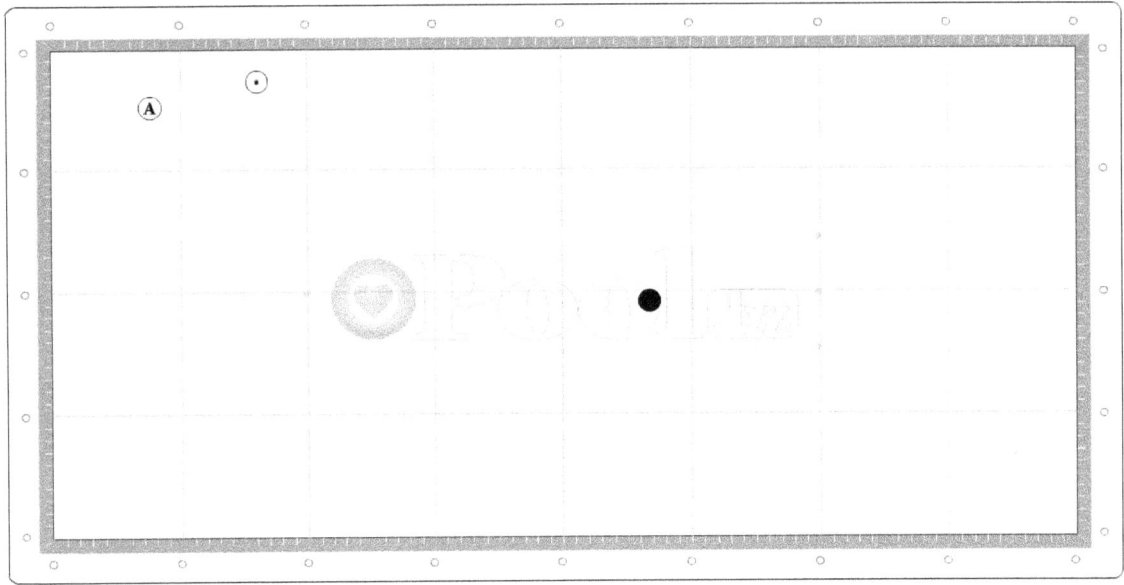

Shot Pattern

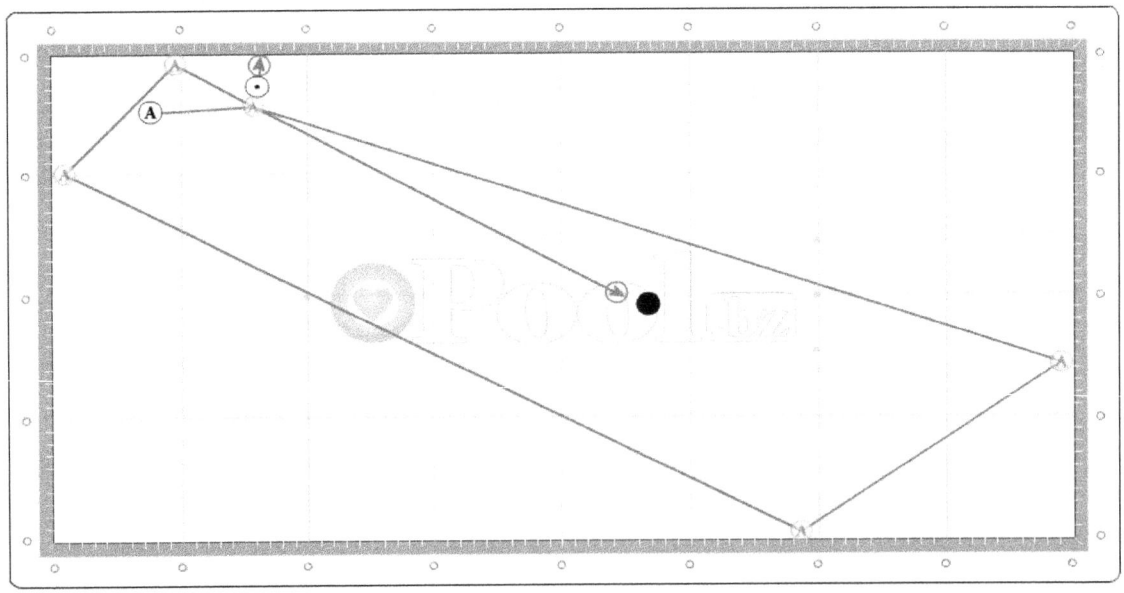

F:2d – Setup

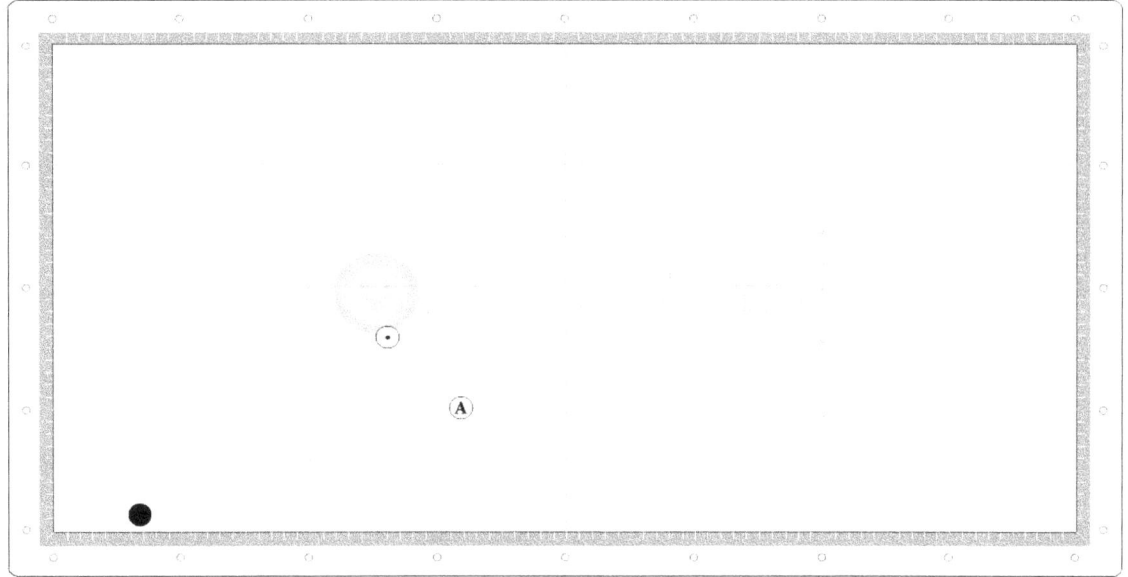

Shot Pattern

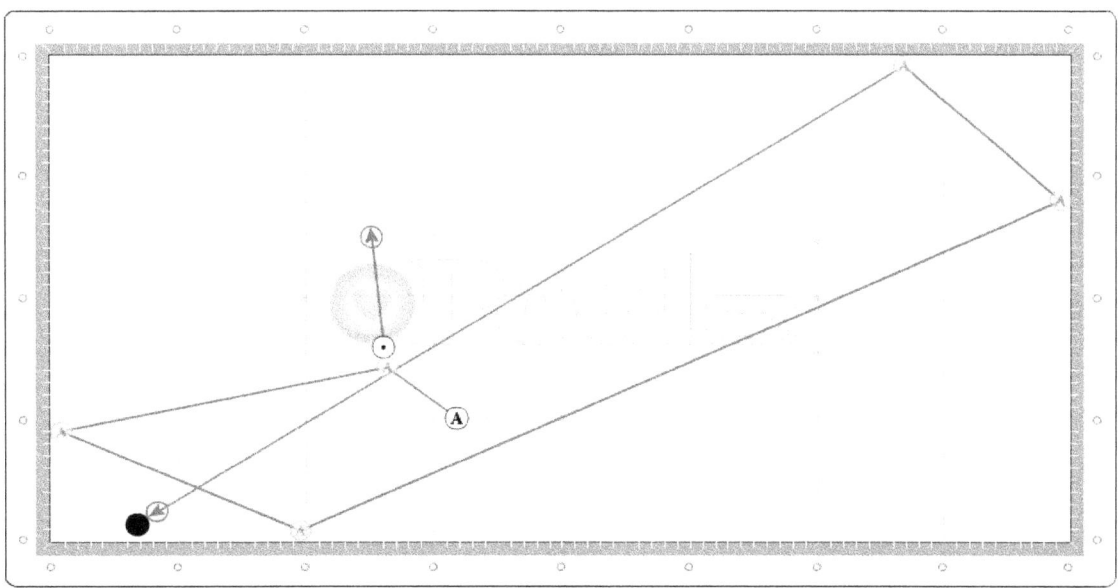

Carom Billiards: Cross-Corner Diagonal Patterns

F: Group 3

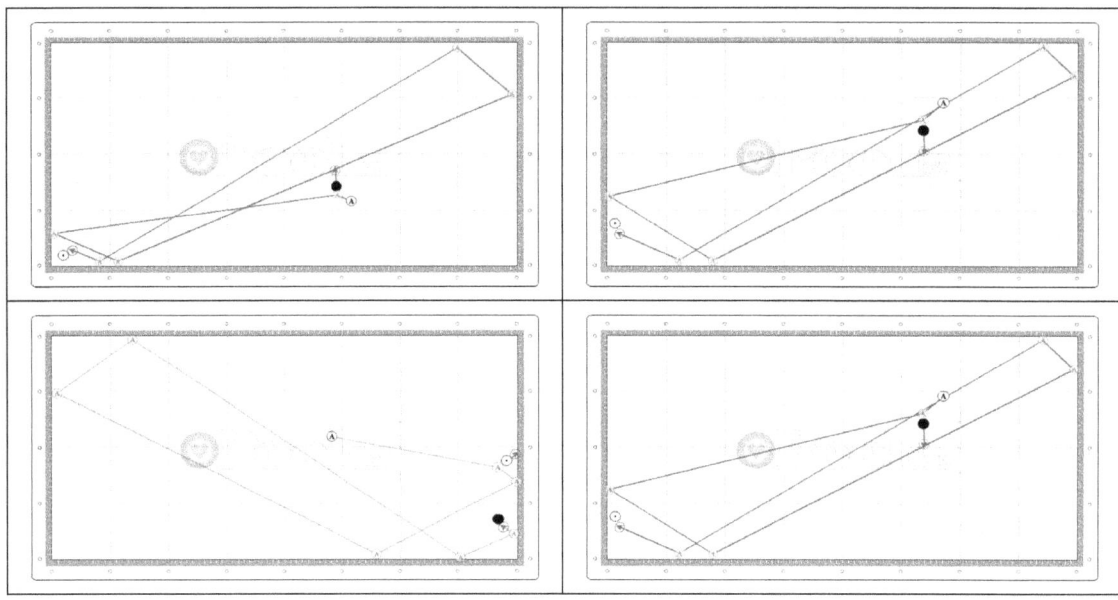

Analysis:

F:3a. _____

F:3b. _____

F:3c. _____

F:3d. _____

Carom Billiards: Cross-Corner Diagonal Patterns

f:3a – Setup

Shot Pattern

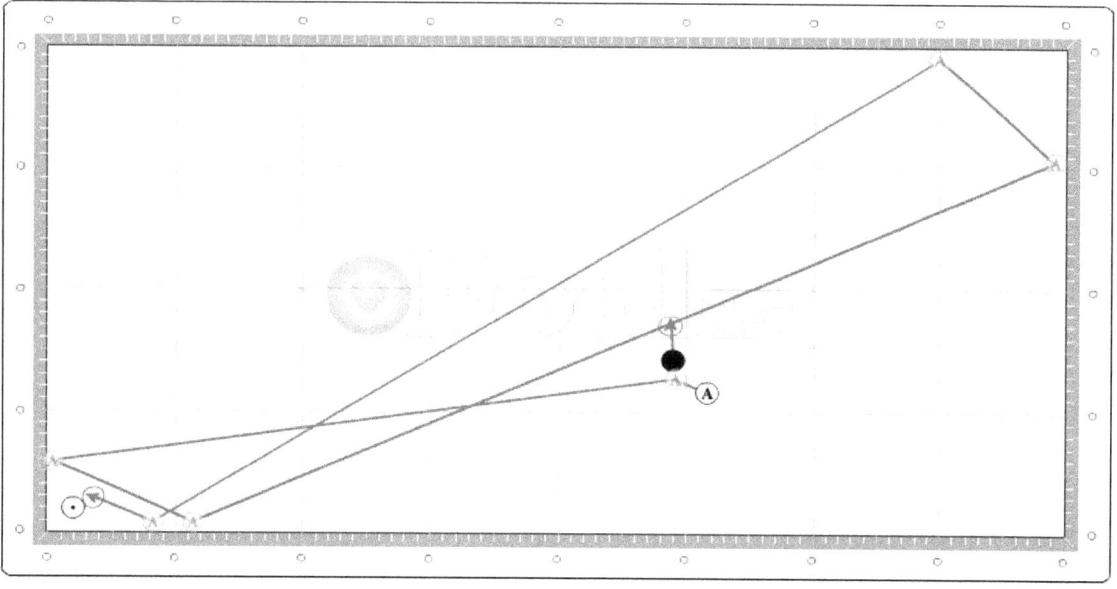

F31b – Setup

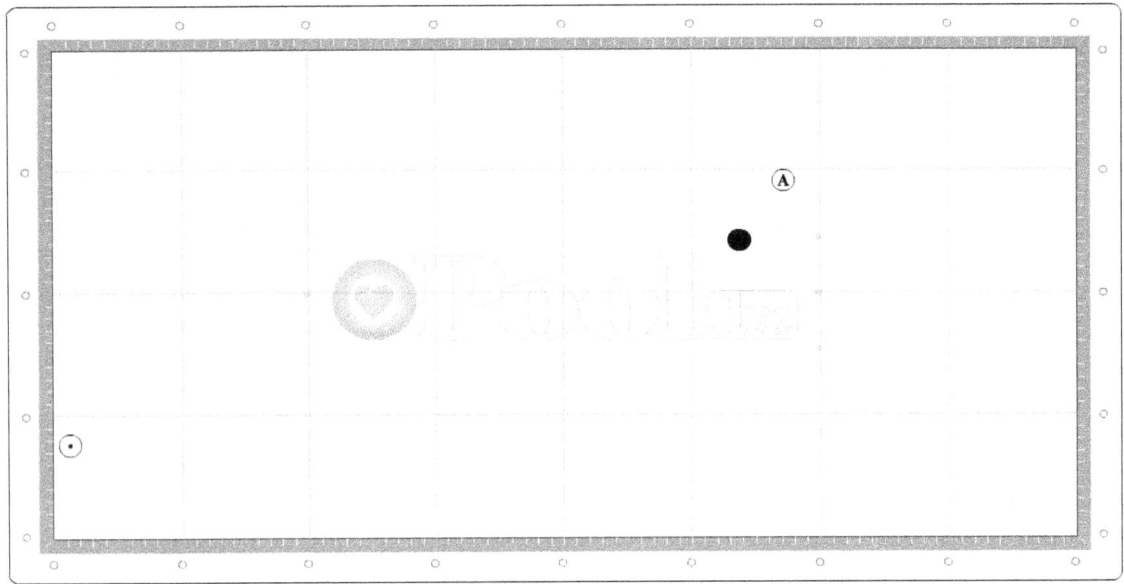

Shot Pattern

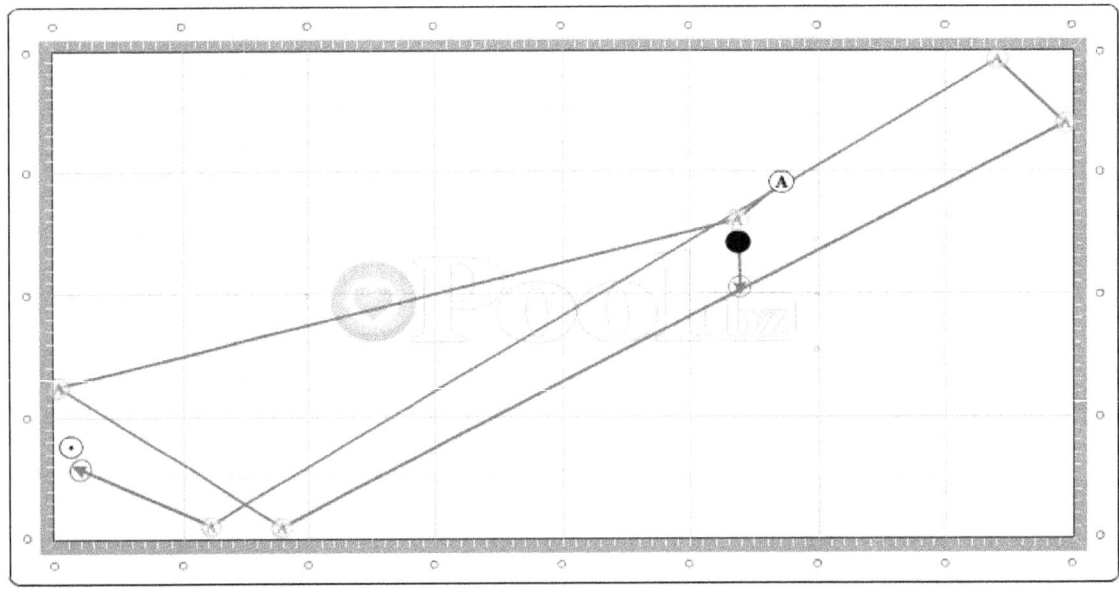

F:3c – Setup

Shot Pattern

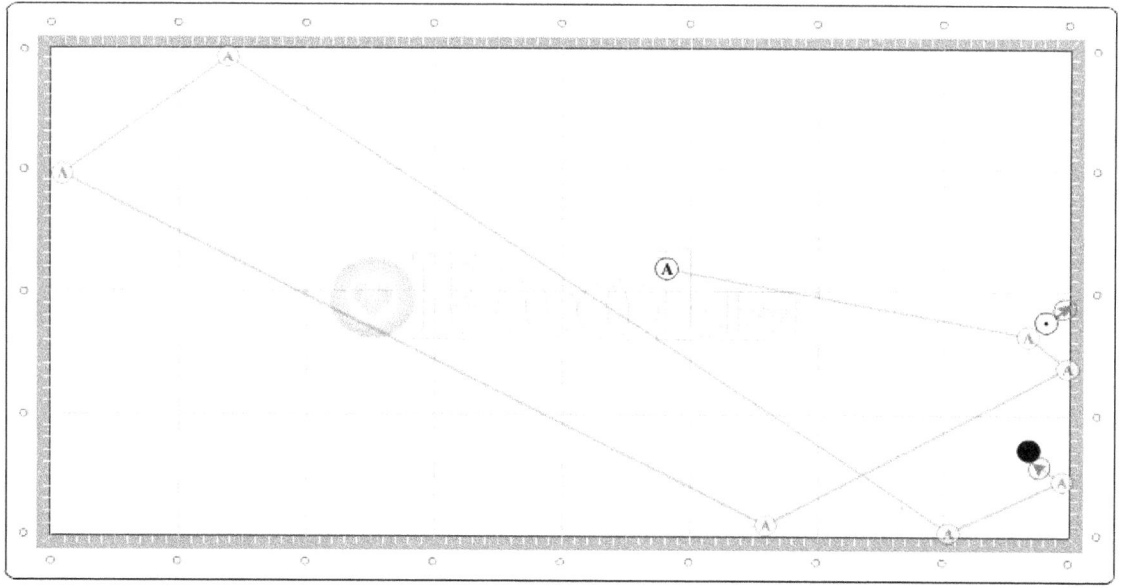

F:3d – Setup

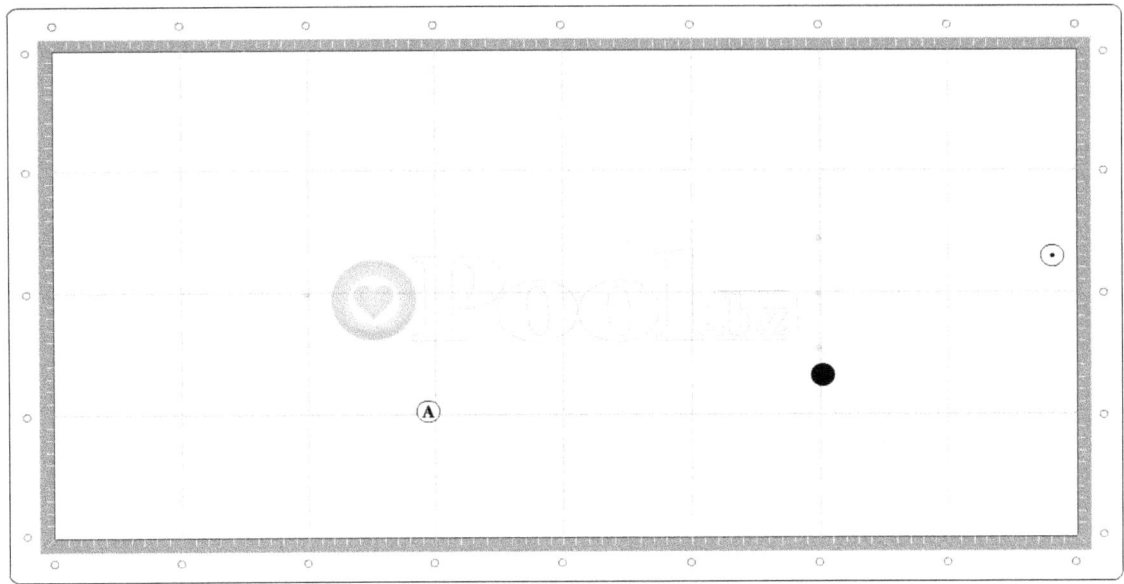

Shot Pattern

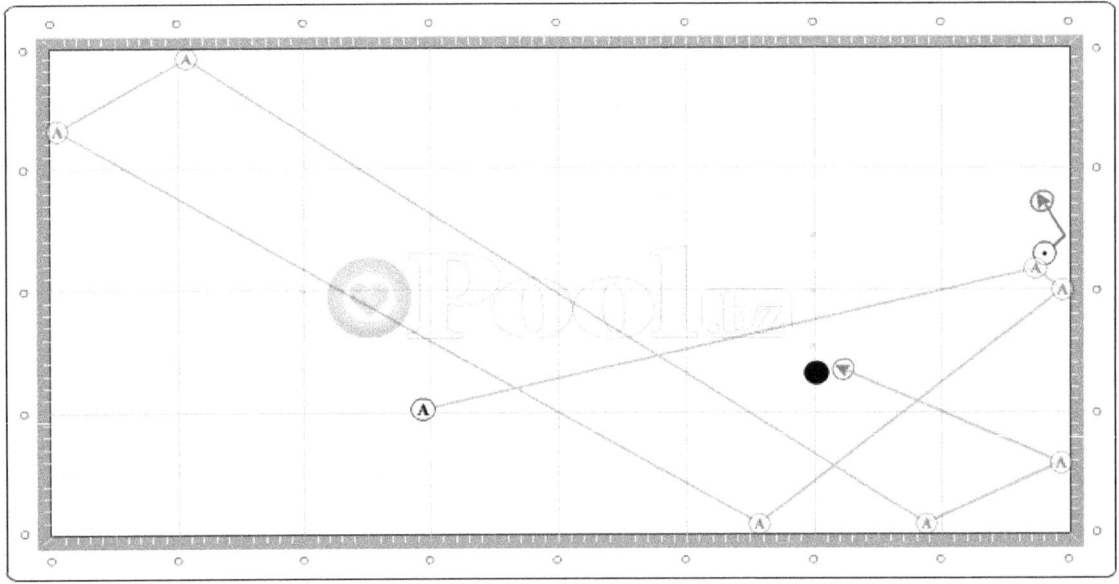